SPRINGS OF ACTION

UNDERSTANDING INTENTIONAL BEHAVIOR

ALFRED R. MELE

New York   Oxford

OXFORD UNIVERSITY PRESS

1992

Oxford University Press

Oxford   New York   Toronto
Delhi   Bombay   Calcutta   Madras   Karachi
Petaling Jaya   Singapore   Hong Kong   Tokyo
Nairobi   Dar es Salaam   Cape Town
Melbourne   Auckland

and associated companies in
Berlin   Ibadan

Copyright © 1992 by Alfred R. Mele

Published by Oxford University Press, Inc.
200 Madison Avenue, New York, New York 10016

Oxford is a registered trademark of Oxford University Press

Library of Congress Cataloging-in-Publication Data
Mele, Alfred R., 1951–
Springs of action : understanding intentional behavior / Alfred R. Mele.
p. cm.   Includes bibliographical references and index.
ISBN 0-19-507114-X
1. Act (Philosophy)   2. Intentionality (Philosophy)
3. Intentionalism.   I. Title.
B105.A35M44   1992.
128'4—dc20   91-17924

2 4 6 8 9 7 5 3 1

Printed in the United States of America
on acid-free paper

For Annamarie, Dino, Mark, and Ron

Contents

PART I

PART II

Preface

In *Irrationality* I made progress toward a causal theory of the explanation of intentional action (1987a). However, my target there was irrational behavior in particular. My aim in the present book is further progress toward such a theory—specifically, toward an explanatory model for intentional behavior in general that locates the place and significance of such mental phenomena as beliefs, desires, reasons, and intentions in the etiology of intentional action. Etiological locations for each of these items will be mapped and the significance of these phenomena explored at length. I shall also have occasion to comment upon additional psychologically explanatory items examined in considerable detail in *Irrationality:* attention, the perceived proximity of a reward, and capacities for self-control. Even with these additions, my discussion omits important psychological contributors to intentional behavior—for example, the emotions—but only so much can be accomplished in a single book.

The majority of this book fits neatly into the philosophy of action. The intended audience, however, is considerably broader. It includes people whose primary interests lie elsewhere in the philosophy of mind and metaphysics as well as moral philosophers and inquiring minds generally. Important recent work on intentionality (in the "aboutness" sense) and the causal relevance of the mental has incorporated extended forays into the philosophy of action (e.g., Dretske 1988; Searle 1983). The same has traditionally been true of investigations of determinism and its practical significance (Honderich 1988 is an excellent recent example); and of course, the springs of action have quite properly been a perennial concern of moral philosophy. The literature in these areas has proved beneficial to me, and I would like to think that this book has something to say to people working in these fields.

Given my intended audience, I have tried to introduce the various issues investigated here in ways that do not presuppose extensive knowledge of the literature. Occasionally, I suspect, specialists will wish that I had got to the focal issue more quickly. But they may skim the relatively brief overviews of familiar territory to locate my central topics of concern and will soon find themselves on more challenging terrain.

My research for this book and some of the writing began in 1986, during my tenure of a 1985–86 Fellowship for College Teachers from the National Endowment for the Humanities (NEH). (The grant supported my work on *Irrationality,* but some of the ideas initially developed for that book seemed to me better left for another occasion.) Subsequent work was partially supported by a 1989 NEH summer stipend and by two grants administered by Davidson College—an Andrew W. Mellon "fresh departures" grant (Spring 1987) and an NEH "coherence in the curriculum" grant (Spring 1988). I am grateful to the granting agencies, to Davidson College, and to Deans Robert Williams and Price Zimmermann for their support and encouragement.

Bits and pieces of the following papers I authored have found their way into this book: "He Wants To Try," *Analysis* 50(1990); "Intending and Motivation: A Rejoinder," *Analysis* 50(1990); and "Intentional Action and Wayward Causal Chains: The Problem of Tertiary Waywardness," *Philosophical Studies* 51(1987) (© 1987 by D. Reidel Publishing Company). The same is true of two coauthored papers: "Mental Causes" (with John Heil), *American Philosophical Quarterly* 28(1991), and "The Role of Intention in Intentional Action" (with Frederick Adams), *Canadian Journal of Philosophy* 19 (1989). Readers familiar with the latter paper will already have surmised that Adams was largely responsible for the control theory advanced there while a good bit of the criticism of John Searle's work fell to me. In fact, my contribution to the piece was largely a paper that I had written earlier for presentation at the 1988 convention of the Pacific Division of the American Philosophical Association. That is the material incorporated here. In the composition of "Mental Causes" there was no such division of labor; I owe my appreciation of the depth of the problem investigated there—and more—to Heil. I have, however, tried to incorporate only parts of the paper that issued from my own PC.

I make more substantial use of "Irresistible Desires," *Noûs* 24(1990); "Exciting Intentions," *Philosophical Studies* 59(1990) (© 1990 by D. Reidel Publishing Company); "Intention, Belief, and Intentional Action," *American Philosophical Quarterly* 26(1989); "Intentions by Default," *Pacific Philosophical Quarterly* 70(1989); "Effective Reasons and Intrinsically Motivated Actions," *Philosophy and Phenomenological Research* 48(1988); and "Are Intentions Self-Referential?" *Philosophical Studies* 52(1987) (© 1987 by D. Reidel Publishing Company). In each case the material has been reworked; and with the exception of "Irresistible Desires," the earlier papers are significantly augmented here.

I am grateful to the editors and publishers for their permission to use material from the essays mentioned. I owe a special debt to my collaborators and good friends, Fred and John, who have granted me permission to use parts of the coauthored ventures.

For instructive comments on various sections and chapters in earlier incarnations, I am indebted to Fred Adams, Louise Antony, Robert Audi, Kent Bach, Myles Brand, Michael Bratman, Carol Caraway, Hector Castañeda, Bob Frazier, Irwin Goldstein, Bob Gordon, Gilbert Harman, John Heil, Tomis Kapitan, Jaegwon Kim, Penelope Mackie, Chris Maloney, Hugh McCann, Brian McLaughlin, Joe Mendola, Paul Moser, Jim Peterman, Piers Rawling, Michael Robins, J. J. C. Smart, J. C. Smith, Mike Smith, Peter Smith, Mark Strasser, and Peter Vallentyne. I am indebted, as well, to audiences at various meetings, including departmental colloquia and conferences of the American Philosophical Association, the Southern Society for Philosophy and Psychology, and the North Carolina Philosophical Society.

Tim Jacks, Brendan O'Sullivan, and Steve Robey—friends and former students—helped in numerous ways. And I am grateful, as always, to Connie and to our children—Al, Nick, and Angela—for their love and support.

Davidson, N.C.   A.M.
May 1991

PART I

1

Introduction

Ordinary explanations of intentional behavior draw upon a rich psychological vocabulary. Our attempted accounts of particular intentional actions appeal to agents' beliefs, desires, hopes, wishes, resolutions, decisions, plans, and the like and sometimes to deliberation or more modest forms of practical reasoning. Occasionally, we advert, as well, to a variety of finely distinguished traits of character or emotions. Traditionally, philosophers have refined and exploited this vocabulary in an effort to produce theories of the explanation of intentional human behavior. One underlying presupposition, perhaps, is that commonsense explanations framed in these terms have enjoyed a considerable measure of success. We understand the behavior of others and ourselves well enough to coordinate and sustain the wealth of complicated, cooperative activities integral to normal human life; and, it seems, the understanding that we have achieved is expressed largely in our commonsense psychological vocabulary.

This book is an exploration of the roles played by a collection of psychological states in the etiology of intentional behavior generally. Intention occupies a pivotal place in that etiology—or so I shall argue. When we ask why Harriet bought a Honda, our primary concern may be with the *reasons* for which she so acted. When we ask how Harriet's reasons for buying a Honda led to her buying a Honda, or how anyone's reasons result in an appropriate intentional action, the explanatory focus shifts. *Intentions* become central, for in them we find the primary link between reasons and actions.

Early in the twentieth-century renaissance of causal accounts of intentional action featuring so-called propositional attitudes, intentions were relegated to the sidelines. In Donald Davidson's "Actions, Reasons, and Causes," for example—a paper that did much to revive such accounts—belief and desire shoulder the explanatory load and such expressions as 'the intention with which James went to church' are understood as referring to no "entity, state, disposition, or event" whatever (1963; 1980,

p. 8).[1] All this has changed (owing partly to later work of Davidson's). Intentions are now taken quite seriously both ontologically and otherwise. However, much can be learned from a close examination of the earlier belief/desire models of the explanation of action—both from their successes and from their failures. In sections 3 and 4, focusing on Davidson's early work in the philosophy of action, I identify central elements in a traditional belief/desire model. This model is criticized and refined in part I of this book. Part II makes a case for incorporating intentions into a further refined model and explores the character of intention and its causal contribution to intentional behavior.

1. Action

Several distinct but promising conceptions of the constitution, identity, and individuation of actions have been defended in the literature. The account of the *etiology* of intentional action that I shall develop in this book is compatible with all of them. At the very least, I shall try to remain neutral on the issues over which the most plausible conceptions in this area divide. I shall not take a stand, for example, on whether actions are to be individuated coarsely, in the manner suggested by G. E. M. Anscombe (1963) and Donald Davidson (1963, 1967), or finely, as Alvin Goldman (1970) urges. In general, the action variable 'A' in this book may be read either as a variable for actions themselves, on a fine-grained conception, or as a variable for actions under A-descriptions. The reader who interprets the action language consistently, should have no problems in this connection.

The uninitiated are owed a bit more detail. Anscombe asks us to consider a man who simultaneously and with the same bodily motions "moves his arm, operates the pump, replenishes the water supply, poisons the inhabitants" (1963, p. 45). Is he performing four actions, she asks, or one? Her answer, with which Davidson concurs, is a single action described in four different ways—one action under four different descriptions. Goldman disagrees: "An act-token is the exemplifying of a property by an agent at a time," and "two act-tokens are identical if and only if they involve the same agent, the same property, and the same time" (1970, p. 10).[2] Since, for example, the property of moving one's arm is not identical with the property of operating the pump, the man's moving his arm and his operating the pump are two distinct actions (or "act-tokens"), *not* a single action under two different descriptions. On Goldman's view, Anscombe has mentioned four distinct actions, some of which are "level-generated" by others (1970, ch. 2). Again, I shall remain neutral.

An alternative to both of the accounts just sketched views the agent as having performed a poisoning possessing various components, including his moving his arm, his operating the pump, his replenishing the water supply, and the pertinent change in the condition of his victims. A variety of "component" conceptions of action have been advanced in the literature (e.g., Beardsley 1975; L. Davis 1970; Ginet 1990; McCann 1972; Thalberg 1977; Thomson 1971, 1977). Their views, though united by a single theme, differ significantly in detail. What I want to leave open is the basic idea that where Anscombe and Davidson find a single action under many descriptions and where Goldman finds instead a collection of actions (act-tokens) generationally related, there may be a 'larger' action having 'smaller' actions among its parts.

The issues just broached are properly viewed in a broader metaphysical context. Competing models of act-individuation are aligned with competing models of the individuation of events generally; and different theories of event-individuation are naturally associated with different theories of—or at least, different vocabularies for expressing—the relationship of the mental to the physical. For Davidson, each mental event is token-identical with a physical event: often (perhaps always; see Davidson 1980, pp. 211–12) the *same* event, *e,* can be picked out both under a physical description and under a mental description. Thus, for example, one and the same event might properly be described as the firing of such and such neurons in S and as S's forming an intention to visit Paris. On a fine-grained view (provided that mental properties are not identical with physical ones), this is unacceptable: Different properties, different events. Fine-grained individuators might say that S's forming the intention *supervenes on* the neural firings; but supervenience is one relation (or collection of relations) and token identity another.

A proper defense of a theory of the individuation of events would require a book of its own. An account of the springs of action can, however, remain neutral on the issue. In the absence of compelling arguments, neutrality has its advantages.

2. Intentional Action

What I have just said about action applies, of course, to intentional action. But there is additional room for broad-mindedness in the latter connection. Any attempt to analyze intentional action faces problems that seem to me intractable, or, at best, capable of being resolved only by stipulation. I shall offer a modest sample of two.

First, it is far from clear whether an agent's A-ing is intentional or nonintentional in some cases in which he realizes that his chances of succeeding in A-ing are very slim.[3] When a basketball player, Connie, tries to sink a last-second basket from midcourt and, executing her plan for doing so, succeeds in sinking the shot, does she *intentionally* make the basket? Opposing answers have been offered, as we shall see in chapter 8. I doubt that a decisive way of settling the issue will be forthcoming. Some of our concepts are simply fuzzy around the edges; and stipulative tidying up can be more trouble than it is worth.

A second problem concerns the following of plans. Some room for departures from intention-embedded plans must be allowed in an analysis of intentional action. But how much? Jill intends to kill Jack by shooting him through the heart; but owing to her inexperience with firearms, she kills him instead by shooting him through the brain. Presumably her killing Jack is properly counted as an intentional deed (other things being equal), even though her behavior does not exactly fit her plan. If, instead, she had missed Jack by a mile but accidentally struck a helicopter, causing it to plummet from the sky and crush Jack to death, her killing Jack would not have been intentional. The knotty problems are raised by intermediate cases. There is no neat and uncontroversial way of sorting the actions into intentional and nonintentional deeds. This is another matter that I shall leave open.

3. Acting Intentionally and Acting for Reasons

So much for neutrality. Next on the agenda are some central features of the belief/desire model of action-explanation to be criticized and refined in part I.

In his seminal book *A Theory of Human Action,* Alvin Goldman suggests that an intentional action might properly be defined as an action that "the agent does *for a reason*" (1970, p. 76). Donald Davidson is prepared to say, at least, that "it is (logically) impossible to perform an intentional action without some appropriate reason" (1980, p. 264). These claims immediately raise an important question. Under what conditions is it true that an action was done *for* a reason?

Goldman and Davidson agree that an action A is done for a reason R only if R is a *cause* of A (Goldman 1970, pp. 76–80; Davidson 1963).

Here they are on firm ground. Arnold has a reason for leaving the lecture hall: He wants to display his dissatisfaction with the lecturer's sexist remarks and believes that leaving the room is a means of doing so. If he does leave the room, do we have here a sufficient condition of his having done so *for* the reason just identified? Plainly not. He might have left the room for another reason altogether. Perhaps he recalled an important dental appointment and left the lecture in order to catch a bus to the dentist's office. The reason for which he leaves the room is, as we might say, the reason that *accounts for* his leaving the room. And it is difficult to see how a reason can account for someone's *A*-ing if it (or the agent's *having* it) does not play a suitable role in the etiology of his *A*-ing. (See Davidson 1963; Goldman 1970, pp. 76–80; L. Davis 1979, ch. 5; Antony 1989. A detailed teleological response to the implicit challenge just sketched is criticized in chapter 13.)

Not just any reason to *A* possessed by an agent will issue in an intentional *A*-ing. Why is it, then, that we act for some reasons and not for others? Davidson maintains that "*R* is a primary reason why an agent performed the action *A* under the description *d* only if *R* consists of a pro attitude of the agent toward actions with a certain property, and a belief of the agent that *A,* under the description *d,* has that property" (1963, 1980, p. 5). He adds, "It is not unnatural . . . to treat wanting as a genus including all pro attitudes as species" (1980, p. 6). Thus, for example, when Larry flipped the switch, his primary reason for doing so was his want or desire to turn on the light together with a belief of his to the effect that by flipping the switch he would turn on the light. One who holds, with Davidson, that reasons are composed of beliefs and desires might attempt to find an answer to the present question in features of these constituents of reasons.

A partial Davidsonian answer may be gleaned from a pair of principles that allegedly "derive their force from a very persuasive view of the nature of intentional action and practical reasoning" (1980, p. 31):

P1. If an agent wants to do *x* more than he wants to do *y* and he believes himself free to do either *x* or *y,* then he will intentionally do *x* if he does either *x* or *y* intentionally.

P2. If an agent judges that it would be better to do *x* than to do *y,* then he wants to do *x* more than he wants to do *y.* (p. 23)

In the preface to his *Essays on Actions and Events,* Davidson remarks that "if reasons are causes, it is natural to suppose that the strongest reasons are the strongest causes" (1980, p. xii). *P1* suggests a partial basis for a reason's causal "strength": The strength of a reason is a partial function of the strength of the *want* incorporated by the reason. Given that the conative components of S's reason to do W and S's reason to do X, respectively, are a certain want to do Y and a distinct want to do Z, given that these wants stand in a mutual relation properly character- ized by the claim that S wants to do Y more than he wants to do Z, and assuming that pertinent subjective probabilities are equal, his reason to do W is *stronger* than his reason to do X.

When relevant subjective probabilities are not equal, the strength of a reason will not be a function of strength of desire alone. Imagine a simple case in which S's reason to do A and S's reason to do B incorpo- rate the same want, a desire to do C: S regards his A-ing and his B-ing as potential but mutually exclusive means to his doing C. Other things being equal, if S assigns a higher probability to his C-ing by B-ing than to his C-ing by A-ing, he will try to do B if he tries to do either A or B. Assuming that he acts on his "strongest" reason, we naturally suppose that the "strengths" of his competing reasons are partially determined by the pertinent beliefs.

Wanting more, for Davidson, is a matter of *motivational* strength: At t, S wants to A at t^* more than he wants to B at t^* if and only if, at t, he is more motivated to A at t^* than he is to B at t^* (t and t^* may or may not be identical). Whereas *P1* links motivational strength to intentional action, *P2* connects evaluative judgment and motivational strength. Together, they entail the following principle connecting judgment and action:

> *P**. If an agent judges that it would be better to do x than to do y, and he believes himself free to do either x or y, then he will inten- tionally do x if he does either x or y intentionally. (cf. Davidson 1980, p. 23)

Presumably, such comparative judgments will be based partly on the agent's assessment of (aspects of) his reasons for doing x and his reasons for doing y.

It is worth observing that one may accept either of *P1* and *P2* while rejecting the other. In chapter 3 I endorse a principle that expresses a central element of the spirit of *P1;* but *P2,* as I have argued at length elsewhere (Mele 1987a) and shall briefly argue again in chapter 9, is untenable.

4. A Point of Departure

I have located several planks in Davidson's early belief/desire model for the explanation of intentional action. The most fundamental of them relates reasons both conceptually and causally to intentional behavior. It may be summarized as follows:

> 1. *The reason basis of intentional action.* An action *A* is an intentional action only if *A*'s agent had a reason for *A*-ing and (his having) that reason was a cause of his *A*-ing.

A closely associated Davidsonian claim addresses the nature of reasons-explanations:

> 2. *Reasons-explanations as causal explanations.* To explain an action by citing the reason(s) for which it is done is to explain the action with reference to its cause.

Further, Davidson advances a position on the constitution of the reasons for which we act:

> 3. *Reasons as belief/desire pairs.* The reasons for which agents act are composed of belief/desire pairs.

Davidson endorses, in addition, a pair of theses relating agents' judgments to their intentional actions:

> 4. *The motivational strength thesis.* "If an agent wants more to do *x* than he wants to do *y* and he believes himself free to do either *x* or *y*, then he will intentionally do *x* if he does either *x* or *y* intentionally" (1980, p. 23).
> 5. *The judgment/motivation alignment thesis.* One is always most motivated to do what one judges it best to do.

The sketch presented in the last few pages of a traditional belief/desire model of action-explanation sets the stage for the remainder of part I of this book. Contentions 1–4 provide points of departure for chapters 2, 3, 4, and 6—and indirectly for chapter 5 as well. Chapter 2 tackles a difficult question that lies at the heart of much recent work in the philosophy of mind: How can a mental state's having the content that it does be relevant to a causal explanation of an agent's behavior? Chapter 3 criticizes and refines Davidson's motivational strength thesis. Chapter 4 addresses the theoretical status of theses of that general kind linking motivation to action. Chapter 5 advances an analysis of irresistible desire with a view to providing a conceptual anchor for a point made in chapter 4 about the control that agents have over their desires. Chapter

6 develops a modified Davidsonian account of the constituents of practical reasons. The judgment/motivation alignment thesis is not addressed
in detail until chapter 9, where it is rejected in connection with an attack
on familiar attempts to reduce intentions to complexes of beliefs and
desires.

Notes

1. Many of Davidson's articles on action have been reprinted in Davidson
1980. In the case of articles reprinted there, all page references are to the 1980
collection.
2. Goldman later substitutes 'act-property' for 'property'.
3. Due to the lack of a neutral third-person personal pronoun in English and
the awkwardness of circumlocutions and systems of switching in a book where
they would have to be in constant use, the conventional masculine pronoun is
here accepted as the least obtrusive format. As gender was in any case irrelevant
to the content, it was not thought desirable to call attention to it. (Here I am
following my copy editor's advice.)

2

Mental Causation

Beliefs, desires, and other intentional attitudes figure prominently in everyday explanations of intentional human behavior. Sally went to New York, we say, because she believed that she would find her runaway son there. Sam left the lounge, we observe, because he wanted to avoid a quarrel with Sue. If our desires, beliefs, and the like really do help to explain our behavior, it is natural to suppose that they do so at least partly in virtue of their content. If Sally had believed her son to be in Los Angeles instead of New York and Sam had wanted to pick a fight with Sue rather than avoid one, they presumably would have acted differently, other things being equal. Commonsense explanations of intentional behavior in terms of beliefs, desires, reasons and their ilk presuppose the explanatory significance of attitudinal content. This presupposition, traditionally, is reflected in philosophical work on intentional action.

Early attempts to explain intentional behavior treated the attitudes as *causally* explanatory. Thus, for example, Aristotle tells us that "the origin of action—its efficient, not its final cause—is choice, and that of choice is desire and reasoning with a view to an end" (*Nicomachean Ethics* 1139a31–33). In its broad outlines at any rate, Aristotle's view has been widely accepted. (Proponents include Aquinas, Hobbes, Spinoza, Locke, Kant, and a slew of present-day philosophers.) Owing significantly to the work of Wittgenstein and Ryle and at least indirectly to the efforts of such behaviorist psychologists as John B. Watson and B. F. Skinner, causal accounts of intentional behavior in terms of the attitudes fell into philosophical disfavor for a time. But they were resurrected in the 1960s and quickly resumed their orthodox status in the philosophy of action.

In recent years, however, a fundamental challenge has surfaced to any theory of the explanation of intentional behavior that accords causal/explanatory significance to intentional attitudes partly in virtue of their having the content that they do. The challenge, briefly put, is to explain how an attitude's figuring in the causal explanation of an action can hinge upon its content. Section 1 identifies a major source of the problem, taking as its point of departure a collection of Davidsonian theses about action, its causation, and its explanation. The remainder of this chapter is devoted to showing that our prospects of meeting the challenge are not nearly as dim as some have portrayed them.

1. Problems

The publication of Davidson's "Actions, Reasons, and Causes" in 1963 (1980, ch. 1) did much to revive the view that the attitudes play a central *causal* role in intentional behavior. A major obstacle at the time to the acceptance of the causal view was the celebrated *logical connection argument,* an argument relying on the premise that cause and effect must be "logically distinct." Since there is a logical or conceptual connection between an agent's wanting (willing, intending, etc.) to A and his A-ing, the latter cannot be an effect, even in part, of the former—or so it was alleged.

Norman Malcolm has advanced a version of this argument that treats intentions as representative of many mental states. There is, Malcolm argues, a

> logical connection between *intending* to do something and *doing* it. If doing it is well within the person's powers, and if he has not given up the intention for some reason or other, and if he has not forgotten his intention, and if no countervailing circumstances have arisen, and if he offers no satisfactory explanation for not fulfilling that intention, and so on— then if he doesn't do the thing, we would conclude that he does not really intend to do it. This way of judging the matter is *required by the concept of intention.*

He adds:

> The logical bond, the conceptual connection between intending and doing, is a loose one; nevertheless it is strong enough to rule out the possibility of there being a merely contingent connection between intending and doing. (1984, p. 88)

Consequently, granting that any causal connection is a "merely contingent" one, there is no causal connection between intending and doing.

Davidson's reply to the logical connection argument is direct and instructive: causation is a relation between events, independently of how we choose to describe them; the logical connections at issue are connections between event-*descriptions* (1980, ch. 1; 1987a). If *A*, the sounding of the alarm, caused *B*, the baby's crying, our describing *A* as "the cause of the baby's crying" (as in, "The cause of the baby's crying caused the baby's crying") plainly cannot change the fact that *A* caused *B*, even though there is a logical connection between subject and predicate in the resulting expression.[1]

For Davidson, *A* causes *B* only if "some law covering the events at hand exists" (1980, p. 18). However, the law need not be framed in terms of *A*-s and *B*-s. Thus,

> the laws whose existence is required if reasons are causes of action do not, we may be sure, deal in the concepts in which rationalizations [i.e., expla-nations of actions in terms of the reasons for which they are performed] must deal. If the causes of a class of events (actions) fall in a certain class (reasons) and there is a law to back each singular causal statement, it does not follow that there is any law connecting events classified as reasons with events classified as actions—the classifications may even be neurological, chemical or physical. (p. 17)

Still, as Davidson puts the point in a later paper, "laws are linguistic; and so events can instantiate laws, and hence be *explained* or predicted in the light of laws, only as those events are described in one or another way" (1980, p. 215, my italics). So how can we explain—"in the light of laws"—actions described as actions by citing reasons de-scribed as reasons?

On one reading of Davidson, his answer appears to be that we cannot. For he accepts the Principle of the Nomological Character of Causality ("When events are related as cause and effect, then there exists a closed and deterministic system of laws into which these events, when appropri-ately described, fit") and the Anomalism of the Mental ("There are no precise psychophysical [or psychological] laws").[2] On Davidson's view, actions under action descriptions apparently cannot be nomologically explained in terms of reasons under reason descriptions; for there are no "precise" or suitably rigorous laws linking reasons so described (or, more generally, *psychologically* described) with events described as actions.[3]

This is quite compatible with a third principle of Davidson's, the Principle of Causal Interaction: "At least some mental events interact causally with physical events" (1980, p. 208; cf. p. 231). For, again, causal relations between events do not depend upon how we choose to describe the events. Thus, in Davidson's shorthand, reasons might cause actions; and if they do, there is a suitable physical law in the background.

A serious problem remains, however. Reasons are supposed to *rationalize* actions (in Davidson's technical sense of the term); and Davidson introduces rationalization as a species of *explanation* (1980, p. 9). Thus, we are faced with an apparent dilemma. Given Davidson's position on explanation "in the light of laws," if reasons cause actions, they apparently do so without explaining them. Or if reasons (described as reasons) *do* explain actions, it would seem that on Davidson's view, they somehow explain them nonnomologically—an idea advocated by friends of the logical connection argument.[4]

Louise Antony, in an instructive paper, suggests that for Davidson, a reason R rationalizes S's action A if and only if (1) S has R, (2) A is reasonable in light of R, and (3) R causes A (1989, p. 166; cf. pp. 156–57). Whether Antony has captured Davidson's position or not (and independently of the accuracy of my own formulation of Antony's interpretation), this account of rationalization or reasons-explanation leads neatly to the focal problem of this chapter. For even if R causes A, that leaves it open whether R's having those mental characteristics in virtue of which it is properly describable as a reason for doing an A is at all relevant to its causing A. On traditional causal models of action-explanation featuring beliefs, desires, reasons, and the like, the causal/explanatory work of these mental items is performed partly in virtue of their having the mental content that they have. On Antony's interpretation of Davidsonian rationalization, we have no assurance that Davidson has preserved this central presumption of the traditional accounts. Is this presumption preservable?

An event X possessing a feature f might cause another event Y without X's possessing f being at all causally relevant to X's issuing in Y. Bill killed Clyde by striking him sharply in the head with one of Don's birthday presents. Various properties of the striking and of the object with which Clyde was struck—an ax—are causally relevant to Clyde's dying; but, at least in a straightforward version of the case, this cannot be said for the object's being a birthday present or for the striking's having been done with something possessing that characteristic.[5] Might the psychological features of reasons be similarly related to the actions that we try to explain by adverting to reasons?

Distinguishing between what may be termed *broad* and *narrow* comparisons of physical items (substances, states, and events) will facilitate discussion. Consider the rear brick wall of my dean's house and a brick-for-brick, molecule-for-molecule identical wall in a possible world W. The dean's wall stands in various relations to things external to it. For instance, it is related to other walls in such a way that it is a wall of a house. The molecule-for-molecule identical brick wall in *W,* let us suppose, stands in different relations to external things. It stands alone, for example (as it always has done), and hence is not a wall of a house. The two walls, I shall say, are *narrowly* identical but *broadly* different. The broad difference between the walls at a particular time *t* in the case as thus far described, is a function of the difference in certain *relational* properties of the walls—those contingent upon features of the walls' respective environments at *t.*[6] We can say that the dean's wall, *narrowly construed,* is constituted by whatever features the wall would share with any molecule-for-molecule duplicate.

Imagine further that whereas my dean's wall was built by Calvin Klein, the narrowly identical wall in *W* was constructed by someone else. Thus, the walls differ in their historical properties. Insofar as they differ in historical respects, I shall say that the walls are broadly different.

This distinction in place, we may distinguish as well between broad and narrow *causal powers.*[7] My eyes were closed a moment ago: I had just awakened from a nap in front of my computer. I had the causal power then to view my computer monitor, in the sense that I could simply open my eyes and view it if I liked. However, the monitor of a molecule-for-molecule duplicate of me in another world was stolen while he slept. Did he have, at the time in question, *t,* the causal power to view his monitor?

In some sense he did. If a computer monitor had been in his illuminated room at *t,* he could simply have opened his eyes and viewed it: he is not blind. In another sense he did not. For he could not, given his circumstances at the time, view his monitor then.

Let us say that the *narrow* causal powers of an entity at a time are entirely fixed by the entity's physical condition, narrowly construed, at that time (its *narrow condition,* for short). *Broad* causal powers are different. They depend partly upon the entity's environment (and perhaps on other things as well). Thus, my doppelgänger and I, for instance, had the same narrow causal powers with respect to the viewing of a computer monitor but different broad causal powers. (One can make the distinction for clarificatory purposes without committing oneself to the "reality" of broad causal powers.)

Return to the question how the psychological features of reasons figure in reasons-explanations of action. For Davidson and many others, practical reasons are belief/desire pairs (where 'desire' is an umbrella term for any conative attitude). Attempted reasons-explanations of behavior identify pertinent beliefs and desires in terms of their content, as in 'Arnie put a dollar on the table because he wanted a bottle of Billy's home-brewed beer and believed that a dollar would get him one'. Now, suppose for a moment that what a human agent does at a time is, in principle, causally explicable only in terms of his *narrowly construed* physical condition at the time and what *supervenes* on that narrow condition (see Fodor 1987, ch. 2). Then if the (minimal) supervenience base of Arnie's having the reason at issue is broader than his narrow physical condition, his having that reason is no part of a causal explanation of his putting a dollar on the table.

To see why the supervenience base will commonly be taken to be broader, we may make a brief visit to Twin Earth. There we find Twin Arnie, an internal-molecule-for-internal-molecule duplicate of Arnie. Billy's home-brewed beer cannot be found on Twin Earth, of course; for an essential property of that beer is that it is brewed by Billy, and Billy and his beer are on Earth, not Twin Earth. But there is a Twin Billy who makes Twin Billy's home-brewed beer on Twin Earth; and Twin Arnie has just put a twin dollar on the table in an effort to purchase one. Arnie has a desire *for* and a belief *about* Billy's beer, whereas Twin Arnie's desire and belief are for and about Twin Billy's beer. In this respect, then, the contents of their beliefs and desires are different, given the popular assumption that intentional features of desires and beliefs are reflected in their content. Yet the twins are internal-molecule-for-internal-molecule duplicates. Therefore, given the assumption just mentioned, the supervenience bases of their having beliefs and desires with the contents at issue are broader than their respective narrow physical conditions.

Perhaps there is a kind of content—*narrow* content—that Twin Arnie's belief and desire share with Arnie's: a kind of content that supervenes on their shared narrow physical condition (Fodor 1980, 1987). But this suggestion may be set aside for now. What drives the present problem about content for traditional theories of the explanation of action is the assumption that an agent's here-and-now causal clout is wholly a matter of his narrow physical condition at the time and what supervenes on it, in conjunction with the contention that mental content is typically *broadly* supervenient. Given that assumption, beliefs and desires whose supervenience bases seemingly stretch out into the world or into the past—or at least their features that supervene partly on historical or environmental conditions—apparently can play no role in the proximal etiology of behavior. It may seem that the only relevant causal powers are *narrow* ones and that this renders the intentional features of states and events causally otiose.[8]

In much of this chapter I shall assume, for the sake of argument, an "externalist" position on content, since the most difficult problems for the causal relevance of the mental arise within an externalist context. I shall suppose, specifically, that the intentional features of beliefs, desires, intentions, and the like are reflected in their content and that the supervenience base of a mental state's having the intentional content that it has is typically broader than any narrow physical condition of the agent.[9] The resolution advanced in this chapter (as I shall explain at the end of section 6) does not *rest on* the truth of externalism, however. It is applicable as well as to the causal relevance of full-blown intentional content *internalistically* construed.

2. Behavior, Broad and Narrow

In some respects, Arnie and Twin Arnie behave identically. They both purchase a beer, for example; and we may suppose that the bodily motions produced by Twin Arnie in the course of purchasing the beer duplicate Arnie's. However, in another respect, their behavior is different. Arnie buys a bottle of *Billy's* home-brewed beer, and he buys it with a genuine United States dollar; but his twin buys a bottle of Twin Billy's beer, with a twin dollar. Are differences of this sort significant for the philosophy of action? Are the differences explicable on causal grounds? And if so, is a causal account of the difference relevant to the project of explaining intentional behavior?

It will prove instructive to examine a case in which the behavioral differences are more pronounced. First, however, I provide some background. What we do *intentionally* depends significantly on the contents of our beliefs and desires. Oedipus intentionally married Jocasta, and Jocasta was his mother; but he did not intentionally marry his mother: he married his mother quite unwittingly. Olive intentionally shot the person who was breaking into her house, and that person was her father; but she did not intentionally shoot her father. It was dark: she thought that a prowler was breaking in. If she had believed that it was her father, she would not have shot. Another example: Wanting to kill Hector and believing the soldier directly in her path to be Hector, Diana hurls her spear at him. She overshoots her mark by fifty feet; but her spear strikes and kills another soldier, who, as it turns out, is Hector. Diana kills Hector—but inadvertently, not intentionally. Her killing Hector is not intentional partly because of the content of her belief.

A related point is in order, a point about the constitution of action. When I unlocked my office door this morning, I moved my right arm, wrist, and hand in some determinate way or other. However, those bodily motions themselves, in abstraction from their relations to other things, do not constitute my action of unlocking my office door. Precisely those motions, narrowly construed, might have occurred without my having unlocked my office door. (Suppose, for example, that the lock into which I inserted the key when producing those motions had been lodged instead in the front door to my house, which lock, for reasons of convenience, is a duplicate of the one in my office door.) What more—or else—is involved in my action of unlocking my office door may be left open for now. The foregoing is sufficient as a basis for a rough-and-ready distinction between what I shall call *narrow* and *broad* behavior. Narrow behavior is mere bodily motion, in abstraction from its causes and effects; broad behavior is richer. Representative instances include an agent's unlocking his office door, making up his bed, and eating his Wheaties.

Consider a boy, Nick, who is taking a third-grade achievement test and intentionally following the instructions. *Following* instructions involves more than merely engaging in behavior that *accords* with those instructions. The distinction here is analogous to a familiar one between a bit of behavior's according with a rule and the agent's following a rule. Ted's bringing his car to a halt at a red light accords with a traffic rule even if Ted, unaware that the light is red, stops for reasons having nothing to do with the rule. We *follow* rules, however, only when our behavior is appropriately *guided* by them. Similarly, Nick follows the test instructions only when his marking the paper as he does is appropriately guided by those instructions. His being so guided depends upon his understanding the instructions, something that requires his having true beliefs about them.

Narrowly conceived, Nick's behavior is just the motions of his arm, wrist, and hand. Broadly conceived, the behavior includes his following instructions, instructions directing him to blacken a series of boxes corresponding to the letters in his name. Given that an agent's following a set of instructions depends upon his being guided by those instructions, the etiology of Nick's instruction-following behavior ineliminably incorporates factors *external* to Nick—the instructions, for instance. It incorporates, as well, Nick's correctly interpreting those instructions. If Nick's production of the marks that he made—marks that accord with the instructions—had in no way depended on his having understood the instructions but had been due instead, say, to a desire to make an *r*-shaped pattern on the sheet, he would not have *followed* the instructions.

Instruction-following behavior is no different, in one important respect, from much intentional human behavior, ordinarily conceived. An agent who has no idea *how* to *A* may *A* accidentally; but he is in no position to *A* intentionally. An idea of how to *A* sufficiently robust to help guide an intentional *A*-ing might be termed a *plan* for *A*-ing.[10] In intentionally *A*-ing, an agent follows some appropriate plan or other. More precisely, when intending to *A* and owing to the presence of that intention, an agent *A*-s intentionally, he executes a plan for *A*-ing.

A Martian who lacks in this sense a plan for bed making is in no position to make up a bed intentionally. Even if in executing a plan for sending a signal from Earth to Mars, he produces bodily motions of precisely the sort that I produced an hour ago when making up a bed and with the same outcome (a tidy bed), he does not intentionally make up a bed. The plan executed by the Martian is not a plan for bed making, even though its execution results—even *reliably* results—in a well-made bed. The difference might be explained by appealing to the historical circumstances of the Martian's having the plan or to the plan's intentional content. Perhaps the plan was learned and continues to be sustained *as* a plan for signaling and was neither learned nor recruited after the fact as a plan for bed making. In light of that etiology, the Martian's plan clearly would not be a plan *for* bed making.

Incidentally, even an agent who impeccably follows a plan for *A*-ing might not *A* intentionally. Hal, who has no idea what a bicycle is, finds a bicycle construction kit with instructions attached, instructions *for* building a bicycle, instructions constituting a plan for that activity and recorded for the purpose of guiding agents in assembling a bicycle. The instructions are framed wholly in terms of lettered parts, numbered slots, and the like (e.g., "Insert tube *B* into slot *C*") and nowhere mention bicycles. After memorizing the instructions, thereby acquiring something constituting a plan for building a bicycle, Hal goes to work. He follows the instructions to the letter and in so doing assembles a shiny new bicycle. Here, Hal intentionally does a number of things, including putting tube B into slot C. But he does not intentionally *build a bicycle* (any more than Oedipus intentionally marries his mother). What stands in the way of his intentionally doing *that* is his ignorance of bicycles, the absence of a requisite state of mind. Someone else, Sal, following the same instructions with the same results, owing, appropriately, to his desire or intention to build a bicycle, would have intentionally built a bicycle.

Given that Sal, but not Hal, *intentionally* builds a bicycle, must there be a difference in their narrow physical conditions at the times of their respective acts of bicycle building that accounts for this actional difference? If so and if it is also the case, as it surely is, that Sal's bicycle building could not have been intentional if he had lacked a concept of bicycle, then Sal's having a concept of bicycle supervenes on (some aspect of) his narrow physical condition. For if it did not so supervene and if his being in that narrow condition accounts for his bicycle building's being intentional, his having a concept of bicycle would not be required for the bicycle building's being intentional. But if his having a concept of bicycle supervenes on his narrow condition, the problem posed about mental content in section 1 is not a problem in this case—a representative instance of broad, intentional behavior. For the challenge there to the causal relevance of a state's having the content that it does rests on the joint supposition (1) that only an agent's narrow physical condition at the time and what supervenes on it figure causally in his behavior and (2) that the supervenience base of a mental state's having the content that it does is typically broader than this narrow condition.

So let us retain the common externalistic supposition, supposition 2. Then perhaps we can, in principle, imagine a Twin Sal who is a narrow physical duplicate of Sal but who nevertheless *nonintentionally* produces a bicycle at the pertinent time. That imagined—we can observe that states bearing broad content, in virtue of their bearing such content, have a role to play in accounting for a representative instance of broad, intentional behavior. Whether or not the accounting, or the role, has *causal* significance remains to be seen.

Perhaps it will be replied that even on the externalistic supposition about intentional content, a twin of the sort mentioned is a conceptual or nomic impossibility. One might contend, to fill in some details, that there is a conceptual or nomic necessity that any narrow duplicate of Sal's narrow physical condition be correlated with external (historical or environmental) conditions of a certain kind—indeed, conditions of such a kind that together with the narrow condition, they constitute a supervenience base for the possession of mental states with the pertinent full-blown content. But if any nomically possible Twin Sal will have what it takes to build a bicycle intentionally and if only agents in possession of a desire or intention to build a bicycle are in a position to produce this broad behavior, why should we suppose that Sal's having such a desire or intention is causally irrelevant to his intentional bicycle building? It might be replied that it cannot be causally relevant, since the proximal basis of an agent's causal clout is restricted to his narrow physical condition and what supervenes on it (Fodor 1987, p. 44)—or that possession of a desire or intention to build a bicycle is a *conceptual* requirement on intentional bicycle building and not something with causal significance. The reply will be challenged later.

3. Conceptual and Causal Relations

Some may unwittingly take unfair advantage of conceptual relations in making a case for the causal relevance of the mental. Others may rashly assume that wherever conceptual relations obtain, causal relations are absent; and, of course, it is possible to confuse relations of the two kinds with one another.

I have a bottle of beer in my hand, and I am about to take a drink. Imagine, if you can, that in some possible world there is a molecule-for-molecule duplicate of me. He has a bottle of beer in his hand, too; but he has no idea what beer is. Beer has just at that moment been introduced into that world by God, who secretly transformed the contents of my twin's bottle into beer. I take a drink; my twin does so as well.

Consider the following concise, but uncompelling, argument for the causal relevance of the mental to intentional action.

1. I intentionally take a drink of beer, or so we may suppose. My twin takes a drink of beer, but not intentionally.
2. This is a difference in the two cases.
3. What my twin and I do are effects of causes.
4. Given that the effects differ, the causes differ.
5. The only relevant difference in the causes is that my molecular state (partly in virtue of its causal history) realizes, say, an *intention* to drink beer, whereas my twin's molecular state does not.
6. So my molecular state's realizing an intention to drink beer (or, more generally, its realizing beer thoughts) is causally relevant to what I do.

One might reply, sensibly enough, as follows. To be sure, an instance of beer drinking is an instance of *intentional* beer drinking only if the agent has beer thoughts (e.g., an intention or desire to drink beer, a belief that this is beer); but this is just a *conceptual* truth. The products of events or states internal to the two agents include, one might grant, beer drinking; and my beer drinking, unlike my twin's, counts as intentional beer drinking because it is caused (nondeviantly) by an internal physical state or event that realizes an intention to drink beer. But this does not establish that the physical item's realizing an intention to drink beer figures in the *etiology* of the effect produced as opposed to merely figuring conceptually in the effect's counting as intentional beer drinking.

The reply here, it should be noted, is *not* that when *A* and *B* are conceptually related they cannot also be causally related. After all, it may be granted, what are being treated loosely as conceptual relations between events are really conceptual relations between event-*descrip-*

tions; and (as noted in sec. 1) two events that are *causally* related may be given descriptions that are conceptually related. The point of the reply is simply that argument 1–6 is not compelling: it does not *establish* the causal relevance to my behavior of my internal molecular state's having the mental features that it does.

One might respond that there being a conceptual relation between intentionally drinking beer and having beer thoughts is not an obstacle to there being a causal relation. After all, there is a conceptual relation between sunburn and exposure to the sun; still, prolonged exposure to the sun does cause sunburn. But some will find this unconvincing. The sun, they will say, has the causal power to produce burns simply in virtue of its internal atomic properties. If X is the sun, we may erase its property of being a sun by eliminating all planets from its environment. Still, X can produce qualitatively identical burns in any bare-skinned people who happen to be floating by. Moral: it is not at all in virtue of having the relational property of being a sun that our sun causes burnt skin. Furthermore, something's having the property of being a sun is required for burns caused by exposure to it to count as sunburn, but that is just a conceptual point.

Now, it might be asked (to put the question in a currently popular way) whether my intention to drink some beer, *qua intention to drink some beer,* is a cause of my behavior. Let us first return to a question touched upon earlier. If, as we are supposing, there is intentional action, philosophers will naturally want a characterization of it, one that enables us, for instance, to distinguish intentional from nonintentional beer drinking. Granting, for the sake of argument, that externalism is true, can an adequate characterization be framed, even in principle, wholly in terms of *narrow* items (items narrowly construed)?

My beer drinking in the initial case, narrowly construed, is, perhaps, constituted by movements of my muscles, arm, mouth, and the like (along perhaps with certain effects: a bottle's rising to my lips, beer's passing into my mouth, down my throat, etc.).[11] Narrowly identical events may occur in my twin's case without his having intentionally drunk beer. Thus, we cannot locate in these narrowly construed events alone anything that entitles us to count my beer drinking as intentional.

This itself does not show that an adequate narrow characterization of intentional action is impossible. On a traditional view, the difference between intentional and nonintentional action rests partly on causal considerations. Thus, for example, it is claimed that an A-ing is an intentional A-ing only if it has an agent-internal cause of a certain sort. But the internal cause of my beer drinking is narrowly identical with that of my twin's beer drinking: our respective physical conditions at the pertinent time are narrowly the same. So, whatever it is in virtue of which I intentionally drink beer whereas my twin does so nonintentionally, the distinguishing factor cannot be located in the narrow, internal physical causes of our respective beer drinkings either.

It looks, then, as though we need to go beyond the narrow realm to find intentional behavior (qua intentional). This should not be surprising, if, as a popular view has it, intentional action is action done for a reason and a physical item's being a reason depends upon its having *broad* features. If, harking back to the criticism of argument 1–6, it is a conceptual requirement on intentional *A*-ing that the agent have *A*-thoughts and if agent-internal narrow physical events or states are (typically) insufficient for the having of pertinent *A*-thoughts, then a proper characterization of intentional action will employ some suitably broad notions.[12]

Supposing that intending to *A,* desiring to *B,* and the like, produce intentional action, but *not* qua intending to *A,* desiring to *B,* and so on, we may still advert to broad, intentional states or events at least in *characterizing* intentional action. Moreover, in adopting a vocabulary suitable for identifying certain effects of internal states or events *as* intentional actions, we may enable ourselves to pick out *causes* of intentional actions qua *intentional*—causes described in such a way as to make intelligible in virtue of what the behavior counts as intentional. These observations will be exploited later.

4. Causal Relevance and Causal History

What about explanation? Does what we believe, desire, and intend make a difference in what we do? If so, is the difference of such a kind as to vindicate the popular idea that much human behavior can be causally accounted for partly in terms of broad psychological states or events?

Imagine that particular collections of intentional attitudes are ascribable to agents partly in virtue of the agents' having a causal history of a particular sort. Consider an agent *S* who has at a particular time *t* a particular collection of intentional attitudes; and suppose that *S* has these attitudes in virtue of being in a particular physical condition with a particular sort of causal history. *S*'s possessing the intentional attitudes that he does at *t,* one might say, *supervenes* on *S*'s being in that physical condition with that kind of etiology.[13] *S*'s physical condition at *t,* a condition having a particular etiology, is a *broad* condition. *S*'s *narrow* condition at *t*, again, is a condition that *S* would share with any molecule-for-molecule twin. It is an abstraction consisting of *S*'s broad condition stripped of its historical properties and any other relational properties involving *S*-external relata.

Supposing that *S* possesses intentional attitudes in virtue of his being in a particular internal physical condition having a certain sort of causal background, it will turn out that it is because the internal physical condition of, say, our intentional bed maker has a particular sort of etiology that he is in a position to exhibit the broad behavior that he does. It is not that the etiology reaches out a ghostly hand to produce action at a distance: its influence is a distal, mediated one. Rather, *owing to that etiology,* among the things true of *S* at *t* are that he has a plan for making up beds and a collection of beliefs and desires in virtue of which he is in a position to make up a bed intentionally. *Owing to that etiology,* we can ascribe to *S* intentional attitudes that help to account for his broad behavior.

I have argued that broad, intentional behavior can occur only if the agent possesses a suitable collection of intentional attitudes. I have supposed, further, that intentional attitudes might be possessed by an ordinary human agent *S* in virtue of *S*'s being in a particular physical state, a state possessing a particular etiology. This is not yet to say that intentional attitudes figure causally in intentional behavior. It is not even to say that there *is* intentional behavior nor that if there is such behavior, it is causally explicable.

One might attempt to block the causal contribution of intentional states by denying that broad behavior is *caused* at all. It might be held that only *bodily motions* are caused and that broad behavior is merely a *projection,* a construction observers (including perhaps the agent) place upon those motions. Intending to *A,* wanting to *A,* and the like might be regarded as *logically* or *conceptually* necessary conditions of intentional *A*-ings and not as items that play a causal role in the production of behavior. It could be granted, then, that while what I have called *broad behavior* must be explained by reference to the contents of mental states, only *narrow* behavior is *causally* explicable. And the exclusion of broad behavior from the realm of items subject to causal explanation apparently undermines the suggestion that intentional attitudes play a role in causal explanations of behavior.

Some remarks of Stephen Stich's are directly relevant. Stich happily grants that "if we are willing to countenance the full range of common-sense descriptions of behavior, then it is false that a person and his replica will always behave identically" (1983, p. 166). He maintains, however, that the only descriptions that "a psychologist will find useful in constructing systematic explanations of behavior" are *autonomous behavioral descriptions,* that is, descriptions such that "if [they apply] to an organism in a given setting, then [they] would also apply to any replica of the organism in that setting" (p. 167). (This entails, of course, that much social psychology is not genuinely psychological, since the descriptions of behavioral explananda employed there are frequently nonautonomous.) Other descriptions are "typically conceptual hybrids" (p. 169).[14]

Broad behavior and the causal relevance of intentional attitudes cannot be pushed aside so easily, however. The historical dimension of an agent's broad physical condition during *t* can be causally relevant even to his *narrow* behavior during *t*. An instance of machine behavior will prove instructive in this connection. Imagine that a certain computing machine *M* has been manufactured by a company that programs half of its machines to produce widgets and half to produce gidgets. *M* has been programmed to produce widgets; and had it not been so programmed, it would have been programmed instead to produce gidgets. Notice that *M,* which is currently producing a widget, has the historical characteristic, *H,* of having been programmed to produce widgets; and its having *H* is explanatorily relevant to its producing a widget at *t.* *M*'s circumstances are such that if it were to lack *H,* it would not, at *t,* be producing a widget; for it would possess rather the historical feature, H^*, of having been programmed to produce gidgets. And in that case it would lack the capacity to produce a widget at *t* and, in fact, would, at *t,* be producing a gidget. Moreover, its possession of *H* is explanatorily relevant as well to the *narrow* behavior of the machine involved in its producing a widget at *t.* For, again, if it were to lack *H,* it would be making a gidget at *t* and would be producing the mechanical motions required for the manufacturing of gidgets, motions altogether distinct from those involved in the mechanical production of widgets.

In this case, the point that the machine would neither be making a widget nor producing the motions that it is producing if it were to lack *H* is not a *conceptual* one required for a certain interpretation of *M*'s behavior. In *some* possible world, *M* makes widgets and produces qualitatively identical mechanical motions even though it lacks *H.* But *M*'s actual circumstances are such that it would not be producing either this broad or narrow behavior if it were without *H.* Its possessing *H* is explanatorily relevant to its behavior, broad *and* narrow, in virtue of the *causal* relevance to that behavior of *M*'s having *H.*

This is not to say, of course, that from statement 1, '*X* would not be producing Y if it were to lack Z' and statement 2, 'statement 1 is not a conceptual truth', it follows that X's possessing Z is causally relevant to its producing Y. Suppose that the manufacturing company C that owns M employs exactly two programmers, Peter and Paul, and that Peter programs machines only for widget making while Paul handles the gidget programming. Suppose also that Mary, Peter's supervisor, is always present and observant when Peter is programming but knows nothing of Paul's activities: we might even imagine that Mary is Peter's Siamese twin. M is presently producing a widget.[15] Now, it might be true that given the details of the story, the closest possible worlds in which M is not presently producing a widget are worlds in which Mary did not observe Peter program M (because Peter did not program it); that is, it might be the case that M would not presently be producing a widget if it were to lack the property of being a C-owned machine whose programming was observed by Mary. But it certainly does not follow from this that Mary's having observed M being programmed is causally relevant to what M is now doing. And of course, the pertinent counterfactual does not express a conceptual truth.

There is, however, an important difference between this last case and the original one. In the original example, the past event that was the programming of M to produce widgets is obviously a cause of M's now being in a state that figures in the etiology of its present widget-making activity. But the same is not true, in the second example, of Mary's observing the programming of M. The latter point accounts for its being false that M's having the property of being a machine whose programming was observed by Mary is causally relevant to its present production of a widget (and the narrow movements involved therein). Similarly, the former observation helps to account for the causal relevance to M's present activity of M's possessing the property of having been programmed to produce widgets.

Imagine now a human agent, Al, who is intentionally making up a bed during t. Prior to performing this chore, Al engaged in practical reasoning. He narrowed the options to two—making up his bed and vacuuming his shag carpet—and he decided to do the former. As it happens, if Al had not decided to make up his bed, he would have decided to vacuum the carpet; and he would have executed the latter decision during t. Now, at the time at which he is making up the bed, Al has the historical feature of having decided to make up his bed at this time. If he were to lack that feature, given the details of the case, he would neither be making up the bed nor producing the bodily motions involved in that activity: instead, he would be vacuuming his carpet and producing bodily motions suitable for that enterprise.

As in the machine case, this last counterfactual observation does not express a *conceptual* point required for a certain construction that observers might place on Al's behavior. In some possible world, Al is intentionally making up a bed at the time, and producing appropriate bodily motions, even though he did not, in that world, decide to do so. (Imagine a world in which Al, who engaged in no deliberation at the relevant time and made no decision, passively acquired an intention to make up his bed.)[16] But Al's actual circumstances are such that if he were to lack the pertinent historical feature, he would neither be making up a bed nor producing bodily motions of a sort appropriate to that task.

Readers who remain doubtful about the status of the counterfactual might be supposing that one could, in one's imagination, erase Al's pertinent historical characteristics—in the case, as described—without in any way changing his narrow physical condition and therefore without changing his narrow behavior. But this is mistaken. Given the details of the case and the truth of even a modest physicalism, if Al were to lack these historical characteristics, he would be in a different narrow physical condition at the time—a condition of a sort that, given a friendly environment, would result in an intentional rug vacuuming and bodily motions appropriate to that activity.[17] The same is true, of course, of machine *M*. Given its circumstances, if it were to lack the historical feature of having been programmed to produce widgets, it would be in a distinct narrow physical state associated with a distinct historical feature.

Perhaps it will be objected that even granting all this, human and mechanical agents' narrow physical conditions are what do the causal work and historical characteristics of agents are therefore causally irrelevant to their narrow behavior. This objection misses an important point, however. A number of distinct narrow physical conditions might have resulted in Al's or *M*'s narrow behavior. Perhaps, if Al had not been in narrow physical state N_i, the state that issued in and sustained his narrow behavior, he would have been in a slightly different narrow physical state, N_j, resulting in qualitatively identical narrow behavior. (For example, N_j might differ slightly from N_i in the magnitude of the electrical impulse that a neuron common to both generates but not in such a way as to result in behavior that is relevantly different.) In that case, what is explanatorily central to his narrow behavior is not the particular narrow physical state that produced it but a broader, historically colored state so constituted that if Al had not been in it he would not have produced that

narrow behavior. The broader state has a more general causal/
explanatory significance not encompassed in that of the particular physical state that resulted in the narrow behavior (see Jackson and Pettit
1988, 1990). Even if broad behavior were excluded from the class of
causally explicable phenomena, one would still be saddled with the
causal relevance of historical features of agents to their narrow behavior.

5. Questions and Answers

Early in section 3 I raised a trio of questions. Are certain differences
between the actions of an earthling and his doppelgänger significant for
the philosophy of action? Are the differences explicable on causal
grounds? And if they are so explicable, is a causal account of the differences relevant to the project of explaining intentional behavior? It is
time for some direct answers. (Since the theoretical setting in which the
questions arose was externalistic, the answers will have an externalistic
flavor as well. But see the concluding paragraph of section 6.)

Consider Sal and Twin Sal again, or my beer-drinking doppelgänger
and me. A notable behavioral difference in the former case is that Sal—
but not Twin Sal—intentionally builds a bicycle, even though the agents
are internal-molecule-for-internal-molecule duplicates whose narrow behavior issues in the same narrow result. Similarly, my doppelgänger and
I produce narrowly identical bodily movements with the result that we
consume beer; but only one of us intentionally drinks beer. Since the
difference between intentional and nonintentional behavior is of central
importance to the philosophy of action, there can be little doubt how the
first question is to be answered.

The second question, as well, is properly answered in the affirmative.
Owing to the distinct *causal histories* of Sal's internal physical condition
at the pertinent time and that of his twin, Sal is in a position to build a
bicycle intentionally; whereas Twin Sal is not. Thus, we can account for
Sal's intentionally building a bicycle while his doppelgänger does not by
appealing to causal considerations. The same is true of my beer-drinking
twin and me.

Turning to the third question, the point just made is entirely relevant
to the project of explaining intentional behavior. It shows, among
other things, that an agent's narrow physical condition and what supervenes on it do not exhaust what is causally relevant to his behavior:
historical features of the agent are relevant as well. Moreover, if, as I
have suggested, an agent's collection of intentional attitudes at a time

supervenes on his broad physical condition at the time, one need not abandon the hope of displaying, in a way perfectly compatible with physicalism, the causal relevance to intentional behavior of a mental state's having the content that it does. My aim here, however, is not to develop a particular theory of the realization of intentional states and their causal powers. Rather, I have in view the much more modest goal of showing that arguments to the contrary notwithstanding, one need not abandon hope for the success of a philosophy of action that accords mental items, partly in virtue of their broad content, a role in causal explanations of intentional behavior.[18]

The position that I have been sketching can be developed more fully. On a commonsense view, as I said, my intention to drink beer results in my beer drinking partly in virtue of its content, partly in virtue of its being an intention to *drink beer.* The same view fearlessly endorses such counterfactuals as 'If Al had not intended to drink beer at *t,* he would not have done so' (while granting, of course, that there are scenarios in which the counterfactual is false). But what is the force of such counterfactuals if the narrow causal powers of the physical states that realize intentions, desires, and the like are not affected by the intentional features of these physical states (Fodor 1987, p. 38)?

It is just the force that the claims were intended to have—or so I shall argue. One may say, in a rough-and-ready way, that the truth of counterfactuals about the actual world is properly tested in the nearest possible worlds in which their antecedents are satisfied.[19] When I asked my neighbor, Betty, whether she would have broken my window if she had not intended to, she said *no.* She did not consider that a molecule-for-molecule duplicate who had no window thoughts might have broken my window anyway and that in some world she is that duplicate. Further, in nearer possible worlds in which Betty did not intend to break my window, she did not break it. In one such world, she decided to set her anger aside; in another, she settled on some other means of getting even.

Not all true counterfactuals support causal claims, however. So even if Betty would not have broken my window had she not intended to, perhaps this by itself shows neither that her intending to break my window was a cause of her doing so nor, a fortiori, that the fact that the physical cause of the action realized an intention to break my window is causally relevant to her breaking it. But if the internal physical cause of Betty's action realized an intention to break my window and if Betty would not have broken my window if she had not intended to, perhaps we can safely appeal to the physical item, under an intentional description, as a cause of her breaking the window in classifying the window breaking as intentional.[20] That done, perhaps we can take steps toward explaining her action by locating the reasons—under reasons-descriptions—that issued in the intention.

I do not want to claim that physical states or events under mental descriptions have causal powers that they lack under physical descriptions. States and events have whatever powers they have no matter how we describe them. So my molecular twins and I have the same causal powers, at least on a *narrow* reading of 'causal powers'.

Nor do I wish to contend that intentions, desires, and the like have causal powers that the pertinent physical states do not. Intentions and desires *add* nothing to these states, on the view under consideration. (Assuming Davidsonian token identity, they *are* these states. Given a more fine-grained view of event-individuation, psychological states and events may *supervene* on broad physical states and events; but one may endorse the latter view without committing oneself to the idea that mental items have a causal clout that is not encompassed in their physical supervenience bases.) Of course, granting the externalism that has motivated much of this chapter, of two narrowly identical physical states, one might have intentional features (features appropriate, say, to a desire to drink beer) that the other one lacks, since those states might have different causal histories. But then one realizes a mental item that the other does not. Narrowly identical states may be broadly different, as I have noted.

Part of what I *do* want to suggest may be put roughly at first: Our intentional properties often make a difference in what we do. We can ask, *holding the narrow features of my physical condition, C, fixed,* whether that condition (or collection of events) would have had narrowly different (proximate) physical effects if C had not realized the mental items that it realized. The answer, I have granted, is *no*. C's narrow causal powers are not affected by C's mental features; that is, holding the narrow features of C fixed and immutable, we cannot change C's narrow causal powers by altering or eliminating its mental properties. But suppose we ask instead whether a particular agent S would have produced narrowly different physical effects at *t*, if he had not been in the mental state that he was in at the time. (Notice that this question, unlike the preceding one, leaves it open whether S would have been in C, narrowly construed, if he had not been in the mental state in question.) Here, a natural answer frequently is *yes*.

The commonsense idea that what we do often depends on what we believe, desire, and intend (even when accompanied by a commitment to physicalism) leaves open the possibility that a molecule-for-molecule duplicate of an agent S produces effects narrowly identical with S's even though he lacks pertinent beliefs, desires, and intentions that S possesses. The idea (in conjunction with physicalism) places a less demanding commitment upon its adherents. Consider Al's making up his bed, to return to an earlier case. Framed in terms of Al's intention to make up his bed, the idea, very roughly, is this:

(A). Al's intending to make up his bed is realized by some physical state or event in him that is a cause of his bed making.

(B). Holding everything fixed at t except Al's intending at t to make up his bed then (and anything else that would have varied at t had Al not intended to make up his bed), if Al had not intended to make up his bed, he would not have done so.

Three points merit consideration. First, (B) does add something to (A). If a statement like (A) were true in a particular case but a corresponding statement like (B) were false, then that the physical item realized a pertinent intention might be of no interest at all. If (assuming the conditions laid down in (B)'s antecedent) Al would have made up his bed even if he had intended, say, to vacuum his carpet, the fact that a significant physical cause of his making up his bed realized an intention to make up his bed might be simply irrelevant to his bed making.

Second, possible worlds in which (standing in his room at the time in question) Al does not intend to make up his bed and does not make it up are seemingly much less remote from the actual world than are worlds in which—although Al's narrow physical condition while standing in the room is identical with his actual narrow physical condition at the time— he lacks an intention to make up his bed (see Horgan 1989). Among the former worlds are worlds in which Al decides to vacuum his carpet rather than make up his bed and acts accordingly. The clearest instances of worlds of the latter sort are those in which Al had never been in contact with beds.

Before turning to the final member of my triad of observations, attention should be called to a wrinkle introduced by the possibility of overdetermination or quasi-overdetermination. The schema of which (B) is an instance is unnecessarily strong in a certain respect. Consider a case in which I decide to drink beer rather than ginger ale and execute my decision. Suppose that if I had not decided to drink beer, I would have decided to drink ginger ale and would have acted on that decision. Suppose also, however, that, unbeknownst to me, a prankster filled all the ginger ale bottles in the room with beer. Thus, I would have drunk beer even if I had not intended to do so.

It is not at all clear, in the case as described, that my intending to drink beer does not figure in a proper explanation of my doing so. Suppose that if Oswald had not shot Kennedy to death when he did, Toswald would have. Toswald, a mind reader, was standing just behind Oswald and had set himself to fire (at *t*) if he saw that Oswald would not do so (at *t*). As it turns out, if Oswald had not fired, Kennedy would have been struck by Toswald's gunfire in just the way he was by Oswald's (and the two gunmen had type-identical weapons and ammunition). So, other things being equal, it is false that if Oswald had not shot Kennedy, Kennedy would not have died when and where he did. Still Oswald's shooting Kennedy caused Kennedy's death.

This is an instance of what might be termed *quasi-overdetermination*. [21] It is not genuine overdetermination, since only one gunman actually fired. Still, if Oswald had not caused Kennedy's death, Toswald would have. The beer/ginger ale case is relevantly similar. If an intention to drink beer (or the physical item that realized it) had not figured in the production of beer drinking, an intention to drink ginger ale (or its physical realizer) would have.

Let us say that an agent *S*'s *A*-ing is *quasi-overdetermined* (i.e., quasi-overdetermined in a way relevant to present concerns) only if the following is true: If the agent-internal component, narrowly construed, of the actual cause of *S*'s *A*-ing had not figured in the production of *S*'s *A*-ing, some *distinct* narrow internal state or event would have. Then we can modify the schema of which (*B*) is an instance as follows:

(*B**). Barring overdetermination and *quasi-overdetermination*, and holding everything fixed at *t* except *S*'s intending at *t* to *A* then (and anything else that would have varied at *t* had *S* not intended to *A* then), if, at *t*, *S* had not intended to *A* then, *S* would not have *A*-ed then. Here, '*t*' ranges over durations, '*S*' over agents, and '*A*' over actions (or actions under '*A*'-descriptions, assuming a Davidsonian model of act-individuation).

My claim, *to a first approximation*, is that the commonsense idea that what we believe, desire, and intend often makes a difference in what we do depends on nothing stronger, in the original bed making/vacuuming case, than that both (*A*) and a pertinent instance of schema (*B**) are true. ((*A*), again, is the assertion that Al's intending to make up his bed is realized by some physical state or event in him that is a cause of his bed making.) In the particular bed making/vacuuming example in question, we can simplify things by building it into the description of the case that my bed making is neither overdetermined nor *quasi-overdetermined*.

The third point: (B^*) is not a *conceptual* truth. It is *conceptually possible* that had I not intended to drink beer in a particular case, I would have been in a narrow physical state identical to my actual narrow state but with a significantly different causal history. In this possible scenario, I may know nothing of beer, act on an intention to consume the contents of a certain bottle, and consume beer in so acting, since, unbeknownst to me, beer was smuggled into the bottle. There is no over-determination here. Nor is my beer drinking *quasi-overdetermined*; for the internal component, narrowly construed, of the cause of my beer drinking in the possible world in question *is identical with* the internal component, narrowly construed, of the cause of my beer drinking in the actual world. Moreover, the remainder of an instance of (B^*)'s anteced-ent is satisfied. Yet, the consequent is false: I drink beer in the possible scenario. Hence, (B^*) is not a conceptual truth. An instance of (B^*) may be false. Given a certain array of *contingent* truths (including truths such that had I not intended to drink beer, I would have been in a narrowly distinct state realizing, say, an intention to drink ginger ale), that in-stance of (B^*) is true.

If the psychological items appealed to in a particular attempt to ac-count for my beer drinking are not, in fact, realized in the internal, physical events that produced my beer drinking, the attempt is unsuc-cessful—the beer drinking has not been explained. But if they are so realized, the person doing the accounting has adverted to a pertinent cause; and depending on the descriptions offered, he might have picked out that cause in such a way that auditors who share his conceptual scheme can see in virtue of what my beer drinking counts as intentional.

Some psychological descriptions of an internal cause of behavior are not terribly useful, of course. Someone might correctly say, for example, "The cause of his beer drinking realized a thought." Others promote genuine understanding, including those citing the reason(s) for which the agent acted *as* the reason(s) for which he acted or the intention that he executed *as* the intention executed.

6. Augmenting the View

I have offered an approximate account of the commitments essential to the commonsense idea that what we believe, desire, and intend often makes a difference in what we do. An important commitment, however, has thus far remained inexplicit.

Consider the following observation by Fred Dretske: "A soprano's upper register supplications may shatter glass, but their meaning is irrelevant to their having that effect. Their effect on the glass would be the same even if they meant nothing at all or something entirely different" (1988, p. 79). In some version of the case, the soprano sings the word 'glass', producing a sound the amplitude and frequency of which are such that her wine glass shatters. Let us say that this intonation of the word 'glass' is realized in a sound having amplitude x and frequency y. And let us suppose that if the soprano had not sung 'glass', the glass would not have shattered. We may imagine, for example, that the soprano, Sally, had been considering whether to sing 'glass' loudly or 'grass' softly and that if she had not decided to sing 'glass' she would have sung 'grass' softly, in which case the glass would not have shattered.

Given these suppositions, it looks as though we have a case parallel in some relevant respects to the bed making/vacuuming case discussed earlier. In particular, we have the following truths:

1. Sally's singing the word 'glass' is realized in her production of a sound that is a cause of the wine glass's shattering.
2. If Sally had not sung the word 'glass', the wine glass would not have shattered.

But does the fact that what Sally sang was the word 'glass' (or a word having that meaning) "make a difference" vis-à-vis the glass's shattering? (Cf. 'The fact that what Al intended was to make up his bed made a difference in what he did'.)

In a sense, it does. For, given the details of the case, if it had been false that what Sally sang was the word 'glass' (or a word having that meaning), the glass would not have shattered. But the difference made is not *projectible* in any interesting way. No explanatorily useful generalization linking singings of 'glass' (or singings of words with the meaning of 'glass') to glass shatterings is supported by the instance, nor would our encountering such a case in the real world (given our background knowledge) tempt us to postulate such a link.

We find here a noteworthy difference between the soprano example and cases of the sort investigated in the preceding section. Sally could have sung 'glass' with any number of different amplitudes and frequencies, only a narrow range of which would result in the glass's shattering. Perhaps it is similarly true that Al's intention to make up his bed, in the earlier example, could have been realized in a range of narrowly distinct neurophysiological states or events. Presumably, however, any of the realizations would do nicely, provided that the realizing neurophysiological item is suitably linked to the output system. We routinely employ the vocabulary of intentions (rather than that of neurons) in commenting on internal springs of a range of behavior. The spring picked out in a particular case of bed making, for example—if we have hit our mark—is realized in neurophysiological events that issue in the pertinent behavior. But we grant that narrowly distinct neurophysiological events can realize an agent's intention to make up his bed, while holding on to the idea (in normal cases) that whatever the realizing events might have been, he would not have made up his bed at the time if he had not intended to. If we are right in this, there is presumably some pertinent intentionalistically framed generalization in the background. Such generalizations play a central role in a familiar brand of functionalism.

Here is a humble truth about actions, one that holds true, presumably, in a wide range of possible worlds: for a great many action-types A, people are considerably more likely to perform a token of type A if they intend to A than if they do not so intend. There is, of course, no comparable truth relating glass breakings to singings of 'glass'. It is false, for instance, that people are considerably more likely to break glass if they sing 'glass' than if they do not sing 'glass'. That what a particular agent intends at t to do then makes a *projectible* difference in what he does then is bound up with the truth of background generalizations (like the humble one just mentioned) of a sort central to a functionalism featuring broad internal states and events.[22] In the case of singings of 'glass' and the pertinent hypothetical effects, no comparable background is to be found.

Some may balk at the claim that the humble truth about action has no analogue vis-à-vis singings of 'glass' and breakings of glass. Consider (G): People are more likely to break glass *by singing* if they sing 'glass' than if they sing nothing at all. Is that a proper analogue? Not at all. (G)'s truth obviously does not rest in the least on special features of the word 'glass' (nor on the meaning of that term). Any term at all can be substituted for 'glass' in (G) without rendering (G) false. This is a significant difference between (G) and the humble truth about action. Substituting 'intend to B (for any B)' for 'intend to A' renders the humble truth false, as does substituting 'hate' for 'intend'.

The central thesis of section 5, as I indicated, was an approximation of the thesis that I intend to motivate—a thesis about the commonsense idea that (often enough) what we believe, desire, and intend makes a difference in what we do. The commonsense idea is, more fully, that what we believe, desire, and intend often makes what I shall call a *systematic* difference in what we do. Major marks of a systematic difference, to take the case of intention again, include our being able (to a significant extent) to predict, understand, and manipulate behavior on the basis of our knowledge of what agents intend. That such prediction, understanding, and manipulation (in everyday senses of the terms) are promoted by our knowledge of agents' states of mind is, of course, widely granted.

An additional mark of there being a systematic connection between mental states and action is our ability to *explain,* in some measure, the latter in terms of the former. The explanatory relevance of mental items to action is, as I have indicated, a commitment of traditional, intentionalistic, causal theories of action-explanation. I have been attempting to convey a firm sense of what that commitment amounts to; but more remains to be said, both here and in section 7.

Consider the following case.[23] Whenever a certain substance C is cooled to 32 degrees, it becomes explosive and turns blue. In its natural uncooled state, C is nonexplosive and red. When C is in the former state, dropping lit matches into it causes it to explode; otherwise, subjecting C to flame does not cause explosions. Here, it may seem, we have an analogue of the soprano case featuring generalizations of the sort absent there. For example, other things being equal, dropping a lit match into *blue C* is much more likely to be followed by an explosion of the substance than is dropping a lit match into *red C*. Further, knowing what we know about C, we can confidently make certain *predictions* about its behavior. And we can *manipulate* its behavior. For example, if we want to produce an explosion, we can cool a vial of C until we see that the substance has turned blue and then drop a lit match into it. Still, we are inclined to suppose, a bit of C's being blue makes no relevant difference at all to its exploding.

One might be tempted to conclude that for all I have said, mental properties of agents might be related to their behavior in essentially the way that the blueness of a bit of C is related to its behavior. The suspicion merits consideration. Suppose that, being experimentally minded folk, we do not simply take it for granted that the blueness of blue C is causally irrelevant to its exploding when subjected to flame and proceed to test that hypothesis. We cool numerous vials of C until the substance turns blue, drop different dyes (green, pink, orange, etc., cooled to 32 degrees) into different vials, and then toss lit matches into the mixes.

Additionally, we dye comparable amounts of *C* blue at various temperatures above 32 degrees and subject it to flame.

If we get explosions across the board in the first case but none in the second, the hypothesis is confirmed. But then, of course, we know that in some nearby nomologically possible worlds, there is no significant correlation at all between *C*'s being blue and its exploding when subjected to flame. Here, then, we find a striking difference between generalizations about *C* and our humble truth about actions. They are remote worlds, indeed, in which it is *false* that for a great many action-types *A*, people are considerably more likely to perform a token of type *A* if they intend to *A* than if they do not so intend.[24] Evidently, the pertinent generalizations about blue *C* and our humble truth about actions are differently grounded. Further, although in light of our knowledge we would be able to predict the behavior of undyed blue *C* and manipulate the behavior of *C* in the way described, we could neither understand nor instructively explain why blue *C* is explosive by adverting to its blueness.[25]

Adding dye (in the imagined manner) alters the physical properties of blue *C* but not in such a way as to eliminate or reduce its explosiveness. Imagine modifying narrow features of the physical states that realize intentions to *A* (intentions to unlock one's office door, drink a Coke, draft a paragraph, and so on) in such a way as to change the contents of those states without eliminating or reducing their capacity to issue in bodily movements of a sort appropriate to *A*-ing. And imagine doing it in a way that shows that in some nomologically possible world our humble truth about actions is false.

Brief consideration of how to get to such a world, as it were, via the route now being imagined will prove instructive. Here is a recipe. First, leave people alone long enough to develop thoughts about objects in their environment and to have formed intentions concerning them. Then have master neuromanipulators start fiddling with their brains. Suppose, for example, that we want to have the brain of a Stone Age man, Fred, manipulated in such a way that a modified version of the physical state that realizes his proximal intention to enter Betty's cave realizes instead a proximal intention to enter his own cave, but without modifying the pertinent narrow causal powers of the original state. If Fred believes that Betty's cave is before him, that he has just walked up the path to her cave, and so on and intends, say, to retrieve a knife that he left there, the masters will have to change that, of course. That package of intentional states goes along with the intention that we want to have modified. So suppose that the masters manipulate Fred's brain in such a way as to alter his relevant beliefs and intentions and that Fred, intending to enter his cave, instead enters Betty's, producing bodily motions narrowly the same as those that would have occurred if the manipulators had not intervened. The specialists can "dye in" new content, as it were, while leaving the physical basis of motor commands intact.

A lot of this sort of thing will need doing—and to a large percentage of the world's population—to produce a world in which the humble truth is false. But so be it. Also, there would be mass confusion, unless the masters were very careful; and our agents might not survive long enough to falsify the humble truth. But we can help out there. When, for example, Fred enters Betty's cave, having intended to enter his own, specialists can manipulate his brain in such a way that he hallucinates *his* cave. They will have to be careful, of course, to get their charges to engage—unintentionally, for the most part—in various life-sustaining courses of action. However, the masters can engineer all sorts of things, taking advantage of neural connections and motor skills originally developed in far different circumstances.

"Basic" actions may seem to pose a greater problem for the manipulators. When Fred forms an intention to run from a tiger encountered in the cave, the masters might manipulate his brain in such a way that he now intends to run from a lion and hallucinates a lion. But he still intends to run. Similarly, his intention to walk into his cave might be changed to an intention to walk into Betty's cave without modifying the pertinent narrow causal powers of the realizing physical state. Still, he intends to walk. Are intentions to run, walk, and the like, immune to manipulation of the required sort?

No. When Fred forms the intention to run from the tiger, the neurospecialists can alter his brain in such a way that he now consciously intends to sneak stealthily away from a lion, even though a portion of the realizing state is such as to issue in motor commands of a sort suitable for running. Again, new content can be dyed in while leaving the physical basis of motor commands intact. And while he is running, Fred can be given pseudofeedback appropriate to a sneaking.

Would the possibility of such a world prove that the contents of our intentions bear no more significantly upon our behavior (broad or narrow) than the blueness of blue C bears upon its exploding when subjected to flame? Not at all. In fact, the remoteness of such a world from the actual world, at least as we understand it, is an indication of the depth of the connections between our mental and physical features. Left to their own devices in an environment like ours, intending beings need to represent their surroundings with considerable accuracy and to respond effectively to those representations in light of their needs and desires. Brain states presumably are recruited for the representational and motivational work of the organism.[26] And other things being equal, the more effective the brain is at representing the environment and coordinating the agent's interaction with it, the more likely the organism is to survive and, eventually, to flourish. Although, in a sense, it may be a cosmic accident that there are intending beings at all, it is no accident that the intenders that there are usually act as they intend to act. Intenders who were no more likely to *A* when they intended to *A* than when they did not so intend would not survive long under normal conditions in an environment like ours.

Before moving on, a promise should be kept. As I mentioned earlier, I have been assuming, for the sake of argument, an externalistic view of content, since that view poses the weightiest problems about the causal relevance of the mental. However, the resolution that I have been advancing does not *depend* on the truth of externalism. Suppose that the supervenience base of any mental state's having the intentional content that it does is limited to the agent's narrow physical condition at the time, even though agents have full-blooded beer thoughts, form intentions to make up beds, and the like. This supposition leaves the commonsense idea just articulated intact. In fact, it would make it intuitively easier to see how the mental can be causally relevant, given the supposed tightness of its connection with agents' narrow physical conditions.

7. Is That All There Is?

The central questions in the philosophy of action are, I think, these: What is an action? What is an intentional action? How are intentional actions, qua intentional, to be explained? If, as I have argued, any succesful answer to the second question will incorporate intentionalistic terminology, the same is true of the third question. Now, I have granted that the loci of agents' narrow causal powers are agent-internal physical events or states, narrowly construed. But in virtue of nonrelational, historical, and environmental features of internal physical events or states, they are appropriately picked out under intentionalistic descriptions. (Alternatively, on an internalistic view of intentional content, pertinent narrowly construed physical items are properly picked out under full-blown intentionalistic descriptions independently of the historical and environmental features.) This is enough for traditional, intentionalistic, causal theories of action, provided that (aspects of) descriptions of the sort just mentioned can figure systematically in suitable true counterfactuals along with pertinent descriptions of a certain range of effects.

Intentionalistic psychology and the philosophy of action are not physics, nor are they neuroscience—which is not to deny that they should be sensitive to, and informed by, both. I have asked, in essence, whether recent work on the causal relevance of the mental tolls the death knell for traditional, intentionalistic, causal theories of action. The answer has been a qualified *no*. Unless, unbeknownst to me, a convincing case for elimination of the mental has been made, we are still in business. If the mental ever is eliminated, intentional action vanishes as well, in which case there would no longer be a subject matter for the philosophy of action and intentionalistic psychology. But is it at all likely that an argument will convince us that we never intentionally do anything? I doubt it.

To be sure, we *might* inhabit a Cartesian demon world in which no human being acts at all. Or perhaps we only *dream* that we are acting. But these possibilities are grist for another mill. The occurrence of broad, intentional behavior, no less than the occurrence of muscle contractions and limb movements, appears well confirmed by experience. Recall the last time you constructed something. You began with a desire and a plan, a plan for producing the desired item; and following the plan, perhaps with some revisions and a few slips along the way, you constructed the desired item. Your constructing the item, in such a case, is an instance of broad, intentional behavior. And should anyone seek it, evidence of such constructive behavior abounds. This is not to suggest that the conceptual apparatus ordinarily employed in describing and accounting for such behavior is unrevisable in principle. Perhaps standard conceptions of desires, beliefs, plans, intentions, and the like are too coarse, or too fine-grained, or in some other respect less apt than intentionalistic successor notions. That there is a difference between intentional and nonintentional human behavior, however, seems indisputable. And that difference speaks in favor of there being causally relevant intentional attitudes.

One of the aims of the philosophy of action and intentionalistic psychology, as I have said, is to explain intentional behavior qua *intentional* behavior. Someone concerned to explain narrow bodily movements alone might search for strict physical laws linking narrow neurophysiological events of certain types to narrow bodily movements of certain types. Psychologists and philosophers endeavoring to explain intentional behavior may happily grant that there are such laws. What they deny is that such laws can tell the whole etiological story about intentional behavior. The rest of the story, whatever it may turn out to be, might not require that there be strict, exceptionless psychological or psychophysical laws.[27] It might require only that important components of the physical causes of actions can be systematically picked out by intentionalistic descriptions that figure, along with intentionalistic descriptions of behavioral effects, in true counterfactuals of a sort that (partly in light of this causal context) help to account for the behavior's *being* intentional.

Philosophers of action are not, of course, in the business of explaining particular actions on a case-by-case basis. Their aim is to produce theories in the light of which actions can be explained. Presumably, particular causal relations between, say, biological realizations of 'proximal' intentions (intentions for the specious present, e.g., my intention to press my 'save' key now) and appropriate bodily movements will be grounded in nomological regularities linking neurophysiological events with the movements of muscles, joints, limbs, and the like.[28] That there are such regularities is not a sufficient basis for traditional, intentionalistic, causal theories of action and its explanation; for the existence of such regularities does not ensure that intentional features of agents make a difference in what they do. But there are also the observations about counterfactuals and systematicity. In the case of proximal intentions, the point, briefly put, is this: nothing in the literature on causal relevance shows that an intentionalistic, causal theory of action-explanation cannot generate illuminating causal explanations of actions in cases in which nomologically grounded causal transactions of the sort in question occur *and* the agents satisfy pertinent instances of counterfactual schema (B^*). Of course, the traditional theories employ an array of intentional notions. Comparable counterfactual schemas are constructable, however, for belief, desire, attention, and their kind; and in each case there are associated background generalizations comparable to the "humble truth" about action and intention identified in section 6.

Why *should* anyone be concerned to explain intentional behavior, qua intentional? Why not set our sights exclusively on the explanation of narrow bodily movements? If, in the distant future, there were a complete science of the brain and body capable of explaining all narrow bodily movements in terms of narrow neurophysiological causes, would intentionalistic psychology and the philosophy of action be otiose? I cannot imagine that at such a time, mental life would be extinct. People would continue to make inferences, for example, and to reason about what to do; and, often enough, they would be aware of so doing (perhaps under other rubrics). To be sure, they would be able to answer questions like, "Why did this limb movement occur?" by citing neurophysiological causes in a purely neurophysiological vocabulary. But they might still be faced with such questions as "What was she (he, I) up to in making that movement?" "What was the point of that movement?" "Why did Sally go to New York?" Perhaps the vocabulary in which questions such as these are answered will be considerably more refined than ours. The descriptions under which many such questions pick out a particular behavior, however, presuppose that the behavior is intentional. And, I have suggested, proper answers to proper questions rightly presupposing this will employ a suitable intentionalistic vocabulary.

Self-understanding and the understanding of others like ourselves encompass the understanding of intentional behavior, qua intentional. Since such understanding requires a conceptual scheme that incorporates intentionalistic notions, there will be a place for the philosophy of action and intentionalistic psychology as long as such understanding is sought. Whether concern for understanding in this sphere is an *essential* part of intelligent, reflective human life may be left open. But it is worth noting that however advanced neuroscience becomes, as long as we continue to attribute moral responsibility to agents for particular deeds, we will need some way of distinguishing between intentional and nonintentional actions; and that will require the application of intentionalistic notions. (This is not to say, of course, that we are morally responsible *only* for our intentional behavior.)

Some readers may harbor the suspicion that at bottom, all that is causally relevant to the production of anything whatever are items countenanced by microphysics. Absolutely everything either is a microphysical item or supervenes on the microphysical, and all items having causal clout are found in this supervenience base. But granting the claim about clout, we can observe that a wealth of macro-items figure prominently in causal explanations offered in chemistry, biology, neurophysiology, geology, meteorology, and the like.

If intentional action and intentionalistic items required for it are not scientifically disreputable, there may still be a place in philosophy for the philosophy of action. And of course, there *ought* to be such a place, given the manifest importance of a proper understanding of our behavior, including our *intentional* behavior. Further, if intentional actions are actions done for reasons and an action is done for a reason R only if (to use Davidson's shorthand again) R is a cause of the action, there ought to be a place for a *causal* theory of action-explanation. The burden of this chapter has been to show that, recent arguments to the contrary notwithstanding, mental items may figure—qua mental, and in a way relevant to causal explanation—in such a theory.

Notes

1. Malcolm is well aware of this line of response. For his rebuttal, see Malcolm 1984, pp. 88–95.

2. The names of the principles are taken from Davidson 1980, p. 208. The formulations quoted are from Davidson 1980, p. 231.

3. Incidentally, actions, for Davidson, are mental events (1980, p. 211).

4. It is open to Davidson to reply that reasons (so described) do nomologically explain actions (so described) but that the laws appealed to at this level of description are not *precise* or *strict* laws (see Davidson 1987a and 1992).

5. One who holds that *a* and *b* are the same event if and only if "they have exactly the same causes and effects" (Davidson 1980, p. 179) might insist that Clyde's actual dying would not be the same event as the dying of Clyde in a possible world in which, say, Don's deadly ax was not a birthday present, on the grounds that the causes would be different (see Davidson 1992). Nevertheless, the dyings or deaths might be "narrowly the same," in a sense defined shortly; and that is sufficient to motivate the issue being raised.

6. I do not intend to be expressing an ontological commitment to properties. What I say here (and elsewhere) can be reformulated in terms of predicates.

7. The notion of causal powers figures significantly in Jerry Fodor's recent work on causal relevance. See Fodor 1987, ch. 2; Fodor 1989, 1991.

8. It is worth noting that this is not an instance of a problem about the causal relevance of supervenient properties generally. There seemingly are genuine macro-causal relations, even though those relations supervene on other, more fundamental ones: consider the increased pressure produced by the rise in temperature of a gas in a rigid chamber. The present problem is a problem about the proximal causal relevance of properties whose supervenience base is broader than the narrow physical condition of the agent at the time. (For a helpful account of supervenient causation, see Kim 1984.)

9. Instructive defenses of externalism (or "anti-individualism") include Burge 1979, 1986, 1989; Davidson 1987b, 1989; Putnam 1981.

10. On plans, see ch. 8.3. In the limiting case of intentional "basic" actions, one's plan is simply a representation of one's prospective action.

11. Again, I am remaining neutral on the issue of the terminus of actions. Did Oedipus' act of killing his father terminate with the end of the striking or with his father's death? For present purposes, it does not matter how the question is answered.

12. Readers who suspect that a trap is being laid might want to contend that the requirement that agents of intentional beer drinking have beer thoughts is not a conceptual one at all but a causal one. But then argument 1–6 is back in the running. Given this contention, on what grounds can it be denied that my molecular state's realizing beer thoughts *is* causally relevant to what I do?

13. This is not to say that just any physical condition having an etiology constitutes an intentional attitude. After all, *every* actual physical condition has

some causal history or other. Which sorts of etiology are sufficient for mental content is a question that I shall leave open.

14. See Tuomela 1989 for a useful critical discussion. See also Adams 1991; Burge 1986; Horgan 1991.

15. Christopher Maloney suggested a version of this example.

16. On the passive acquisition of intentions, see ch. 8.3.

17. 'Modest physicalism' (i.e., noneliminative and nonreductive physicalism), for my purposes may be characterized in a way that leaves both Davidsonian token identity and competing modest physicalist views open. Modest physicalism maintains that every substance, event, and state of affairs either is a physical substance, event, or state of affairs or is supervenient on (or realized in) one.

18. In the last three paragraphs, I assumed that there being a Twin Sal who, unlike Sal, nonintentionally makes a bicycle is a genuine nomic possibility. But suppose that this scenario is nomically impossible. Suppose that it is nomically necessary that anyone whose narrow condition duplicates Sal's must also have broad physical characteristics in virtue of which it is true both that he, like Sal, possesses a concept of bicycle and that his bicycle building is intentional. Such broad characteristics, as I argued, have causal significance for both broad and narrow behavior. And if, as I suggested, an agent's collection of intentional attitudes supervenes on his broad condition, the causal relevance of the mental items is underwritten by that of the broad physical conditions that constitute the supervenience base of that collection in conjunction with the alleged nomic necessities.

19. See Stalnaker 1968 and Lewis 1973. I am making no commitment here to modal realism. Talk of possible worlds, for my purposes, may be understood as a heuristic device.

20. Two observations are in order. First, I am assuming that the window breaking is intentional and, consequently, that it is not a product of causal waywardness of a sort that is incompatible with its being intentional. (On causal waywardness, see ch. 11.1–2.) Second, I am not abandoning the neutrality on event-individuation to which my neutrality on act-individuation in chapter 1 commits me. Not all ways of picking out physical events under intentionalistic descriptions imply the token identity of mental events with physical events. Consider the description 'the physical event that realizes his proximal intention to *A*'. As I use the expression, to say that a physical event *realizes* a proximal intention to *A* is neutral as between that event's being token-identical with the agent's proximally intending to *A* and the event's being an item distinct from the agent's proximally intending to *A* on which the latter supervenes.

I have tried to formulate the problem of causal relevance in two different vocabularies: one suited to coarse-grained individuation and token identity, the other suited to fine-grained individuation and the rejection of token identity. For example, I have asked (in the former vocabulary) whether intentions, *qua inten-tions,* figure in the etiology of action and (in the latter vocabulary) whether, given that the supervenience base of a particular intention is broader than the agent's narrow physical condition, the agent's having that intention makes a difference in what he does.

21. This is sometimes termed "preemption." See, e.g., Lewis 1986, pp. 160, 171–72.

22. For recent instructive defenses of functionalism of this familiar sort, *broad* functionalism, see Jackson and Pettit 1988 and 1990.

23. Essentially this case is presented in Van Gulick 1992.

24. Here is a sketch of one such world, *WD*. *WD* is partially populated by a handful of human beings and a very powerful mind-reading demon who makes it his business to thwart the overwhelming majority of human intentions for actions requiring bodily movement but without preventing the beings from acting. Thinking (as the reader might be) that beings who lack a sense of personal efficacy would never become intenders, the demon (by means of mind control) systematically causes people to believe that their intentions have been executed: their apparent success rate is comparable to our actual success rate. Additionally, he engages in widespread item switching, so that, for example, agents who intend to eat one sort of food end up eating another, people who intend to drink a beverage of one kind instead drink beverages of other kinds, and so on; and he employs various crafty techniques for other sorts of intended behavior, including intended basic actions. Further, the demon is careful, of course, to ensure (at least for a while) that his victims do not starve or accidentally kill themselves. As it turns out, *WD*'s human inhabitants typically stand no better a chance of *A*-ing when they intend to do so than when they do not so intend. Indeed, the demon's purpose in all this, as he reveals to a demonic friend, is to prove that my "humble truth" about action is false in some possible worlds. (The friend expresses a suspicion that the beings have a better actual success rate in various "mental" actions. But the demon observes that they are not terribly thoughtful beings, that they do not often intend to perform mental actions, and that their intentions for such things range over only a tiny subset of the mental action-types available to us.)

25. Suppose that things had turned out otherwise. No matter what the temperature of the substance, the blue *C* exploded and the red *C* did not—or the blue *C* exploded 95 percent of the time and the nonblue *C* only 1 percent. Then we would have to start taking very seriously the hypothesis that the blueness of blue *C* does play a role in its explosiveness, even if we found it puzzling how that could be. Some philosophers, apparently, find themselves in a comparable situation concerning the causal relevance of the mental.

26. For one possible account of recruitment, see Dretske 1988.

27. Instructive discussions of strict and nonstrict laws include Davidson 1980, pp. 219–23, 230–31, 240–41, 250; Davidson 1992; and McLaughlin 1985.

28. On proximal intentions and their role in the etiology of action, see ch. 10.

3

Wanting and Wanting Most

Wanting or desiring has traditionally occupied a central role in explanations of intentional action. Obviously, we do not do—or even try to do—everything that we want to do. Sometimes an agent's wants compete. When that happens, the "strongest" wants prevail—or so it is standardly claimed.

Two decades ago, Donald Davidson offered the following formulation of a principle relating wanting to acting that seemed to him "self-evident":

> *P1.* If an agent wants to do x more than he wants to do y and he believes himself free to do either x or y, then he will intentionally do x if he does either x or y intentionally. (1970; 1980, p. 23)[1]

Something like *P1* is central to a distinguished tradition according to which intentional attitudes (beliefs, desires, intentions, and the like) figure importantly in causal explanations of action, one that continues to have a powerful influence on the philosophical and psychological literature on intentional behavior.[2] However, for reasons that emerge in section 2, *P1* is false. My primary aim in this chapter is to develop a successful alternative formulation of the principle that *P1* was designed to capture.

The burden of this chapter is not merely to introduce precision where it was wanting but also to display more fully than has been done the bearing of desire upon action. There are, in the literature on desire, objections to the very project that I shall be undertaking. For the most part, discussion of those objections will be reserved for chapter 4. Often, ground-level objections are most profitably assessed after the details of the view under attack are in place.

1. Wanting

A familiar attempt to falsify *P1* and close relatives misses the mark. It is sometimes suggested that our intentional behavior is occasionally at odds with what we want most to do, because we are occasionally moved to act not by our wants but rather by such items as our moral judgments. However, someone who is moved to A by a judgment is plainly *motivated by* the judgment, in which case the judgment has a motivational dimension. In a suitably broad, Davidsonian sense of 'want', an agent who is moved by a judgment is moved by a want. As I shall provisionally use the verb 'want', to want to A is to have some motivation to A, the content of which features a representation of the agent's (current or prospective) A-ing.[3] I shall use the noun 'want' in a correspondingly broad sense. Distinctions that are blurred by this usage can be recaptured by differentiating among types of wants or desires—for example, appetitive versus nonappetitive wants, egoistic versus altruistic wants, affective versus nonaffective wants. I shall use 'want' and 'desire' interchangeably.

Two common distinctions merit mention. The first is a distinction between *occurrent* and *latent,* or *standing,* wants.[4] Angela, when she entered college, decided to do her best to graduate with honors. Graduating with honors has now been a high priority of hers for three years. Consequently, we might quite happily say that 'She wants to graduate with honors' is true of Angela even at times at which so graduating is the furthest thing from her mind—for example, while she is wholly absorbed in a conversation about saving the whales or dreamlessly sleeping. At such times, Angela lacks an occurrent desire or want to graduate with honors. Presumably, however, given what might be termed her *standing* want to graduate with honors (following Goldman 1970, pp. 86–88), she is disposed to have occurrent wants for that goal under a range of conditions. Indeed, her standing want is plausibly treated as being just such a disposition. If, as seems clear, the route from dispositions of that kind to intentional A-ings includes occurrent wants manifesting those dispositions, *P1* is most charitably construed as a principle linking *occurrent* wants to intentional actions. In what follows, 'want' and 'desire' should be read uniformly in the occurrent sense.

The well-worn expression 'occurrent want' is misleading. Occurrent wants are not occurrences (i.e., events). They are states. Acquiring or forming an occurrent want is an event; but that is another matter. Occurrent wants differ from their counterpart dispositional states, "standing wants," in that the latter are dispositions to acquire the former. Not all occurrent wants, incidentally, need be wants that we *consciously* possess. Jill might have spoken as she did partly because she wanted (occurrently) to hurt Jack's feelings, even though she was not at all conscious of wanting to do that. If common sense and clinicians can be trusted, the desires that move us to act sometimes include desires not present to consciousness at the time. The occurrent/nonoccurrent distinction, then, is not a conscious/nonconscious distinction. Indeed, we are conscious of some of our standing wants. Stanley is disposed to want (occurrently) to smoke when he sees others smoke. While reading a newspaper article on smokers' habits, it occurs to him that he is so disposed; he is conscious of being so disposed. But he has at the time no relevant occurrent want.

The second distinction is between *intrinsic* and *extrinsic* desires.[5] When we want something—for example, to do A or to possess B—we may want it either for its own sake (i.e., intrinsically) or for its believed conduciveness to something else that is wanted (i.e., extrinsically). Some desires, incidentally, are *mixed* in this regard: Jill might desire to play tennis now both for its own sake (as an *end,* we might say) and for the sake of her health. Desires of each kind are relevant to our intentional behavior. Having an intrinsic (or a mixed) desire to entertain this evening a good friend whom he has not seen for years, Irwin might form or acquire a variety of extrinsic desires for actions that he believes would promote his achieving the goal. Less happily, wanting to be rid of his excruciating toothache, Jack might form or acquire a desire to schedule and undergo a root canal. If all goes well for Irwin and Jack, their desires will be satisfied; and the satisfaction of these desires will be due in part to the effects of the desires upon the agents' behavior.

It is commonly, but not universally, granted that an agent can have a desire to A while also desiring more to do something, B, that he recognizes to be incompatible with his A-ing. Thus, it seems, Paul may now have a desire to play tennis with Peter at five o'clock this evening even though Paul wants more to rest his swollen ankle all day. Frank Jackson (1985) finds this suggestion unacceptable. Suppose that Paul deliberated about the issue. According to Jackson, he "was deliberating about what [he] *wanted* to do" (p. 106, my italics); and what he wanted to do, as it turned out, was to rest his ankle, not to play tennis. Someone might, Jackson mentions, try to make out a distinction between types of wants that permits an agent to have wants of one type ("type 1") that he knows cannot be jointly satisfied, while precluding this happening in the case of wants of the other type ("type 2"). But, Jackson asks, in virtue of what would type 1 wants ever count as *conflicting* with one another? "That there was a conflict" between two type 1 wants, he says, "would be transparent" if the agent's having either were incompatible with his having the other; "but the view in question is precisely that this is not the case" (p. 108). Jackson insists, moreover, that "it is type 2 . . . wants that are meet for fulfilling and satisfying" (and, presumably, *not* type 1 wants).

Jackson's contentions are problematic on several counts. First, many instances of deliberation are less "about" what one *wants* to do than about what *to* do (see ch. 12). That, on the basis of deliberation about what to do, Paul decided to refrain from playing tennis in order to rest his ankle does not itself imply that he had at that time no desire to play tennis. Further, even if Paul's deliberation were, in some sense, about what he wanted to do, why not suppose that it was specifically about what he *wanted most* to do? His concluding (truly) that he wants most to rest his ankle all day in no way obviously precludes his having a want to play tennis (while recognizing that he cannot both play tennis and rest his ankle all day).

To illustrate a further problem, we shall need some *interpretation* or other of a distinction between type 1 and type 2 wants. Let us say that an agent has, at t, a want of type 2 to A at t^* if and only if, at t, he wants to A at t^* more than he wants to do anything that he takes to be incompatible with his A-ing at t^*. (Three minor points: [1] The analysans is satisfied by default when the want to A is the only relevant want possessed at the time; [2] t and t^* need not be different times; [3] 'at' may be read as 'at, during, or throughout'.)[6] Let us say, as well, that an agent has, at t, a want of type 1 to A at t^* if and only if he has, at t, a want to A at t^*, a want that may or may not also be a type 2 want. If it is supposed that at some point Paul has a desire to play tennis with Peter at five o'clock and a desire to rest his ankle all day, realizing full well that he cannot do both, in virtue of what can these desires or wants conflict? An obvious and familiar answer is that they conflict precisely in the sense that they are not jointly satisfiable. This is a *practical* conflict, a conflict that can have undeniable practical significance.

Finally, it is false that only type 2 wants are "meet for fulfilling and satisfying." Since all type 2 wants, on the present interpretation, are type 1 wants, any satisfied type 2 want is a satisfied type 1 want. Additionally, type 1 wants that are not also type 2 wants are satisfiable. In refraining from playing tennis, Paul might satisfy his (mere) type 1 want, say, to honor his wife's request that he not play tennis today. Even if the desire to honor the request provides little incentive to refrain from playing, it is satisfied by Paul's not playing.

The preceding distinction between type 1 and type 2 wants or desires points up a possible source of confusion. In saying that someone wants to *A,* we occasionally mean, I suppose, that he *preponderantly* wants to *A* (roughly, that he wants to *A* more than he wants to do anything that he takes to be incompatible with his *A*-ing). Sometimes we mean only that he has a desire, preponderant or otherwise, to *A.* If nothing counted as a want unless it were a preponderant want, no individual would ever knowingly have conflicting wants (in the sense of 'conflicting' adumbrated).

Several further observations about wanting are in order. First, 'wants' in '*S* wants to *A*' creates an opaque context; and *P1* and its ilk rely upon this opacity. Suppose that Oedipus wants to marry Jocasta more than he wants to remain in Thebes and that he believes himself free to do either (in fact, both). *P1* entails that Oedipus will intentionally marry Jocasta if he either intentionally marries her or intentionally remains in Thebes. If 'wants' did not create an opaque context in '*S* wants to *A*', we could infer from the information in hand about Oedipus' wants and what we know about Jocasta that Oedipus wants to marry his mother more than he wants to remain in Thebes. And from this in conjunction with *P1* it follows that Oedipus will intentionally marry his mother if he either intentionally marries his mother or intentionally remains in Thebes. Since Oedipus does intentionally remain in Thebes, the upshot is that he intentionally marries his mother—which is false! Though Oedipus intentionally marries Jocasta, he marries his mother quite unwittingly.

Second, '*S* wants to *A*' and '*S* wants to *B*' do not jointly entail that *S* wants to *A* and *B*. Wanting is not agglomerative in this way. I want to go to the midnight movie and I want to go to the midnight concert. But although I want to do each, I do not want to do *both*.

Even when an agent is acting simultaneously on a want to *A* and a want to *B*, he need not want to do *A and B*—that is, he need have no want whose content features a representation of his *A*-ing *and B*-ing. *S* may want now to be walking home now and want now to be thinking about his next lecture now without also wanting now to be doing *both* now. The two wants may each function separately. I see no reason to suppose that in the case at hand, *S* must have a further want aimed at the conjunction of his thinking about his next lecture and his walking home. (This observation raises a difficulty addressed in section 4.)

Finally, 'wants . . . more' in *P1* should be given an explicitly motivational reading. A number of philosophers have distinguished between an evaluative and a motivational interpretation of 'wants more'. As Gary Watson puts the point, "In the [evaluative] sense, if one wants to do *x* more than one wants to do *y*, one . . . ranks *x* higher than *y* on some scale of values or 'desirability matrix'. In the [motivational] sense, if one wants to do x more than y one is more strongly motivated to do x than to do y" (1977, pp. 320–21). If evaluation and motivational strength are always in perfect alignment, the distinction may be of little practical significance. But if they sometimes come apart, it is the *motivational strength* of our wants that has the tighter grip upon action.[7] However the notion of motivational strength is to be cashed, the currency can crudely be identified as action-causing power.

2. Problems for *P1*

At the risk of seeming pedantic, I open this section with a collection of very simple counterexamples to Davidson's *P1*. My aim in raising the objections advanced here is to identify some desiderata for a successful formulation of the underlying principle. An additional desideratum will emerge in section 4.

CASE 1. Barney wants to fly to New Orleans more than he wants to fly to Miami. Fortunately, he can do both. He intends to fly to Miami and then, after a week's time, fly to New Orleans, since this is the least expensive way to fly to both cities. However, Barney's flight to Miami is so traumatic that he never flies again. Although he wanted to fly to New Orleans more than he wanted to fly to Miami, Barney intentionally flew to Miami and did not fly to New Orleans. Hence *P1* is false.

This counterexample may easily be circumvented by adding appropriate temporal indices to *P1*. (Notice that there are two temporal indices for wants. There is the time at which a want is present and the time—however indefinite it may be—at which a want aims. We want at, or during, or throughout t to A at, or during, or throughout t^*, where t^* may or may not be identical with t.) Though Barney wants to fly to New Orleans more than he wants to fly to Miami, he presumably wants to fly to Miami *first* more than he wants to fly to New Orleans first. Or, more pertinently, at the time at which he sets out for Miami, he presumably wants to fly there *then* more than he wants to fly to New Orleans then. And apparently, once Barney is traumatized, he wants not to fly to New Orleans more than he wants to fly there.

Other counterexamples to *P1* raise problems that the addition of temporal indices cannot resolve.

CASE 2. Tom wants to anger Jerry even more than he wants to insult him and decides to anger Jerry *by* insulting him. Tom intentionally insults Jerry, but he does not intentionally anger him; for, as it happens, Jerry is not angered by the insult. Here Tom acts intentionally at *t;* but although he wanted to anger Jerry more than he wanted to insult him and believed himself free to do either (indeed, both), he intentionally did the latter without also intentionally doing the former. Here again we see that *P1* is false.

CASE 3. Tom wants to anger Jerry *while also* insulting him more than he wants to perform either of the conjuncts. At midnight, Tom intends to insult Jerry then by making a derogatory remark about Jerry's attire and to anger him then by smashing Jerry's favorite vase. Tom insults Jerry in the intended way; but his attempt to smash the vase is unsuccessful, and Jerry is not angered. So what Tom intentionally did at midnight was something that he wanted to do *less* than he wanted to do something else that he believed himself free to do. *P1* is false.

Cases 2 and 3 trade upon the obvious truth that attempts are sometimes unsuccessful. We shall see shortly that they are easily accommodated by a revised version of *P1*. Another problem with *P1* is more revealing.

CASE 4. Fred wants to juggle four balls more than he wants to juggle three balls, but he also wants to juggle three balls and balance a carrot on his nose more than he wants to juggle four balls. (He believes that he cannot balance the carrot while juggling four balls.) Although he wants more to juggle four balls than three and believes himself free to do either, he intentionally juggles three balls (and he intentionally balances a carrot on his nose), but he does not juggle four balls. Hence, *P1* is false.

The success of case 4 as a counterexample derives from *P1*'s particular comparative form. Someone who wants to *A* more than he wants to *B* might want to *B and C* more than he wants to *A;* and he may consequently *B* intentionally (and *C* intentionally) rather than *A*. Of course, since the agent wants to do the compound action *B* and *C* more than he wants to do *A* and believes himself free to do either, *P1* implies that he will intentionally do *B* and *C* if he does either *B* and *C* or *A* intentionally. But it also implies that he will intentionally do *A* if he does either *A* or *B* intentionally. Suppose that the agent does *B* intentionally (and *C* intentionally). Then *P1* implies that he does *A* intentionally. Thus, on the supposition that the agent cannot do both *A* and *B, P1* yields an impossibility. At bottom, *P1* is incoherent.

Some readers may wonder whether Case 4 itself and the schematic description of the problem that it poses for *P1* are coherent. Consider an analogous case in which an agent ranks various options on an evaluative scale. On a certain aesthetic scale, Barney gives his juggling four balls now a 4, his juggling three balls now a 3, and his juggling three balls while balancing a carrot on his nose now a 9. This is obviously a coherent assignment of values. Moreover, it is possible that Barney's desires for these actions accord with his aesthetic assessment of them. Hence, it is possible that Barney's desires for these various actions stack up in just the way that I have supposed Fred's do, in which case the collection of wants attributed to Fred is a coherent one.

CASE 5. At time *t*, Gil wants to smoke (starting then) more than he wants to jog (starting then) and he wants to jog (starting then) more than he wants to grade papers (starting then). Further, he believes himself free to perform each of the actions at issue. *P1* tells us (1) that Gil smokes intentionally if he either smokes or jogs intentionally and (2) that he jogs intentionally if he either jogs or grades papers intentionally. Predictably, Gil starts smoking at *t*. And because he would not dream of jogging while smoking, he does not also start jogging when he starts smoking. However, simultaneously with his starting to smoke, Gil starts grading papers as well (intentionally, of course). Hence, statement 2 is false. *P1* gives us the right result in one application and an incorrect result in another.

Case 5, like case 4, points to a problem with *P1*'s comparative form. Unlike case 4, however, this one does not feature a conjunctive want. There is no need to suppose that Gil has a want whose object is his smoking *and* grading. We may suppose instead that given how the three wants stack up and that Gil is ill disposed toward jogging while smoking, his additional behavior is independently driven by the third desire in the hierarchy. (I shall return to this suggestion in section 4.)

CASE 6. Psychologist Icek Ajzen has claimed that whenever an agent contemplates the possibility of his making an *unsuccessful* attempt to *A*, "the attitude toward trying [to *A*] will be determined not only by the attitude toward (successful) performance of the behavior [i.e., *A*-ing] but also by the attitude toward a failed attempt" (1985, p. 31). One need not endorse the claim in its full generality to glean from it a problem for *P1*. Consider Wally. Wishing to make a good impression on his friends, he wants to bench-press two-hundred pounds more than he wants not to do this. (He wants, I shall say, to "*A*" more than he wants to "*B*".) Wally knows that he has succeeded in about half of his attempts to bench-press two-hundred pounds; and he believes that the probability of his accomplishing the lift, if he makes the attempt, is about .5. If Wally can properly be said to possess the pertinent 'freedom' belief, *P1* implies that he will intentionally *A* if he either *A*-s or *B*-s intentionally. However, even though he wants to lift the weight more than he wants not to lift it, he may, owing partly to his aversion to making an unsuccessful attempt, want not to *try* to lift the weight more than he wants to try to lift it. In that event, it seems, he will intentionally not lift the weight—since, assuming the pertinent 'freedom' belief, he will intentionally refrain from trying to lift it. (We can safely ignore the remote possibility that while intentionally not trying to lift the weight, Wally somehow manages to lift it—presumably nonintentionally.) And this is incompatible with *P1*'s implication that Wally will intentionally lift the weight, if he either intentionally lifts the weight or intentionally does not lift it.

CASE 7. Sam, who has only one dollar with him, is considering buying a lottery ticket. To simplify exposition, I shall suppose that the lottery is an *instant* lottery: the winning tickets, concealed in a machine with the others, are marked 'winner'. Two prizes are available, a million dollars and a hundred dollars; and Sam knows that he has a one-in-two-million chance of winning the former prize and a one-in-a-hundred chance of winning the latter prize. Sam understandably wants to win a million dollars more than he wants to win a hundred dollars then; and he takes himself to be free to do either. Suppose (1) that Sam, a good Bayesian, wants to buy a one-in-a-hundred chance at the hundred-dollar prize more than he wants to buy a one-in-two-million chance at the million-dollar prize. Add (2) that Sam wants to win a million dollars then more than he wants to purchase the chance at a hundred dollars then. What result does *P1* yield, assuming that Sam takes himself to be free to do these things? Given supposition 1, *P1* implies (3) that Sam will intentionally purchase a chance at a hundred dollars if he either buys this chance or buys a chance at a million dollars intentionally. Given supposition 2, *P1* implies (4) that Sam will intentionally win a million dollars if he either wins a million dollars or buys a chance at a hundred dollars intentionally. Now assume (a) that Sam purchases a chance for one and only one of the prizes and (b) that he wins a million dollars only if he intentionally buys a chance at that prize. Assumption (a) in conjunction with supposition 3 implies (5) that Sam intentionally buys a chance at a hundred dollars. But suppositions 4 and 5 imply (6) that Sam intentionally wins a million dollars. And the assumptions, conjoined with supposition 5, imply (7) that Sam does not intentionally win a million dollars. So Sam intentionally wins a million dollars, and he does not intentionally win a million dollars. Something has gone wrong.

It is perhaps tempting to suggest that winning a million dollars in a fair lottery is not something that can be done intentionally and that this example consequently does not falsify *P1,* on a *charitable* reading of the principle. *P1,* one might claim, is *meant* to apply only to actions that can be intentionally performed and to wants for such actions. Thus, for example, it might be suggested that *P1* is not intended to apply to such pairs as buying a one-dollar chance at a hundred dollars (which can be done intentionally) and winning a million dollars in a fair lottery (which cannot). Consequently, one might contend, the example and the problem that it generates are irrelevant to *P1.*

This does not provide a perfectly general resolution of the difficulty, however, since cases can be constructed that have the same problematic structure and involve only alternatives that can be performed intentionally. Here is a case in point: Sue, who is well aware of her 60 percent success rate from the basketball free throw line and her 90 percent success rate on lay-ups, has promised to participate in a shooting game in which one must buy either a $160 ticket to win $100 for sinking a free throw or a $9 ticket to win $1 for sinking a lay-up. (The price of the ticket is refunded to winners.) For reasons that need not concern us, Sue (1) wants to win $100 then more than she wants to win $1 then, (2) wants to buy a $9 chance at the $1 prize then more than she wants to buy a $160 chance at the $100 prize then, and (3) wants to win $100 then more than she wants to buy a $9 chance at the $1 prize then. And she possesses the pertinent 'freedom' beliefs.

I should remind the reader, additionally, that my aim in this section is to identify desiderata for a satisfactory successor to *P1.* Not only does case 7 falsify the principle as formulated but it poses an important problem to be surmounted.

Cases 1–5 identify three problematic features of *P1:* the absence of temporal indices, the strength of its consequent vis-à-vis failed attempts, and its particular comparative form. Diagnosing the flaws in *P1* that open the principle to the objections raised by cases 6 and 7 is more difficult. Since my aim in this section is more diagnostic than critical, the cases merit further attention. Locating the sources of *P1*'s failures will promote our prospects of finding a successful replacement for the principle. I shall reserve further comment on case 6 for section 3 and turn directly to case 7.

Can the lottery counterexample be circumvented by adding suitable temporal indices to *P1*? Given a properly indexed version of *P1*, the only wants of Sam's that are relevant are wants for actions that he believes himself free to perform at the time. Thus, for example, that Sam wants at *t* to win a million dollars sometime in his life is relevant to a temporally modified *P1* as it applies to what Sam will do at *t* only insofar as Sam takes himself to be free at the time to win a million dollars then. Even then, if, although Sam wants to win a million dollars sometime or another, he has (at *t*) no desire to win a million dollars *then,* the former want will be irrelevant. Now, one cannot, at *t,* want to *A* then more than one wants to *B* then and want to *B* then more than one wants to *A* then. (One can want certain features of a prospective *A*-ing more than one wants certain features of a prospective *B*-ing while also wanting various features of the latter more than one wants comparable features of the former; but that is another matter.) And in case 7, Sam wants to purchase a one-in-a-hundred chance at a hundred dollars more than he wants to purchase a one-in-two-million chance at a million dollars. So if, given what he knows, Sam's wanting at *t* to win a million dollars then more than he wants at *t* to buy a one-in-a-hundred chance at a hundred dollars then ensures that at *t,* he wants to buy a one-in-two-million chance at a million dollars then more than he wants to buy a one-in-a-hundred chance at a hundred dollars then, the first two wants mentioned in the antecedent cannot, consistently with the details of the case, stack up in the envisaged way. In short, the case would be internally inconsistent.

Is the specified result ensured, however? Given what he knows, can Sam want at *t* to win a million dollars then more than he wants at *t* to buy a one-in-a-hundred chance at a hundred dollars then and yet not want at *t* to buy a one-in-two-million chance at one million dollars then more than he wants to buy a one-in-a-hundred chance at a hundred dollars then? Perhaps Sam's ticket-buying wants turn out as they do because he is a good Bayesian. But even a good Bayesian who knows what Sam knows can also want at the time to win a million dollars then more than he wants to buy a one-in-a-hundred chance at the smaller prize then. After all, buying the latter chance pales by comparison with winning a million dollars. The relative strength of Sam's ticket-buying wants is presumably not explained by his having at *t* a relatively weak desire to win a million dollars then. Rather, we may suppose that in Sam's case the buying wants stack up as they do because of the strength of his desires for the prizes *in conjunction with* the pertinent subjective probabilities. The effect of his subjective probabilities upon him is such, we may suppose, that Sam wants to buy a chance at the hundred-dollar prize more than he wants to buy a chance at the larger prize—even though he wants to win the latter prize much more than he wants to win the former. We can imagine Sam saying, sincerely and truly, "Of course I want to win a million dollars now more than I want to buy a ticket for the hundred-dollar prize now; who wouldn't? But since the odds against my winning the big prize are so great, I want to have a go at the hundred more than I want to try for the million."

We should grant that Sam might want most at the time to win a million dollars then even though he wants to buy the chance at a hundred dollars more than he wants to buy the chance at a million dollars and believes himself free or able to do each. But it does not follow from Sam's being in this condition that he will win a million dollars—or even *try* to win a million—if he performs any of the envisaged actions intentionally at the time. So, obviously, we do not want a principle that would have this consequence. Now, we might search for a principle that can explain the strength of 'means-wants' partly in terms of the strength of 'end-wants' and link both sorts of wants (some directly, others indirectly) to action. But this departs from the spirit of *P1*. That principle is not designed to explain the strength of wants; rather, it is designed merely to link our wants (in virtue of their strength) with our intentional actions. Accounting for want-strength is a task for another principle. (A variety of proposals have been offered in the psychological literature on the determinants of "resultant motivation." Feather 1982 is a useful collection of essays on the topic.)

The fundamental problem with *P1* in the present case is that the principle treats Sam's want to win a million dollars now as being on all fours with his ticket-buying wants—or, more generally, that it treats all wants for present action the same. *P1* permits—indeed requires—what amounts to an illegitimate double counting of wants. As soon as Sam's desire to win a million dollars now does its part in determining how his ticket-buying wants stack up at the time, the former desire has played out its hand with respect to the determination of which sort of ticket Sam will purchase then. To proceed to pit the desire to win a million against the desire to buy a chance at the smaller prize is to count the former desire twice—to reenter it into the competition after the race has been run. *P1* must be modified in such a way as to exclude double counting of this sort.

3. A Partial Remedy

Many of the objections raised in the preceding section can be avoided by reformulating *P1* as follows:

> *P1x.* If, at *t,* an agent takes himself to be able to *A* then and wants to *A* then more than he wants to do anything else that he takes himself to be able to do then, he intentionally *A*-s then, or at least tries to *A* then, provided that he acts intentionally at *t.*

Incorporating temporal indices handles the problem posed by case 1; and in cases 2–5 the agent either does or tries to do what we may suppose he wants most to do. The double counting problem remains, however. Assuming that, in case 7 (or a variant), Sam wants to win a million dollars then more than he wants to do anything else that he takes himself to be able to do then, *P1x* implies that he intentionally wins a million dollars then, or at least tries to do so then, provided that he acts intentionally then. Nevertheless, Sam may understandably forego buying a chance at the million-dollar prize and intentionally purchase a chance at the hundred-dollar prize.

The problem here actually runs deeper than the label 'double counting' suggests. Suppose that in a variant of the case, Sam is psychologically so constituted that whenever the subjective probability of achieving a desired monetary goal is less than .000001, he has no desire whatever to take what he deems to be necessary means and that Sam's desire to win the million-dollar prize in no way prompts (or enhances the strength of) a desire to buy a chance at the prize. Still (this time in the absence of *double* counting) Sam desires to win a million dollars then more than he desires to buy a one-in-a-hundred chance at the hundred-dollar prize then. Assuming that among the things that he takes himself to be able to do then, there is nothing that Sam wants to do more than (or as much as) he wants to win a million dollars then (and that he takes himself to be able to win it), *P1x* implies that he will win the million then, or at least try to do so, if he does anything intentionally at the time. And, again, we may safely suppose that the implicate is false in this case.

P1x must be augmented not merely to block double counting but also, and more fundamentally, to exclude instances of wanting more (or most) of the "wrong" sort. Now, what sort is that?

Here the notion of the *positive motivational base* of a desire, which I introduced elsewhere for another purpose (Mele 1987a), will prove useful. "The *positive motivational base* of a desire," as I defined the notion, "is the collection of all occurrent motivations of the agent that make a positive contribution to the motivational strength of that desire" (p. 67). For example, when Peter lit a cigarette a few minutes ago, his desire to do so presumably had a desire to smoke in its positive motivational base. And when Bob subsequently left the room, the positive motivational base of his desire to leave (I surmised) included a desire to avoid breathing Peter's smoke. As I observed, for clarificatory purposes:

> Not every occurrent motivation that figures in the causation of a particular desire is in the positive motivational base of that desire. For example, in the course of deliberation undertaken with a view to the achievement of a desired end, E, S may discover that his doing A is a necessary condition of his achieving E, and he may consequently desire to do A. This latter desire may prompt a bit of deliberation about how best to put himself in a position to do A, resulting in a desire to perform some basic action, B. In such a case, S's desire to do A may be a causal antecedent of his desire to do B without making a positive contribution to the *strength* of S's desire to do B; for the strength of the latter desire may be wholly derivative from the strength of S's desire for E. Conversely, an occurrent motivation may be in the positive motivational base of a desire without contributing causally to the formation or retention of that desire. Suppose that having already acquired the desire to do B, S discovers that B-ing will contribute to the satisfaction of his desire for C. If this strengthens his desire to do B, his desire for C will be in the positive motivational base of the former desire. And not only is the latter desire not a cause of the formation of the former, it need not even causally *sustain* S's desire to do B. S's continuing to desire to do B may be causally independent of his desire for C. (p. 67; see pp. 67–69 for the *negative* and *total* motivational bases of a desire)

Consider a desire D that an agent S has at a time t to A then. Suppose that as things stand at the time, D's capacity to issue in an intentional A-ing or an attempt to A then is contingent upon D's being in the positive motivational base of a distinct desire of S's to do something, B, then that S takes to be conducive to his A-ing. Desires such as D may be termed *buffered* desires. From the facts (1) that in a case of the sort at hand, some agent wants to do A more than he wants to do anything else that he takes himself to be able to do then and (2) that the agent acts intentionally at the time, it does not follow that he intentionally does or tries to do A. This is a moral of the lottery case: although Sam wants to win a million dollars more than he wants to do anything else that he takes to be open to him at the time and although he acts intentionally, he does not win—or even try to win—the million. The point is not, of course, that buffered desires to A (e.g., Sam's desire to win the million dollars) can play no role in the production of an intentional A-ing (or of an attempt to A). Rather, their playing a role is dependent upon their contributing to other desires, or, more specifically, upon their being in the positive motivational base of other desires—desires with a tighter potential grip upon action.

Buffered desires need not all be simple or nonconjunctive. Suppose that Sam, in case 7, has a conjunctive desire to buy a chance at the million-dollar prize *and* win that prize. (In that event, Sam presumably wants to buy the chance *and* win the prize more than he wants to buy the chance.) Now, if the capacity of Sam's conjunctive desire to issue in an intentional buying and winning (or an attempt at that) is contingent on the desire's being in the positive motivational base of a distinct desire of Sam's to do something then that he takes to be conducive to his performing the conjunctive deed—most plausibly, his buying a chance at the million-dollar prize—the conjunctive desire is a buffered desire. (What is true of this conjunctive desire would be true as well, other things being equal, of a conjunctive desire of Sam's to win the million dollars *by* purchasing a chance at it.)

Let us say that a desire D that an agent S has at t to do an A then is a *nonbuffered* desire—or, less distractingly perhaps, a *buffer-free* desire— if and only if it is *false* that as things stand at the time, D's capacity to issue in an intentional A-ing or an attempt to A then is contingent upon D's being in the positive motivational base of a distinct desire of S's to do something then that S takes to be conducive to his A-ing. Buffered desires are relevant to intentional behavior insofar as they can enter into the positive motivational bases of other desires. Buffer-free desires have a more direct relevance. A principle relating only agents' strongest *buffer-free* desires to intentional action (buffered desires being treated as having only the indirect relevance just marked) will avoid double counting and related problems.

P1x may now be reformulated as follows:

> *P1a.* If, at t, an agent takes himself to be able to A then and wants to A then more than he wants to do anything else that he takes himself to be able to do then—where the wants at issue are buffer-free wants—he intentionally A-s then, or at least tries to A then, provided that he acts intentionally at t.

P1a does not divorce buffered wants from action. The proponent of *P1a* may quite happily grant that buffered wants (in conjunction with subjective probabilities) have a role to play in generating buffer-free wants and in determining their strength. To be sure, one would like to understand how buffered wants fill this role. Again, however, it is not a function of Davidson's *P1* to account for the bearing of wants upon wants; rather, *P1* is designed to link wanting to acting. And *P1a* is offered for the same purpose.

I promised in section 2 to render a diagnosis of the problem with *P1* exploited by case 6, the weight lifter example. Although for many powerful folks in a wide range of situations—and Wally on some occasions—the desire to bench-press two-hundred pounds need not be accompanied by a distinct desire to *try* to lift the weight in order for an attempt (successful or otherwise) to ensue, Wally's situation requires such a desire, if he is intentionally to lift the weight. Wally's desire to lift the weight, given the details of the case, is a *buffered* desire. The problem with *P1* identified in the discussion of case 7 emerges in case 6 as well. Incidentally, given that Wally wants not to try to lift the weight more than he wants to try to lift it (and supposing that these are the only pertinent buffer-free wants that he has at the time), the implication of *P1a* is clear.

A point just made is worth emphasizing. Desires to *A,* where *A* is not a *trying* to do something, need not always be accompanied by a desire to *try* to *A* in order to result in an intentional *A*-ing. Generally, if we are not entertaining doubts about the prospects of our succeeding in *A*-ing (*A* being something that we want to do), we have no desire specifically to try to *A.* Thus, not all buffer-free desires are desires to *try* to do something.

I should mention as well that although buffer-free wants often have other wants in their positive motivational bases, this is not always the case. In the preceding example, Wally's reasons for trying to lift the weight incorporate desires (e.g., his desire to impress his friends by lifting the weight) that are in the positive motivational base of his buffer-free desire to try to lift it. Many buffer-free desires to *A* are similarly related to the agent's reasons for *A*-ing and to desires encompassed by those reasons.[8] But one can easily imagine situations in which a buffer-free want has no distinct wants in its positive motivational base. Someone's *wholly intrinsic* desire, in a carefree moment, to whistle a tune is an obvious case in point, if he has no other desires at the moment. (The positive motivational base of any intrinsic desire is, we may say, at least partly internal to the desire itself; see Mele 1987a, p. 68.)

I turn now to a modification common to *P1x* and *P1a.* The reader will notice that I have substituted 'takes himself to be able' for *P1*'s 'believes himself free'. The substitution is motivated by considerations of clarity. In particular, the meaning of 'free' in 'believes himself free' is by no means obvious; and 'believes' in the same expression may or may not be understood to include *tacit* belief. Now, the supposition that whenever we *A* intentionally we occurrently believe that we are able to *A* is psychologically unrealistic. Often, when we intentionally perform an action *A*, nothing prompts the occurrent thought we are able to *A*: the issue simply does not arise. I have been intentionally typing this section for some time now; but I acquired the occurrent belief that this is something that I am able to do only a couple of minutes ago, when a philosophical question prompted a thought about my ability to do what I was doing. It is not as though I made a remarkable *discovery,* of course. I knew all along, we might loosely say, that I was able to type this section. But, it seems, I had no occurrent belief to that effect until just recently. As I shall understand the expression, at a particular time *t* an agent "takes himself to be able" to *A* then if and only if, at *t,* he both possesses a representation of his (current or prospective) *A*-ing then and does not believe that he cannot (owing to external or internal circumstances or both) *A* then. Since this account of taking oneself to be able does not require that the agent *occurrently assent* to a proposition to the effect that he is able to *A* at *t, taking* oneself, at *t,* to be able to *A* then is weaker than *believing* oneself, at *t,* to be able to *A* then—on one common construal of belief.[9] (For an account of ability, see ch. 5.)

I conclude this section with a brief commentary on trying. Typically, someone who wants to try to *A* wants also to *A*. Alleged exceptions that I have encountered are unconvincing. Here are two representative examples. Little Johnny tries to throw a ball over his father's head as a means of getting the ball to his father, without wanting at all to throw the ball beyond his father. Sally tries to shatter her shatterproof gizmo in order to prove to a friend that the gizmo is shatterproof; she is not desirous in the least of shattering it. Both agents, it is alleged, want to *try* to perform the actions in question.

Given their respective purposes, however, Johnny and Sally are implausibly regarded as trying to do the deeds mentioned. Rather, it seems, Johnny, in an attempt to get the ball to his father, is behaving as he would behave if he *were* trying to throw it over his father's head, and Sally is acting as she would (or might) act if she *were* trying to shatter the gizmo (cf. McCann 1986b, p. 211, n. 20; Wilson 1989, pp. 152–53). And if they are not trying to perform the deeds at issue, there is no reason to suppose that they *want* to try to perform them.

More promising instances of trying to *A* without at all wanting to *A* are imaginable. Suppose that Brett promises to pay Belton fifty dollars if Belton tries to solve a certain chess problem within five minutes. It is a mate-in-two problem, a kind of problem that Belton has found very difficult; and Belton thinks it very unlikely that he will solve it. He thinks it particularly unlikely because the problem is a picture puzzle on a page of a chess book, and Belton has no movable chess pieces with which to experiment: He must do it all in his head. Brett assures Belton that he need not actually solve the problem; but he insists that Belton must *try* to solve it (in five minutes time) and not just pretend to be trying. To forestall the objection that Belton will want to solve the problem because only his discovering the solution can guarantee that Brett will deem him to have tried, let us suppose that Belton is convinced that Brett is psychic (or omniscient) and can tell whether he has tried, independently of Belton's succeeding. Now, if and when Belton does try to solve the problem, there is a sense in which his mental activity is directed toward discovering the solution, the way to achieve checkmate in two moves. Belton's consideration of various possible moves must be guided by the thought of bringing a piece into a mating position. His consideration of chess moves will be organized around mating the king. In some sense, then, mating the king—which *is* solving the puzzle (provided it is accomplished in two moves)—is a *goal* in Belton's thinking about chess moves when he is trying to solve the problem. Still, I see no need to suppose that this goal must be *desired* (or wanted; again, I make no distinction) by Belton. Perhaps he is indifferent to his actually mating the king. Nevertheless, wanting the fifty dollars, he wants to *try* to solve the puzzle; and he may act on that want.

The content of Belton's desire to try to solve the puzzle approximates that of a desire to solve the puzzle; but it is such that the desire (not necessarily Belton) would be satisfied by an attempt—successful or not—to solve the puzzle, whereas the satisfaction of a hypothetical desire to solve the puzzle would require the agent's actually solving it. One might object that desires to try to *A*—genuinely to try and not just to pretend to try—are functionally indistinguishable from desires to *A* and, consequently, that there can be no mere desires to try to *A*. But setting the inference aside, the *premise* is disputable. Arguably, a functional feature of a range of desires is that partly in virtue of a particular desire's presence, the agent is disposed to experience satisfaction when the desire itself is satisfied (i.e., when what is desired is achieved). Desires to try to *A* can fill this role in situations in which desires to *A* would not. The example of Belton is a case in point if he fails to solve the problem.[10]

Fortunately, *P1a* is not undermined by the possibility of someone's wanting to try to *A* without also wanting to *A*. Notice that *P1a* does not imply that if *S* tries to *A, S* wants more to *try* to *A* than he wants to do anything else that he takes himself to be able to do. That *would* be problematic, since, wanting more to A than he wants to do anything else, S might try and fail to A while wanting more to B than to *try* to A. (Suppose that he has no desire specifically to *try* to A, in which case it is true by default that he wants to B more than he wants to try to A.) *P1a* takes us from motivation to action, not vice versa.

Now, when (suppressing temporal references and supposing that the wants at issue are buffer-free wants) an agent wants to try to A more than he wants to do anything else that he takes himself to be able to do, *P1a* implies that he intentionally tries to A, or at least tries to try to A, provided that he acts intentionally. But this does not commit the onto-logically cautious to the view that there are tryings to try. If there are no "second-order" tryings, the second disjunct of the consequent of *P1a* simply is never instantiated in cases in which what one wants most is to *try* to do something.

4. Competing Wants and Coordination

Consider the following attempted schematic counterexample to *P1a*. At t, S wants to A then more than he wants to B then and wants to A then more than he wants to C then. However, the respective strengths of S's want to B and S's want to C are such that together, they outweigh S's want to A. Furthermore, although S can do *both* B and C then, doing both does not occur to him: he has no representation of his doing both. S takes himself to be able to do any one of A, B, and C; but he neither takes himself to be able to do both B and C nor to be unable to do them. And since doing both B and C does not occur to him, it is not the case that he wants to do both. Thus, by default, S wants to A more than he wants to B and C. And we may suppose that he wants to A more than he wants to do anything else. So *P1a* implies (supposing that all the wants mentioned are buffer-free ones) that S will intentionally A at t, or at least try to A then, if he intentionally does anything at the time. But (or so the critic of *P1a* alleges) this result is unacceptable. Since the collective strength of S's desire to B and S's desire to C is greater than that of his desire to A, he will do (each of) B and C intentionally—or at least try to do them—if he does anything intentionally at the time.

Is this a successful counterexample? It is best to proceed slowly. No-tice first that the strengths of wants are not additive in any simple way. Archie's desire to drink beer now and his desire to eat a hot fudge sundae now may each be stronger than any desire that he has to do *both* now. And the strength of Edith's desire to have cookies and milk now might significantly exceed the sum of the strengths of her desire to drink milk and her desire to eat cookies. Some activities are less attractive together than they are individually, and vice versa.

Still, one might suggest, we can surely imagine that in the case at hand the strengths of S's desire to B and his desire to C together exceed that of his desire to A. But with what is the strength of S's desire to A being compared? If we are comparing it with the strength of some *nonexistent* desire—specifically, a nonexistent desire of S's to do both B and C—we are concerning ourselves with something that cannot influence S's behavior: nonexistent desires have no motivational clout. And surely, we do not want to say that if the strength of S's desire to B plus the strength of his desire to C is greater than the strength of his desire to A, he will intentionally B and intentionally C if he intentionally does any of the actions at issue. For one thing, doing *both* B and C may be relatively motivationally unattractive to him. If one counters by suggesting that we consider a case in which S *would* desire to do B and C more strongly than he desires to do A if only he *had* a desire for the compound action, we are back to square one. Nonexistent desires cannot influence behavior.

Davidson's *P1* and my *P1a* imply that in the case at issue, S will intentionally A (or at least try to A) if he intentionally does (or tries to do) any of A, B, and C. This is a plausible consequence if, to put the point dramatically, desires compete individually with one another for control over intentional behavior. The supposition that competition is individual, however, does not commit one to holding that desires cannot team up, as it were, against other desires. Rather, the point is roughly that the members of a teamed pair of desires defeat an opposing desire that is stronger than each member of the pair, not directly, but via agglomeration: when, desiring to X and desiring to Y, an agent comes to desire to X and Y, the compound desire can defeat an opposing desire to Z even though this last desire is stronger than each of the first two. (Additionally, a teamed pair of desires might, in a sense, defeat a competing desire D by giving rise to a further desire that is stronger than D but is not an agglomeration of the pair—hence, 'roughly'.)

Although *P1a* survives the putative counterexample, it does not apply to the full range of intentional actions. Case 5 illustrates the point, although I did not adduce it specifically for that purpose. Here, I provide another illustration. Suppose that at t Gil wants to smoke a cigar then and that he has at the time a pair of mutually competing wants: he wants to review some page proofs then, and he wants to prepare a lecture then. Suppose, further, that Gil wants to smoke more than he wants to do either of the things just mentioned. If it so happens that Gil wants to smoke *and* do one of the actions at issue more than he wants to smoke and do the other, then, assuming that Gil has no other relevant wants, *P1a* applies straightforwardly to the case. But suppose that Gil has no such compound want. Then, even if he wants to review page proofs more than he wants to prepare a lecture (and has no pertinent wants at the time other than those already mentioned), *P1a* does not imply that he will (try to) do the former. It implies only that he will (try to) smoke (assuming that he takes himself to be able to do so and that he does something intentionally at the time). Still, in addition to smoking, Gil may well intentionally review the page proofs.

This does not show that *P1a* is *false*, of course. But it does indicate that there is room for a more broadly applicable formulation. One suggestion is that *P1a* be augmented by a version of the principle itself that is designed for cases in which, at *t*, in addition to performing or trying to perform the intentional action *A* that he wants most to perform, an agent also performs an independent intentional action. (Again, assume that the wants at issue are buffer-free ones. Henceforth, the reader should understand this assumption to be in place, unless otherwise indicated.) The idea, very roughly, is that if, at *t*, an agent both *A*-s intentionally and performs some independent action intentionally, then, if he wants to *B* more than he wants to do anything else that he takes himself to be able to do at the time—*excluding A* and any actions with which *A* competes—he does or tries to do *B* (and similarly for additional independent intentional actions performed by the agent at the time).

The idea can be stated more formally with the assistance of the following notions: (1) an action *A* is *subjectively open* at *t* for an agent *S* if and only if, at *t*, *S* takes himself to be able to *A* then; (2) *S*'s intentional *A*-ing and *S*'s intentional *B*-ing are *mutually independent actions* if and only if they are not parts of the same intentional action, neither is identical with or part of the other, and neither is performed as a means to the other; (3) *S*'s intentionally *A*-ing at *t competes* with *S*'s intentionally *B*-ing at *t* if and only if either he takes himself to be unable to do both *A* and *B* or his doing either would make his doing the other sufficiently unattractive that he would neither intentionally do nor try to do each.

I offer notion 1 merely to secure a space-saving expression for 'takes himself to be able to. . . .' The second notion serves a more significant purpose. In cases of the sort presently under consideration, an agent is simultaneously embarked upon two or more separate courses of action. The function of notion 2 is to characterize this separateness.

Notion 3 also requires brief comment. Let us add to the earlier case of

Gil a desire at t to jog at t. Suppose that at t Gil wants to smoke then more than he wants to jog then (as in case 5) and that he wants to jog then more than he wants to do either of the academic tasks then. And suppose that, at the time, simultaneously smoking and jogging is not a live option for Gil: his doing either would make his doing the other sufficiently unattractive that he would not do both or even try to do both. But if he were either to read page proofs or prepare a lecture, he would still smoke (and he does not mistakenly take himself to be unable to do either pair). Hence, notion 3 implies that the jogging—but neither of the academic tasks—competes with the smoking.

P1a can now be augmented by means of a principle concerning intentional deeds of S at t that are independent of his A-ing (what he wants most to do) and of his trying to A. (A-ing can, of course, be a conjunctive action—e.g., eating cookies and drinking milk.)

> *P1b.* If, at t, of all actions subjectively open to S at t that do not compete with S's A-ing at t (what S wants most to do) and that are independent of S's A-ing at t, S wants most to B then (where the wants at issue are buffer-free wants), S B-s then, or at least tries to B then, if, at t, in addition to intentionally A-ing or trying to A, S performs an independent intentional action.

The pair, *P1a* + *P1b*, can be similarly augmented to handle additional intentional actions of S at t that are independent of his A-ing, his B-ing, and their conjunction. Indeed, *P1a* is itself applicable to any number of independent intentional actions (including tryings) performed by S at t, provided that in each successive application we do two things: (1) exclude from the relevant domain of subjectively open actions the actions identified in the consequents of the preceding applications and all actions with which they compete and (2) suitably augment, à la *P1b*, the proviso with which *P1a* concludes. Let us call the conjunction of *P1a* and the observation just made *P1**.

Notice that *P1** says nothing about the practical outcome of cases in which there is nothing that the agent wants most, where 'most' is read exclusively. It is to this issue that I now turn.

5. Motivational Ties

Must a rational ass equidistant from two equally attractive bales of hay starve for lack of a reason to prefer one bale to the other?[11] Must a human being who wants *F* neither more nor less than he wants an alternative *G* fail to pursue either option? Surely, one suspects, some practical resolution is possible. Surely, ties of either sort need not result in death or paralysis. But why?

My concern here is with human beings and wanting or motivation, not with asses and reasons. My guiding question in the remainder of this chapter is roughly this: How is intentional behavior possible in instances of motivational ties?

The tighter the connection between motivation and intentional action, the more intriguing our question becomes. Consider again Davidson's *P1*:

> If an agent wants to do *x* more than he wants to do *y* and he believes himself free to do either *x* or *y*, then he will intentionally do *x* if he does either *x* or *y* intentionally.

If an agent realizes that *x* and *y* are mutually exclusive alternatives and he wants to do neither more than the other, he might do something else entirely, of course—something that he wants to do more. But if there is nothing else that he wants more to do, what happens? One might suggest that the agent will at least want to do *either x* or *y* more than he wants to do *neither*: perhaps even though he wants *x* and *y* equally, he has another want, a want to do either, that is stronger than any competitor. But, of course, he cannot just do *either; if he is to do either, he must do one or the other. But which, given that he wants them equally? If he simply *picks* one or adopts some randomizing selection procedure such as tossing a coin and then acts accordingly, must the motivational tie have been dissolved? Or might he intentionally do *x* (or *y*) while still wanting equally strongly to perform the alternative? Might something other than his wanting to do one more than he wants to do the other account for what he does?

Davidson's answer to the last two questions appears to be *no*. He maintains that "only if an agent values one line of action more highly than any alternative does he act intentionally in the present, or harbour intentions for the future" (1985a, p. 200). And, for Davidson, the valuing at issue is to be understood motivationally: "I think of evaluative judgments as conative propositional attitudes" (p. 206). He claims, as well, that when—there being no intrinsic grounds for preference—we resort to extrinsic grounds, such as the result of a coin toss, our "need to choose has caused [us] to prefer the alternative indicated by the toss" (p. 200). Taking 'prefer' to imply 'want more', the claim suggests that for

Davidson, the practical outcome of a motivational tie of the sort at issue depends upon the tie's being broken—upon the agent's coming to want to perform one of the actions more than he wants to perform the other. Is that right?

In this age of mass production, we seem often to be faced with alternatives equivalent in all relevant respects. I see several shirts of the same size, style, and color in the bargain basement or several toothbrushes similarly related; and I buy *one*. But why *that* one? Did I want most to buy *it*? How can that be the case, if I recognized that none of the shirts, or toothbrushes, was any better or worse than the others?

One might suggest that in all such cases the agent judges it best to purchase the item selected and is accordingly most motivated to buy it. However implausible this suggestion may seem, it is worth pursuing if only briefly.

In a well-known paper, psychologists Richard Nisbett and Timothy Wilson report the results of a study in which 52 subjects were invited to evaluate "four identical pairs of nylon stockings" (1977, pp. 243–44).[12] Stockings at the far right of the display were judged superior to "the leftmost by a factor of almost four to one." Here, the position of an item in an array apparently has a marked influence on evaluation; and we properly expect motivational strength to follow suit.

Other things being equal, the individuals who judged the rightmost stockings to be of the highest quality, would buy them, if they were to buy any of the four pairs. But even someone who judged the stockings to be of equal value might, with good reason, purchase the rightmost pair. Nisbett and Wilson speculate that the evaluative favoring of the rightmost stockings may be accounted for by the subjects' carrying "into the judgment task the consumer's habit of 'shopping around', holding off on choice of early-seen garments on the left in favor of later-seen garments on the right" (1977, p. 244). Even a shopper who judges an array of inspected items to be *qualitatively identical,* however, may reasonably want to purchase the last one inspected more than the others, simply because it is at his fingertips. And his buying the one he does might accord with some evaluative principle of his concerning efficiency.[13] This, of course, is why Buridan's ass is placed between two *equidistant* bales of hay.

Let us consider, then, a case in which an agent is equidistant from a pair of items even while he is inspecting them. Suppose that he wants a copy of a certain book and that he spies a pair, each wrapped in cellophane, on a shelf. He picks both up, one in each hand; and he looks at each in turn, starting at the left. If he finds no qualitative differences, what happens next? Well, perhaps he takes the book looked at last to the cashier, owing to something like the aforementioned consumer's habit. And if we can reasonably appeal to habit in this way, we lack here a clear instance of a motivational tie; for, owing to his consumer's habit, the agent may be more motivated to select the book that he did than he would otherwise have been and more motivated to select this one than the alternative.

Does the very *inspection* of the items confront our agent with a motivational tie? Not necessarily. Perhaps he carried into the inspection task his "reader's habit" of starting at the left. And, owing to that habit, he might have been more motivated at the time to start at the left than at the right.

One might think that if we grant habits of the sort in question a role in determining motivational strength, we can achieve a motivational tie by counterbalancing the agent's habit with his giving a slightly higher evaluative rating to the book first viewed. But this presupposes a conception of the operation of the habit that may well be too crude. Perhaps the habit enhances motivation to select the item last inspected only when the agent gives no other item in the array a higher evaluative rating.

It is evident by now that clear instances of motivational ties are not as easy to come by as one might have thought. One source of the problem merits special emphasis. An evaluative tie is not sufficient for a motivational tie. For example, even if our book buyer does not take either copy of the book to be superior to the other, he may be more motivated to buy the one viewed last, owing to the motivational influence of habit. Of course, evaluative ranking of purchasable items is one thing and evaluative ranking of *acts* of purchasing another. For reasons of efficiency, I may judge it better to buy the stockings that I am now holding than to buy the qualitatively identical ones that I saw earlier twenty feet to the left, even though I take the stockings to be equally good. But I see no compelling reason to maintain that our book buyer explicitly judged it best to purchase the book that he did. Wanting more does not entail judging better, as familiar examples of akratic behavior indicate.[14]

6. Practical Resolution of a Motivational Tie

Ironically, relatively clear instances of motivational ties might be easier to find when alternative objects are *not* identical (in the mass production sense). Alan, who wants to see a movie tonight, has narrowed the options to two films scheduled to be shown simultaneously at the same theater complex. He finds the prospect of seeing each equally attractive and, we may suppose, he is no more motivated to see one than the other.

Imagine that Alan decides to drive to the theater this evening and to resolve the issue there by tossing a coin if a look at the movie posters and the like leaves him undecided. Later, while standing in line at the theater, Alan resorts to a coin toss. Setting aside questions about the etiology of Alan's assignments of heads and tails, let us suppose that movie A wins the toss and that Alan purchases a ticket for A.

I have already mentioned Davidson's claim that when, in a situation like Alan's, we resort to a strategy like his, our "need to choose has caused [us] to prefer the alternative indicated by the toss" (1985a, p. 200). Taking 'prefer' to imply 'want more', this suggests that Alan's coin toss, in conjunction with other features of the case, has one or both of the following results: (1) Alan's motivation to see A tonight (or to purchase a ticket for A) increases; (2) Alan's motivation to see B tonight (or to purchase a ticket for B) decreases. Both are genuine possibilities, and a motivational shift may well be a normal feature of cases of the sort at issue. (Probably most agents would want in advance to abide by the result of the toss more than they want not to do so; and this condition may generally be expected to issue in a motivational shift of the kind identified when the agent notes how the coin has landed.) But I shall suggest that there is another possibility as well, a theoretically interesting one that is excluded by Davidson's contention.

Before the further possibility is identified, we would do well to inquire about the grounds for Davidson's claim. The functional connection between wanting and action has at least two dimensions. First, the representational content of an agent's want to A identifies a practical goal (or subgoal), the agent's A-ing, so that "action-wants" provide some practical direction, as it were. Second, wants have an inclinational or conative dimension. They incline agents to act on them. If we suppose (1) that we intentionally A only if we are moved to A; (2) that wants (qua wants) move us to act in virtue of their motivational strength alone (*what* they move us to do, however, depends on their content); and (3) that only wants are capable of moving us to act in the pertinent sense of the term (or, more cautiously, that any motivational state is so only in virtue of its incorporating a want or wants and that a motivational state's capacity to move us to act is encompassed in the capacity of the incorporated want or wants to do so)—then we are well on our way to Davidson's view about the motivational outcome of random selection. For, given these suppositions, if the motivational strength of the pertinent wants were equal in a case like Alan's, there would be nothing to account for his being moved to act by one of the competing wants rather than the other.

Although supposition 1 is certainly in need of elaboration, I shall simply grant it for the sake of argument.[15] Now, supposition 2 is, I think, true of wanting, standardly conceived. And a popular philosophical convention treats 'want' as a blanket term for all motivation. But it may be that when the standard conception and the convention are combined as in supposition 3 something goes awry.

Consider this conjecture. Faced with the motivational tie at issue, Alan selects a coin-tossing procedure for settling what he will do. Having settled upon this procedure (and assignments of heads and tails)[16] and tossed the coin, he forms a purchasing intention in accordance with the result of the toss; and, as it happens in this particular case, he acts on that intention *even though the motivational tie persists*. If, as I shall argue at length in subsequent chapters, the capacity of intentions to move agents to act is not wholly encompassed in the (relative) motivational strength of incorporated wants, the conjecture might be true.

Here is a hypothesis. When a desire to A that one has at t issues (in the "normal way") in an intentional A-ing at t, it does so by issuing in, and sustaining, an intention to A (or an intention to try to A), of which the following is true: acquisition of the intention initiates the A-ing and the intention, once it is in place, sustains and guides the A-ing.[17] Further, an agent who intends to A (beginning) at once—an agent who, as I shall say, *proximally intends* to A—will A intentionally (beginning) straightaway, unless something prevents his doing so or thwarts his efforts. (This latter suggestion is hardly a bold one.) Sources of prevention and of thwarted efforts include the agent's lacking the ability to A, the unfriendliness of his environment, his bungling an attempt, and his being more motivated to do at the time something, B, that is incompatible with his A-ing. However, being *equally* motivated to perform some competing action is not a preventive or thwarting condition.

This conjunctive hypothesis does not require that proximal intentions generally—or even *effective* proximal intentions particularly—incorporate preponderant motivational strength. It leaves open, for example, the possibility that intentions move us in virtue of their having some executive quality that is not reducible to desire-strength.[18]

The latitude provided is attractive. An agent who makes the transition from merely wanting to A—even preponderantly—to intending to A is commonly regarded as having made progress toward action. And this progress cannot be articulated wholly in terms of motivational strength. Someone who, wanting to *A* more than he wants to do anything incompatible with his *A*-ing, forms an intention to *A* need not now want more strongly to *A* (either absolutely or relative to alternatives) than he did a few moments earlier. (Indeed, owing in part to the enhanced salience of the prospect of *A*-ing attendant, in a particular case, upon forming the intention, one's absolute motivation to *A* might even diminish a bit. Consider a long-term bachelor who, having finally decided to marry Susan, is now feeling considerably more anxious about the quality of married life than he was just prior to reaching the decision, with the result that his motivation to marry Susan is slightly attenuated.) Still, it certainly looks as though, in forming an intention, the agent has made practical progress. And even if his (absolute or relative) motivation to *A* *were* to increase, why should *this* be counted as progress, given that he was already preponderantly motivated to *A* anyway?

Against the background of a view of action that accords beliefs, desires, intentions, and the like a causal role in the production of intentional behavior, we should expect the progress characteristic of the transition from wanting to intending to have some *causal* significance. Now, the formation or acquisition of an intention need not augment the agent's *cognitive/representational* condition in a way required for the production of intentional behavior. After all, the pertinent know-how, beliefs, plans, and the like are sometimes present already, awaiting the agent's decision. I have suggested that motivational strength need not be altered either. Still, it seems, even in the absence of a change of either sort, there is practical progress in the move from wanting to intending— progress whose causal significance, if any, must be located elsewhere, perhaps in some further, executive, dimension of intention.

Brief consideration of a case not involving a motivational tie will prove useful. Sally is preponderantly motivated to avenge an insult, and she knows this. However, she has moral qualms about behaving vengefully in this instance; consequently, she is attempting to decide what to do. Eventually, Sally decides to indulge her desire for vengeance, even though she thinks that doing so is morally improper; and she acts accordingly. Here, Sally's practical progress consists in her now being *settled* upon taking a course of action—one that she was already preponderantly motivated to take.

If Sally's progress lies in her coming to be settled upon a course of action, the same may be said of Alan. The result of the coin toss settles for him the matter that had been unsettled. And, one naturally supposes, his being settled upon purchasing the designated ticket will issue in his purchasing it, provided that nothing prevents this.

One might be tempted to infer from Alan's purchasing the ticket for A that he wanted to purchase that ticket more than he wanted to purchase a ticket for B. But the question before us now is whether this inference is *required*—whether we can make sense of Alan's behavior *only* on the supposition that he wanted most to purchase an A ticket. I have suggested an alternative; and if the alternative is a genuine one, it has significant implications for the theory of motivation. Most important, not all states that move us to action need be understood as moving us to A in virtue of their incorporating *preponderant* motivation to A.

I have been suggesting that faced with a motivational tie between options A and B, an agent might intentionally A without having come to want to A more than to B. My focus has been on the connection between the motivational condition of an agent and the behavior that it promotes. Call that a *forward* connection. It might be claimed that some *backward* or historical connection, in a case like Alan's, requires that the agent want to A more than to B. More concretely, one might contend, for example, that an agent's recognizing the result of a randomizing procedure as A-favoring, in a case of the kind in question, provides him with a new reason to A and that other things being equal, this will strengthen his desire to A relative to his competing desire to B.

Unpacking 'other things being equal' here is not easy. (It rarely is.) And without some qualification, the claim would obviously be false. For example, seeing that the coin has come up heads, S might unexpectedly experience disappointment and now want the losing alternative more. Further, setting aside cases of this kind, why can't the acquisition of the new reason issue in an intention to A while not issuing in a preponderance of motivation to A? After all, the point of the toss is to settle matters; and if matters would be settled by the formation or acquisition of an intention even in the absence of a change in relative desire-strength, why suppose that the intention-promoting new reason must (also) be a desire-enhancing reason? Why can't acquisition of the new reason go directly to the heart of the matter, as it were, without (also) bringing it about that the agent wants more to A than to B?

Even if a reading of the ceteris paribus clause could be found, however, on which the claim about enhanced desire-strength is true, that would not imply that whenever agents faced with a motivational tie employ a randomizing procedure and then intend and act accordingly, they want to perform the action performed more than the relevant alternative. That inference is blocked by the ceteris paribus clause. What is needed is an additional premise, or argument, to the effect that when other things are not equal in instances of motivational ties in which agents resort to a randomizing procedure, agents intentionally *A* only if their desire to *A* is strengthened relative to the competing desire—which leads us quickly back to *forward* connections. If (1) the hypothesis expressed earlier about the connection between intention and intentional action is correct and (2) intending to *A* (as I shall argue in chapter 9) does not require wanting to *A* more than one wants to perform any relevant alternative, cases are easily imagined in which one's motivation to *A* is not increased relative to the pertinent alternative by an *A*-favoring flip of the coin and one nevertheless intentionally *A*-s. (Recipe for constructing cases: identify something about *S* or his circumstances that precludes a shift to wanting to *A* more than to *B* upon viewing what he knows is an *A*-favoring toss but without preventing him from intending to *A*, which intention he acquires.) The issue at hand turns upon forward connections and the nature of intentions, not upon the effects of randomizing procedures on desire-strength in normal cases.

Again, I am willing to grant that *normally,* in cases of the sort in question, agents want most to do what they do. Even when an arbitrary picking is substituted for a coin toss, an agent might, after picking, want to perform the action picked more than the alternative. If the picking is identified with the formation of an intention, he might want more to act as he intends than to act otherwise. Then again, motivated by a desire to do either *A* or *B* in an instance of a motivational tie, perhaps an agent may simply arbitrarily select one alternative without possessing or acquiring at the time a selection-referring or intention-referring desire (e.g., a desire to execute his intention to *A* or a desire to conform his behavior to his selection of an alternative). Perhaps in some instances of motivational ties, picking or intending an alternative *A* settles matters without the assistance of a desire whose content refers to the agent's picking or intending *A* and without his wanting to *A* more than he wants to *B*. In any event, I have not been able to locate a convincing argument that the practical resolution of a motivational tie between an *A*-ing and a *B*-ing requires that the agent come to want one more than the other. And I have sketched grounds for thinking that no such argument is forthcoming. On the conception of intention to which I have alluded (a conception defended in part II), there is no *need* for a preponderant want of the identified kinds in the production of intentional action. In the absence of such a need, an agent may intentionally *A* while wanting just as much to do something, *B*, that he deems an open alternative to an *A*-ing.

7. Wants, Intentions, and Motivational Strength

In a very broad sense of 'want,' intentions are at least partially constituted by wants. Earlier, I provisionally characterized wanting to A, in a
broad, technical sense of the term, as having motivation to A, the content of which features a representation of the agent's (current or prospective) A-ing. If intending to A encompasses the possession of motivation
to A, as is standardly thought, then intending to A encompasses wanting
to A, on the characterization at issue. (Obviously, an intention to A has
the requisite representational property.) Now, even if wants not incorporated in intentions move us to act in virtue of their motivational strength
alone, the supposition that intentions incorporate wants does not entail
that *intentions* move us only in virtue of the motivational strength of the
incorporated wants. Again, intention may have a motivational feature
not wholly encompassed in the strength of incorporated wants.

One might attempt to find resources for rebutting this last suggestion
in a certain conception of motivational strength. It has often been observed that the motivational strength of a want cannot be determined by
the felt intensity of the want, if our intentional behavior is to accord
uniformly with our strongest wants: sometimes, our most affectively
intense wants are not the wants on which we act. Nor is want-strength
universally fixed by agents' assessments or evaluations of the objects of
the wants, as garden-variety instances of akratic action show (Mele
1987a, chs. 3 and 6). Some might be tempted by a certain quasi-
functional account of motivational strength according to which the motivational strength of a state is simply a measure of its capacity to produce
appropriate intentional behavior. On such an account, if the capacity of
an agent's intention to A to result in an attempt to A is greater than the
capacity of his competing desire to B to result in an attempt to B, the
intention has more motivational strength than the desire.

Notice what the thesis that wants move us to act in virtue of their
motivational strength alone (supposition 2 on p. 71) amounts to, on this
account of motivational strength: wants move us to act in virtue of their
capacity to move us to act. This is far from satisfying. Matters would be
improved significantly if features of wants on which that capacity rests
were identified. Of course, on the account of motivational strength at
issue, the *motivational strength* of wants cannot, without vicious circular-
ity, be offered as such a feature.

Suppose that other things being equal, intentions to A have a greater
"capacity" to produce appropriate intentional behavior than do *mere*
wants to A, that is, wants that are neither identical with, nor incorporated

into, intentions.[19] This supposed fact need not be accounted for by maintaining that intentions possess to a greater degree some determinate feature that they share with mere wants. The difference in question might be explicable, for example, on the alternative hypothesis that intentions and mere wants have different functional roles in the production of intentional action. Perhaps, as I suggested earlier, the specifically actional function of mere wants is to prompt and sustain suitable intentions, while that of intentions is to initiate, sustain, and guide intentional action. The motivational element in each state might play a different functional role. In that case, it would be misleading to suggest that there is some single motivational property, namely, action-causing strength, that an agent's intentions and mere wants have in varying degrees. And if motivational commensurability of the sort at issue is rejected, the door is wide open to the possibility that occasionally, wanting equally strongly to *A* and to *B* and recognizing that we cannot do both, we intentionally *A*.

In the absence of a compelling reason to maintain, roughly, that we intentionally do only what we want most to do, we should leave it open that motivational ties may, in some instances, be practically resolved while the tie remains. Of course, we will want to have at our disposal some account of how this can happen. The pertinent hypothesis offered about a functional connection between intentions and intentional actions is developed in part II.

Notes

1. Compare *P1* with psychologist J. W. Atkinson's claim: "The act which is performed among a set of alternatives is the act for which the resultant motivation is most positive. The magnitude of response and the persistence of behavior are functions of the strength of motivation to perform the act relative to the strength of motivation to perform competing acts" (1957, p. 361).

2. Mook (1987) provides an excellent survey of recent psychological work on the topic.

3. This characterization is redundant if all motivation to *A* features a representation of the agent's (current or prospective) *A*-ing. However, we sometimes identify a state as motivation to *A* even when we take it to involve no such representation. For example, if a young child habitually strikes other children who anger him, we may say that his anger at little Billy is, for him, motivation to strike Billy, even though we regard the anger not as incorporating a desire to hit—nor a representation of hitting Billy—but as *issuing* in a desire with that representational content. (A finer-grained conception of wanting would distinguish it from intending. See sec. 7 and chs. 8.3; 9.4–5; 10.2–3)

4. See, e.g., Goldman 1970, pp. 86–88; Alston 1967.

5. See Brandt and Kim 1963, p. 426; Goldman 1970, pp. 50–51, 105–6; Wright 1963, p. 103.

6. Regarding the claim about wanting more by default, some might object that (1) '*S* wants *A* more than he wants *B*' entails (2) '*S* wants *B*'. Now, perhaps it is true that utterances of form 1 *conversationally imply* that *S* has some desire for *B*. But there is nothing stronger than conversational implicature here—in particular, no logical entailment. Consider a coach's assertion to his team: "They want to win more than you do; in fact, you don't want to win at all." What follows the "in fact" is not a retraction of the initial assertion: it serves to reinforce the claim.

7. In Mele 1987a, chs. 3 and 6, I argue that they do sometimes come apart.

8. On reasons for action, see ch. 6.

9. I shall understand taking oneself to be *unable* to *A* as follows. At a time *t*, an agent "takes himself to be unable" to *A* then if and only if, at *t*, he believes that he cannot (owing to external or internal circumstances, or both) *A* then. Thus, if, at *t*, an agent possesses a representation of his (prospective) *A*-ing then, he takes himself (at *t*) to be able to *A* then, unless he believes (at *t*) that he cannot *A* then. Taking oneself, at *t*, to be able to *A* at the time is, one might say, the default condition of possessing such a representation.

10. For a more detailed version of the argument of the last few paragraphs, see Mele 1990c.

11. This question is traditionally associated with Buridan. However, Ullmann-Margalit and Morgenbesser report that the example of the ass does not appear in his known writings (1977, p. 759n.). For interesting recent discussions of "Buridan cases," see Bratman 1985, 1987.

12. For additional details and discussion, see Wilson and Nisbett 1978.

13. This point is not offered as an objection to Nisbett and Wilson's (1977) conjecture. The conjecture concerns the *rating* of purchasable items; my point is about the *purchasing* of the items and attitudes toward the purchasing acts. This distinction will be addressed shortly.

14. For a defense of this thesis, see Mele 1987a, chs. 3 and 6.

15. On supposition 1, see Mele 1987a, pp. 12–14.

16. In some cases, assignments of heads and tails will themselves raise problems about motivational ties. But let us simply suppose that Alan is in the habit of assigning heads to the alternative he represents first and that his representing *A first* is not motivationally explained.

17. Compare Myles Brand's contention that "desiring is an intention-former" (1984, p. 127) and Hector Castañeda's claim that "wantings are characteristically inclinations to intend" (1975, p. 284). See also ch. 9.

18. On the executive nature of intentions, see chs. 9 and 10.

19. The distinction drawn earlier between buffered and buffer-free wants may be applied straightforwardly to *mere* wants or desires, as just characterized.

4

*P1** and the Plasticity of Motivational Strength

P1, P1*, and the like do not place us at the mercy of our desires. Even if, to oversimplify the underlying idea, we always act as we want most to act, we may have considerable control over what we want most. Unless a desire is irresistible, it is, in some sense, up to us whether we act on it.[1] This is not to say that it is up to us whether our intentional actions coincide with what we want most. Rather, the point is that in the case of desires that are not irresistible, we have some control over motivational strength.

In *Irrationality* (Mele 1987a) I argued that normal agents are capable of influencing the strength of their desires in a wide variety of ways. Desires, by and large, do not come to us equipped with immutable strengths. The plasticity of motivational strength is presupposed by standard conceptions of self-control (see Mele 1987a, chs. 2–6; Mele 1990e).

This plasticity may be viewed by some as a threat to the explanatory value of the notion of motivational strength for a reason identified in section 2. The notion's value, in any case, has been attacked on related grounds. The truth that *P1* and its ilk are designed to capture, it is sometimes claimed, is a *conceptual* one and therefore can have no empirical or explanatory content. It is also claimed, in the same vein, that talk about motivational strength is actually only disguised talk about intentional action and that the alleged conceptual truth at issue, therefore, is a vacuous one that cannot even suggest a research program.[2]

The present chapter is addressed to such worries as these about the standing of the notion of motivational strength in a theory of the explanation of intentional action. I shall argue that the worries rest on a mistake about the theoretical status of *P1* and its kind.

1. Some Determinants of Motivational Strength

Desire-strength is subject to multiple influences. Attention to some of them will shed light on the plasticity of motivational strength. In *Irrationality* (Mele 1987a) I found particularly useful in this connection work on impulsiveness and delay of gratification by psychologists George Ainslie, Walter Mischel, and their respective colleagues.

Ainslie marshals weighty evidence for a view that I summarized as follows:

> 1. "The curve describing the effectiveness of reward as a function of delay is markedly concave upwards" ([Ainslie] 1982, p. 740). That is, a desire for a "reward" of a prospective action, other things being equal, acquires greater motivational force as the time for the reward's achievement approaches, and after a certain point motivation increases sharply.

> 2. Human beings are not at the mercy of the effects of the proximity of rewards. They can bring it about that they act for a larger, later reward in preference to a smaller, earlier one by using "pre-committing devices," a form of self-control (1975, 1982). "Rewards that are due at different times will be chosen in proportion to their actual amounts, as long as the choice is made far enough in advance" (1975, p. 472). And if someone who chooses early believes that his "preference for the better alternative is apt to change," he will be motivated to exercise self-control (1982, p. 743). (For example, he can bind himself à la Odysseus or employ techniques that increase the motivational force of the preferred alternative.) In some cases, exercises of self-control are both required and successful.[3] (Mele 1987a, p. 85)

Mischel and his colleagues, in a series of studies that I shall briefly discuss in chapter 9, advance a compelling case for the thesis that the manner in which children attend to, or represent, reward objects has a marked influence on the strength of their motivation to pursue the rewards.[4] Thus, for example, children told to focus on the "consummatory" qualities of such alternative rewards as pretzels and marshmallows opted for the less-valued reward much earlier than did children instructed to "transform" the desired treats in imagination into brown logs and white clouds, respectively.

Ainslie's and Mischel's studies indicate that desire-strength, at least in some cases, is subject to intentional control. We might, for example, intentionally exert control over the strength of a desire for a piece of chocolate pie by picturing the dessert as a large wedge of chewing tobacco in order to attenuate the strength of our desire for it. Alternatively—or additionally—we might promise ourselves a reward with a view to enhancing motivation to eschew the dessert. In both cases, successful intervention into our own motivational condition is possible.

If behavioral therapists and our own experience may be trusted, we are often able to bring the strength of our desires into line with our better judgments. Consider a superficially simple case. James is more strongly motivated to continue lying in bed than he is to start his daily routine. However, he judges that it would be best to get up at once; and acknowledging his sluggishness, he utters a self-command: "James, get going—now!" Responding to the command, James climbs out from under his covers and heads for the shower.

The motivational strength of James's desire to continue lying in bed *was* greater than that of his desire to rise; but apparently, owing in part to his better judgment, he was also more strongly motivated to take measures to get himself to rise than he was to take no such measures.[5] Since the measure that James takes is successful, one result, presumably, is that he became more motivated to rise than to remain in bed.

A related point also merits attention. Just as the strength of one's wants for the present can be influenced by new perceptual information, they can be influenced by a variety of other fresh mental states. Here is a straightforward instance of perceptual influence. Fran, a football quarterback, is preponderantly motivated to throw the ball to Ahmad now; but as he begins his throwing motion, he sees a defender dart into the intended path of the ball. One result is a change in Fran's motivational condition: he is now most motivated to look for another receiver. In a case of another sort, Lynn, owing partly to habit, is preponderantly motivated to take a second helping of dessert; but as she reaches for the pie she recalls her New Year's resolution, with the result that she now wants more not to take a second helping. Don, who is simultaneously looking for another dessert, is so impressed by Lynn's self-control that he now wants most to forgo an extra dessert himself.

2. The Status of *P1**

If motivational strength is as plastic as all that, one might ask, what explanatory value can it have? How will we be able to gauge the relative strengths of competing desires—a desire to *A* and a desire to *B*, say— except on the basis of whether the agent does *A* or *B*? Here we encounter a familiar criticism of *P1* and its kind, one resting on the idea that desire-strength can only be defined in terms of intentional action. If one defines the *strongest* desire of an agent at a time as the desire that issues in action then, how, it is pointedly asked, can we *account for* the occurrence of an action by appealing to the strength of the desire that allegedly produced it? If the sole criterion of relative motivational strength is what the agent does, how can the motivational strength of his wants *explain* what he does?

There are, as I observed in *Irrationality,* indicators of the relative strength of competing desires other than the agent's subsequently acting on one or the other of them:

> An agent's own reports on the matter are relevant, as are past effective choices among options similar to those with which he is now presented. Moreover, the relative motivational strengths of an agent's present desires for competing *future* actions (e.g., buying a house before his infant daughter starts kindergarten versus buying a yacht within five years) cannot *now* be gauged on the basis of which future action he performs; but present goal-directed behavior of his can be quite telling. Indeed, an agent's present behavior concerning temporally distant action-goals is generally a better indication of the relative strength of his *present* motivation to perform the future actions than is his subsequent performance of one of the competing future actions. (Mele 1987a, p. 15)

A much more fundamental observation is, however, in order. The supposed definitional or criterial dependence of motivational strength on subsequent intentional action allegedly speaks against the usefulness of principles like *P1**. But the difficulty of defining intentional action independently of desires or wants merits equal attention.

Intentional action is purposive action. Sometimes, if Aristotle is right, the goal or purpose is the performance of the action itself (*Nicomachean Ethics* 1144a18–20). More often, intentional action has an external goal. In either case, an intentional action is in some way guided or directed by the agent's representation of the goal or object of the action. But *mere* representation is not enough. We represent all sorts of things that we do not pursue or do or even *try* to pursue or do (see Brand 1984, pp. 45–46, 238–39; Mele 1987a, pp. 12–13).

This is where wanting, in the broad sense, enters the picture. An agent intentionally *A*-s only if he has a pertinent purpose; and wanting, in the broad sense in question, is an essential ingredient in having a purpose of the relevant sort. (Typewriters and telescopes have purposes of another sort.) Indeed, the very activity of interpreting a bit of behavior as intentional involves a presumption of a pertinent want on the part of the agent. In supposing that an agent is *intentionally* insulting his *boss,* we presume that he has some want or desire to insult his boss (or a desire to do something else to which he takes insulting his boss or trying to insult his boss to be a means; or, depending on one's position on double effect, he has a desire to do something, *X,* that he is willing to do at the expense of insulting his boss).[6] If, wanting instead to insult his assistant, and mistaking his boss—disguised as Santa Claus—for his assistant, he berates the costumed person, he is not intentionally insulting his *boss*. We do not—as the objector would have us imagine we do—identify a bit of behavior as intentional and *only then* bring in the notion of wanting, if we feel inclined to produce a motivational redescription of the behavior. Rather, identification of a bit of behavior as intentional already involves a motivational presumption. And once we grant motivation or wanting a genuine place in our conceptual scheme, motivational *strength* gains a foothold as well. For, surely, if we are motivated beings, we are more strongly motivated to do some things than others: in human beings as they actually are, motivation is not egalitarian.

"Why," *Q* asks, "did *S* intentionally *A*?" Typically, it will not do to respond that *S* wanted to *A* (in the broad sense of 'want' articulated in chapter 3) more than he wanted to do anything else at the time. That *S* wanted most to *A* (in that sense of 'want') will generally be taken for granted.

Often, in asking why someone did something, we are asking for the *reason(s)* for which he acted. But sometimes an identification of the reason(s) leaves us unsatisfied. Suppose that we know that *S* had exactly one reason *R1* to do *A* and another reason *R2* to do *B*, a competing action. Suppose further that we learn that *S* intentionally *A*-ed and that *R1* was the reason for which he *A*-ed. We might still reasonably ask why *S A*-ed. We might want to know why *S* did *A* rather than *B*. Knowing the reason for which *S A*-ed does not satisfy our curiosity (unless we take *R1* to be obviously superior to *R2*). So what must we discover in order to see why *S* did *A* rather than *B*?

Suppose that we learn why, in light both of *S*'s pertinent reasons and of other features of the case, *S wanted* more at the time to *A* than to do anything else, including *B*, then. Would this satisfy us? Once we understand *why* an agent wanted most at the time to perform the action *A* that he performed, would we be satisfied that we understood why he *A*-ed? I think that we would, at least normally. And when such information does satisfy us, there is a background presumption at work, namely, that the agent *A*-ed *because* (in some sense) that is what he wanted most to do at the time. If his wanting most to *A* were *irrelevant* to his *A*-ing, the explanation that we have of his wanting most to *A* would also be irrelevant to his *A*-ing or, at best, tangentially relevant.

I am not here retracting my claim that 'He wanted most to A' generally is not a satisfactory response to the question 'Why did he A?' It may well be true that a particular agent A-ed because that is what he wanted most to do; I do not deny that. We often want more than truth, however, in the responses that our queries elicit. If one were uncertain whether S A-ed intentionally, the answer at issue would be informative. But when it is taken for granted that the A-ing was intentional, then 'Because he wanted most to A,' though it might not fall short in truth, offers little illumination.

Not only do the preceding remarks suggest that $P1^*$ and its kind have some explanatory significance for intentional action, but they suggest, as well, a partial identification of their significance. The principles articulate background presumptions about intentional action in the context of which we offer explanations of particular intentional actions in terms of such psychological items as beliefs, desires, and reasons. Precisely because we presuppose the existence of a tight connection between motivational strength and intentional action, our acquiring information about why an agent wanted most to do what he did promotes in us an understanding of why he did it.

So, again, what should we make of the aforementioned plasticity of motivational strength? Plainly, this plasticity does not count against the *truth* of $P1^*$. This principle places no constraints on changes in the strengths of a person's wants. One might claim that the plasticity of motivational strength makes it illegitimately easy for proponents of $P1$ or $P1^*$ to respond to alleged counterexamples in which an agent supposedly does something other than what he wants most to do at the time and that the principles are therefore devoid of explanatory significance. But if the explanatory significance of the principles lies, as I have suggested, in their articulating background presumptions in attempted "folk psychological" explanations of intentional actions, this objection misses its mark. (Notice that even principles that are, to use Davidson's expression, "self-evident" may have explanatory significance of this sort.) The target ought to be much broader, namely, entire theories of the explanation of intentional behavior that give an important role to intentional states—or at least theories of this sort that presupposes a principle of the kind that $P1^*$ is designed to express.

An investigation of the merits of intentionalistic psychological theories of action-explanation is well beyond the scope of the present chapter (though not of the present book). My point here is only that a fair assessment of the principle relating wanting and acting that Davidson attempted to express in $P1$ and that I have tried to capture in $P1^*$ must give considerable weight to the virtues and vices of the best theory of the explanation of intentional action in which the principle plays a significant constitutive role. The principle itself is not designed to explain intentional actions. It is rather the theory in which the principle is embedded that is supposed to do the explanatory work. My primary aim in this chapter has been to locate the function in such a theory of the principle that Davidson's *P1* was designed to express and, in so doing, to defuse familiar objections to principles of that kind.

Notes

1. An analysis of irresistible desire is offered in chapter 5.

2. See, e.g., Charlton 1988, ch. 7.3; Gosling 1990, pp. 174–85; Locke 1982; and Thalberg 1985. For a brief response to Thalberg, see Mele 1987a, pp. 11–15.

3. See Ainslie 1975, 1982. See also Ainslie and Haendel 1982; Ainslie and Herrnstein 1981; Navarick and Fantino 1976; Rachlin and Green 1972; Solnick et al. 1980. For further discussion, see Mele 1987a, pp. 84–86, 90–93.

4. For discussion of the studies, see Mele 1987a, pp. 88–93. The studies include Mischel and Baker 1975; Mischel and Ebbesen 1970; Mischel, Ebbesen, and Zeiss 1972; H. Mischel and Mischel 1983; W. Mischel and Mischel 1977; Mischel and Moore 1973, 1980; Moore, Mischel, and Zeiss 1976; Patterson and Mischel 1976; Yates and Mischel 1979.

5. The possibility of an agent's being in a motivational condition of the sort in question is defended in Mele 1987a, ch. 5. An agent's wanting more to *A* than to *B* is compatible with his being more motivated to exercise self-control in support of his *B*-ing than to refrain from so doing.

6. Typically, if, motivated by a desire to *A* and a belief that *B*-ing is a means to *A*-ing, *S* intentionally *B*-s, *S* will have an "extrinsic" or instrumental desire to *B*. (On extrinsic desires, see ch. 3.1.) In some exceptional cases of intentional *A*-ing, there may be no desire at all to *A*. In one version of the Belton example in ch. 3.3, Belton, motivated by desires to win money and to try to solve the chess problem, solves the problem intentionally even though he has no desire to solve it. Still, Belton's intentional solving of the problem is explained in part by relevant desires, including his desire to try to solve the problem. Similarly, in familiar cases of double effect, even if some foreseen but unwanted actional side-effects of intentional actions are properly counted as intentional actions, they are side-effects of desired actions. (On double effect, see ch. 6.6 and the final paragraph of ch. 10.1.)

5

Irresistible Desires

An appreciation of the extent to which our desires are subject to our control is essential to a proper understanding of normal human agency. I suggested in chapter 4 that unless a desire is irresistible, we have some control over its motivational strength. However, the precise content of the suggestion is left open in the absence of an account of irresistible desire. We face, then, a difficult question: What is an irresistible desire?

Irresistible desires are mentioned with unsurprising frequency in discussions of free agency and moral responsibility. Actions motivated by such desires are standardly viewed as compelled, hence unfree. Agents in the grip of irresistible desires are often plausibly exempted from moral blame for intentional deeds in which the desires issue. Yet relatively little attention has been given to the analysis of irresistible desire. Moreover, a popular analysis is fatally flawed.

My aim in this chapter is to construct and defend a new, successful analysis of irresistible desire. Although, to render the discussion manageable, I shall keep the issues of freedom and responsibility to one side, readers will see them in the background at every major turn.

1. An Unsuccessful Approach: Not Being Open to Persuasion

The proverbial irresistible force cannot be resisted by anything. However, this model is inappropriate for irresistible desires. When we ask whether a desire is irresistible we are asking whether the person whose desire it is can resist it. Moreover, since it is prima facie possible that a desire resistible by someone at one time is not resistible by him at another, the irresistibility of desires should be relativized not only to agents but to times as well.

A popular criterion of the irresistibility of a desire is the agent's not being open to persuasion in relation to the desire. Witness Wright Neely's account: "A desire is irresistible if and only if it is the case that if

the agent had been presented with what he took to be good and sufficient reason for not acting on it, he would still have acted on it" (1974, p.
47; italics deleted; cf. Glover 1970, pp. 97–107, 173).

Three problems with this analysis merit mention. First, the subjunc-
tive conditional opens it to simple counterexamples of a familiar type.
Suppose that although S acted on a certain desire, he would not have
done so if he had been presented with a reason of the sort that Neely
mentions—but only because his being presented with such a reason
would have resulted in an incapacitating heart attack. Plainly, this supposition is compatible with the desire's having been irresistible by S.[1]

Second, the analysis entails that the desires that motivate a central
species of incontinent action are irresistible. In central cases of akrasia, or
"weakness of will," agents judge it best, all things considered, not to A
and yet intentionally and freely A. These agents (or some of them, at any
rate) take there to be good and sufficient reason for not acting on their
desires to A, but they act on them nonetheless.[2] However, incontinent
agents are commonly distinguished from victims of irresistible desires.
The former, we say, succumb to desires that they *could have* resisted.[3]

A third problem is equally revealing. Even in extreme cases of phobia
or addiction we can usually imagine some reason such that if the agent
had possessed that reason for not acting as he did, he would not have so
acted. But it does not follow that in these cases the desires on which the
agent acted were resistible by him at the time of action. Suppose, for
example, that Fred has agoraphobia and that his fear is so strong that he
has not ventured out of his house in ten years, despite our many attempts to persuade him to do so. We decide finally that we just have not
been presenting Fred with the right reasons and we threaten to burn his
house to the ground if he does not open his door today. When it becomes
evident that the threat will not work, we start throwing flaming brands
through his windows. Fred, panic-stricken, tears open his front door and
runs screaming into the night, having finally been presented with what
he takes to be a good and sufficient reason for leaving his home.

Fred's situation is comparable to that of the woman who, under ordinary circumstances, cannot even budge a three-hundred-pound weight
but who, upon finding her child pinned under a four-hundred-pound
timber manages, due to a sudden burst of adrenalin, to raise the timber
from his body. Surely, it would be misleading to say that she can lift four-
hundred pounds, if we leave it at that. Rather, we should say that in
ordinary circumstances she cannot do this (no matter how hard she
tries), although in a certain kind of exceptional circumstance she can.
Similarly, it is possible that under ordinary circumstances Fred cannot

resist his desire to remain in his house no matter how hard he tries to do so, even though a raging fire would drive him out. Thus, a distinction between irresistibility under ordinary circumstances and irresistibility under exceptional circumstances is in order. Neely's account is too strong for the former.

This distinction cuts two ways. It is imaginable that a person who in ordinary circumstances cannot resist his desire to A can do so in exceptional circumstances. It is also imaginable that an agent who can resist his desire to A in ordinary circumstances cannot do so in certain exceptional circumstances. We might imagine, for example, an alcoholic who, though he is generally able to resist his desires to drink, cannot do so when he is extremely nervous or depressed.

Distinguishing ordinary from exceptional circumstances does not promise to be easy. However, it is not necessary to tackle the problem here; for my concern is with the irresistibility of a desire under the circumstances that obtain at the time at which the desire is irresistible, whether those circumstances be ordinary or exceptional.

2. Toward an Account of Irresistible Desire

The ordinary, folk-psychological conception of an irresistible desire is roughly this:

> *IDa.* A desire is irresistible if and only if the agent is powerless to prevent that desire from being effective.

Neely's analysis of irresistible desire may be construed as an attempted account of this powerlessness. In the present section I begin to develop an alternative account.

What does it mean to say that an agent is powerless to prevent something, *X,* from happening? If it means or implies that he cannot perform actions that result in *X*'s not happening, then *IDa* is overly exclusive. Suppose that Dolores has an irresistible desire to throttle the cocker spaniel whose barking has just awakened her. She leaps from her bed and runs down her dark hallway. In her mad dash toward the dog, she trips over little Delbert's snowshoes and suffers an incapacitating injury. Dolores's dash results in her not throttling the dog. Therefore, it is false that she could not perform actions that result in her not beating the dog. But, of course, this is quite compatible with her having had an irresistible desire to spank the spaniel.

If there is a sense in which Dolores prevented her desire to beat the dog from being effective, her doing so was plainly unintentional. Perhaps, then, the prevention that figures in *IDa* is *intentional* prevention. Consider the following reformulation:

> *IDb.* A desire is irresistible if and only if the agent cannot *intentionally* prevent that desire from being effective.

Suppose that Dirk has a desire to work on his car tonight and a competing desire to go to an evening movie instead. Suppose further that he decides that repairing the car would be more enjoyable and consequently spends his evening tinkering with the engine. Dirk's desire to view a movie needs no resistance, and he makes no effort to resist it. Even if there is a sense in which Dirk's working on the car prevents his desire to view the movie from being effective, Dirk does not intentionally prevent the desire from being effective. He takes no action to combat the desire.

The stage is now set for any number of examples in which an agent who can easily perform some alternative to his *A*-ing cannot intentionally prevent his desire to do *A* from moving him to *A*. Suppose, for example, that Delphine wants to do *A* less than she wants to do some incompatible action, *B*, and that she does *B* rather than *A*. Suppose also, however, that, unbeknownst to Delphine, there is a powerful demon on the scene who would have thwarted any attempt by Delphine to prevent her desire to *A* from moving her to *A*. Under these circumstances, Delphine could not have intentionally prevented the desire from moving her even though she easily performed *B* intentionally, an action that is incompatible with her *A*-ing.

Delphine's desire to do *A* is irresistible in a sense. If she cannot defeat the demon, she cannot intentionally make a successful effort of resistance against the desire; and we may safely suppose that the demon is just too powerful to be defeated by Delphine. But the desire is not irresistible in the stronger sense that *IDa* and *IDb* are *meant* to capture. For Delphine's desire to do *A* does not preclude her performing an intentional action that is an alternative to her *A*-ing.

IDb focuses on the agent's inability to conquer a desire. This focus is recommended by the *expression* 'irresistible desire' and its cognates; but we have just seen that the *concept* of an irresistible desire has a broader application. Even if one cannot intentionally conquer a desire to do *A*, one might be able to perform an intentional action that is an alternative to one's *A*-ing. Here, a distinction between *conquering* (in direct combat, as it were) and *circumventing* a desire is in order. Even an uncon-querable desire might be circumventable. And the presence of an uncon-querable but circumventable desire to A leaves room for the perfor-mance of an intentional action B that is an alternative to one's A-ing. To be sure, an *attempt* to circumvent a desire is an attempt to prevent that desire from being effective. And if Delphine makes any attempt to prevent the pertinent desire from being effective, she will fail. But, of course, she can simply intentionally do B, thereby circumventing her desire to do A without either intending or trying to circumvent it.

One might be tempted to draw the moral that in analyzing irresistible desire, one should concentrate on the agent's inability to perform inten-tional actions that are alternatives to the action urged by the target desire. But this would be too hasty. Although, ultimately, the inability just mentioned is important to the concept of irresistible desire, much of the substance of a successful analysis can be discovered by close atten-tion to the unconquerability of a desire. In the next two sections, I shall develop successors to *IDb* that focus on successful resistance and the inability to resist a desire successfully. The analysis is refined in section 5 to handle cases like Delphine's.

3. Resistance

'Resistance' does not entail success. There are successful and unsuccess-ful instances of resistance. Nevertheless, when we say that a desire is irresistible, we do not mean that the agent is unable to make an effort of resistance: he may well be able to make an *unsuccessful* effort.

Just what successful resistance entails will be taken up shortly. My immediate concern is with attempted resistance. An agent's attempt to resist a desire is an attempt to manipulate his motivational condition, his environment, or both to bring it about that he does not act on the desire being resisted. For example, an agent may promise himself a reward for successful resistance, force himself to picture in a particularly unattrac-tive way the goal that he is tempted to seek, lock himself in his room, or leave the scene of a heated argument when he thinks that he is about to lose control of himself. Resistance strategies such as these may be termed *skilled* strategies.

There is also what we might call "brute" resistance—roughly, what we have in mind when we speak of someone resisting a desire by sheer effort of will. Brute resistance against a desire to do A consists, roughly, in forming or retaining an intention not to *A* in order to bring it about that the desire does not issue in an *A*-ing. For example, if, while I am tempted to smoke, I form the intention not to smoke in order to bring it about that my desire does not issue in my smoking, I have made an effort of brute resistance against my desire to smoke.[4]

The ability to make a successful effort of resistance has at least two components, one *representational* and the other *executive*. (A third, motivational component will be addressed shortly.) Consider, for example, the simple technique of counting to ten before acting in order to avoid behaving impulsively out of anger. A person who is ignorant of the technique lacks, in an important sense, the ability to utilize it: his deficiency with respect to the technique is epistemic or *representational*. On the other hand, a person who is familiar with the technique but at a given time is so moved by emotion that he cannot bring himself to count to ten before acting, lacks at the time *executive* ability with respect to the technique. Even brute resistance is dependent upon representational and executive elements. If, for example, a person is so befuddled by passion that he is unable to conceive of any alternative to his *A*-ing, he cannot resist his desire to *A* by forming an intention not to *A;* and one who is well aware of alternatives to his *A*-ing may be unable to intend any of them, as, for example, a person with a severe fear of flying may be unable at *t* to intend to board an airplane at *t*.

Suppose that someone is familiar with the technique of counting to ten but that in a certain appropriate situation, the possibility of using the technique does not occur to him. Does it follow from his not thinking of the technique at *t* that he is unable at *t* to use the technique then?[5] Consider an analogous question about motivation. Suppose that—as is often held—one will intentionally *A* at *t* only if one has some motivation at *t* to *A* at *t* and suppose further that at *t* *S* has no motivation to *A* at *t*. Does it follow from this that *S* is unable at *t* to *A* intentionally at *t*? Now, if *S* is *unable* at *t* to have motivation to *A* at *t,* we may well want to say that he is unable at *t* to *A* intentionally then; for ex hypothesi, he is unable at *t* to satisfy one of the necessary conditions of his *A*-ing intentionally at *t*. But his merely lacking motivation at *t* to *A* at *t* is compatible with his then being able to have motivation at *t* to *A* at *t* and with his being able at *t* to *A* intentionally at *t*. Suppose, for example, that *S* has no motivation at *t* to eat at *t,* since he has just finished a large meal. Still, barring exceptional circumstances, he is *able* at *t* to eat (intentionally) then. He lacks not the ability to eat at *t* but the inclination. (Notice that if he were to have at the time a reason to eat even though he is no longer hungry—perhaps a desire not to offend his host in conjunction with a belief that his host would take offense at his ceasing to eat now—he might well want extrinsically to eat, and eat.)

The analogous position in the representational realm is, for example, that an agent's *inability* at *t* to represent his *A*-ing then renders him unable at *t* to *A* intentionally then but that his merely *not* representing a prospective *A*-ing is compatible with his being able at *t* to *A* intentionally at *t*: he might be able at *t* to represent his *A*-ing then.[6] Let us say that an agent is *representationally unable* at *t* to *A* intentionally at *t* if and only if at *t* he is unable to be in a representational state required for his intentionally *A*-ing then (e.g., he is unable to represent, at *t,* any means to his *A*-ing then, in a case in which *A*-ing is something that he can do at the time only if he intentionally does something, *B,* that is a means to his *A*-ing; or he is unable to represent, at *t,* his *A*-ing then). And let us say that an agent's intentionally *A*-ing at *t* is *representationally open* to him at *t* if and only if he is not representationally unable at *t* to *A* intentionally at *t*.

It will be useful later to have an account of a motivational analogue of representational openness. Let us say that an action *A* is *motivationally open* to an agent *S* at *t* if and only if *S* is able at *t* to satisfy the motivational prerequisites of his intentionally *A*-ing at *t*.

The foregoing may give the impression that an agent's being able to resist a desire is a purely internal matter—that it is wholly independent of anything external to the agent. This misimpression must be corrected. Suppose that an agent correctly believes that he can succeed in resisting his desire to kill himself today only if he contacts his therapist, so that she can dissuade him. He may be able to execute a plan of action for contacting his therapist—for example, phoning her office and, if that fails, her residence. But if she happens to be unavailable, our agent, ex hypothesi, cannot resist his desire. In the event of her unavailability, there is a common use of 'able' in which it is correct to say that the man is not able to resist his desire. This inability is a partial function of his therapist's being unavailable. When the successful execution of a strategy depends upon factors external to the agent, executive ability is not strictly internal to the agent. Sometimes executive ability has both internal and external components.

It is not immediately clear what constitutes the successful execution of a resistance strategy. The execution of a resistance strategy against a desire to do an *A* during *t* is successful only if it results in the desire's not moving the agent to *A* intentionally during *t*. But is this enough? Suppose that the strategy produces the desired result as a consequence of a bizarre sequence of events that are no part of the agent's plan of attack.

For example, an agent decides to take a cold shower as a means of resisting a certain sexual desire and in the course of executing his strategy he suffers an incapacitating injury in the tub, with the result that he does not act on his sexual desire.

If, in this case, it is correct to say that our agent successfully executed his resistance strategy and therefore that he was able at the time to execute the strategy successfully, the ability to execute a resistance strategy successfully is not a sufficient condition of the resistibility of the desire in question.[7] For—at least as resistible desires are ordinarily conceived—the relevant ability is a capacity for *nonaccidental* successful resistance against them. Surely, the possibility that one will accidentally kill or otherwise incapacitate oneself in the course of executing a resistance strategy available to one is not sufficient for the resistibility, in the standard folk-psychological sense, of the desire at which the strategy is aimed. If the accident had not occurred, one might have proceeded to act on the desire that one was attempting to resist; and one might have been *irresistibly* moved so to act by that desire.

To circumvent the problem that the possibility of wayward causal chains of the kind at issue poses for resistance-centered accounts of irresistible desire one needs a nonaccidentality condition of some sort. One might either attempt to build the condition into the meaning of 'successful resistance' or construe successful resistance more loosely and add a distinct nonaccidentality condition. In the interest of stylistic simplicity, I shall do the former:

> *NA.* An agent successfully executes a resistance strategy against a desire of his to do *A* at (during) *t* if and only if he executes the strategy in such a way that in executing it, he *intentionally* brings it about that that desire does not move him to *A* intentionally at (during) *t*.

Progress will be facilitated by a working reformulation of *IDb* that incorporates the results thus far obtained in this section. First, however, it will be useful to develop some light machinery for the temporal indexing of desires. What I shall call a *t-desire* is a desire to do something at or during *t,* where *t* may be as general as "some time or other" or as specific as "3:48 P.M. sharp." Every desire to do something is a *t*-desire.[8] What is important for present purposes is the distinction between a *t*-desire's being (ir)resistible *prior* to *t* and its being (ir)resistible at (during) *t*. The following analyses are addressed to the latter situation alone. (To say that a *t*-desire *D* that is irresistible by *S* at *t* was resistible by him at an earlier time is to say, very roughly, that at the earlier time it was within *S*'s power to respond to *D* in such a way that he would not have acted on it at *t*.)

Consider the following reformulation of *IDb*:

IDc. A *t*-desire *D* to do *A* is irresistible by *S* at (during) *t* if and only if, at (during) *t*, (a) no successful strategy for resisting *D* is both representationally and motivationally open to *S* or (b) if a strategy for resisting *D* is open in both ways to *S*, he is unable to execute it in such a way that in executing it, he intentionally brings it about that *D* does not move him to *A* intentionally at (during) *t*.

Given the nonaccidentality inherent in intentional behavior, *IDc* resolves the aforementioned problem with wayward causal chains. Of course, the analysis of intentional action is a subject of considerable controversy, and readers' interpretations of *IDc* will be conditioned by their understanding of intentional behavior. Since an attempt to defend an account of what it is to act intentionally is beyond the scope of the present chapter, I shall say only that I favor a rather broad conception, according to which intentional action is, roughly, action appropriately motivated by reasons.[9]

4. Ability and Irresistibility

A popular approach to the analysis of the ability to *A* intentionally is what I shall call the *conditional success* approach. The proponent of this approach attempts to analyze '*S* is able at *t* to *A* intentionally at *t*' partly by locating conditions minimally sufficient for *S*'s *A*-ing intentionally at *t*. Here is an example:

A1. *S* is able at *t* to *A* intentionally at *t* if and only if *S* would *A* intentionally at *t* if, at *t*, he wanted more to *A* at *t* than to refrain from *A*-ing at *t*.

Note that '*A*' may represent the successful execution of a resistance strategy.

There are two noteworthy problems with this analysis. First, even if *S* would *A* intentionally if he had a preponderant want to do so, he may be unable at the time to have such a want (or even to want to *A* *as much as* he wants not to *A*).[10] And *this* inability would render *S* unable at *t* to *A*

intentionally at *t*. Consider, for example, someone with severe claustro-
phobia. His fear may be such that he is psychologically unable at *t* to
have a preponderant want to enter the elevator before him. And he may
consequently be unable at *t* to enter the elevator intentionally at *t*.
Nevertheless, his being unable so to act is compatible with its being the
case that he would intentionally enter the elevator at *t* if, at *t,* he had a
preponderant want to do so then.

The problem just located poses a serious difficulty for the whole conditional success approach to the analysis of ability. Whatever analysans is
offered, its proponent must include a statement to the effect that the
agent is able to satisfy the conditions of success mentioned there. If this
second instance of ability is itself to be spelled out in terms of conditional success, there will be another instance of ability to unpack; and
the regress threatens to continue indefinitely.

The second problem with *A1* is that we sometimes fail to do what we
are able to do, even when we want very much to do it and have no
competing desires whatever. Consider a professional bowler, Amy, who
occasionally misses a moderately difficult spare of a sort that she usually
makes (for example, a five–seven split). In normal cases, such misses
are due to an avoidable flaw in her delivery, not to inability or insufficient motivation.

If we reject the conditional success approach, how should the ability
to do something intentionally be analyzed? Further consideration of
the bowling example will prove instructive. What do we mean when we
say that Amy, who missed a five–seven split, was able to make the shot
(intentionally)? One possibility is this: that she had at the time the
physical and psychological skills and capacities that one needs to have
a reasonable success rate vis-à-vis the making of five–seven splits.
But suppose that in the case in question the five pin is much heavier
than usual—say, one thousand pounds. Then even though Amy presumably had the aforementioned skills and capacities, she was not able
to make the split in question. Amy's having the ability to make (intentionally) the five–seven split with which she was faced depends upon
her having the physical and psychological skills and capacities necessary for making *that* split.

Is the possession of these skills and capacities sufficient for the ability
to make the split in question? That depends upon how we understand
the pertinent skills and capacities. Suppose, for example, that although
Amy is otherwise able to make the split that faces her, she is for some
reason psychologically unable to want to make the split. If our conception of the pertinent capacities is sufficiently broad to include the capac-

ity to want to make the split, this example is compatible with the suggestion that the possession of the skills and capacities necessary for making this split (intentionally) is sufficient for having the ability to make the split (intentionally). Similarly, if the pertinent skills and capacities include necessary representational capacities, the possession of the necessary skills and capacities will preclude representational inability. The notion of physical and psychological skills and capacities, *broadly* interpreted, includes the skills and capacities that render prospective actions representationally and motivationally open (in the senses I have defined) to agents. Henceforth, I shall construe the notion broadly.

One might think that the account now being suggested of ability is too strong. If Amy has the skills and capacities necessary for intentionally making her split, how can she miss? If she has the necessary skills and capacities in this strong sense, won't she satisfy *all* the necessary conditions of her making the shot? And if this is so, won't she satisfy a *sufficient* condition of her making the shot? But, the objection continues, being *able* to A intentionally is not sufficient for intentional A-ing.

One mistake here is not difficult to locate. Someone who has the skills and capacities necessary to A intentionally and wants most to A need not succeed in A-ing. Intentional A-ing depends upon the agent's utilizing the skills and capacities effectively; and an agent who is able to do the latter may nevertheless fail to do so. For example, there may be an avoidable hitch in Amy's delivery. From the supposition that she has the skills and capacities necessary to avoid the hitch, it does not follow that she will avoid it. Amy's bowling skill might be imperfectly manifested on that occasion.

Notice also (setting aside Amy's case) that an agent who has the skills and capacities necessary for intentionally A-ing, including the ability to satisfy the motivational prerequisites of his A-ing, may simply not want to A. Such an agent's ability to A, articulated in terms of skills and capacities, plainly is not sufficient for his intentionally A-ing.

The preceding discussion of ability suggests the following characterization:

> A2. S is able at (during) t to A intentionally at (during) t if and only if, at (during) t, S has the physical and psychological skills and capacities necessary to A intentionally at (during) t.

These skills and capacities should be construed broadly, so as to include both representational skills and capacities and necessary motivational capacities. *Executive* ability in particular may be identified with the possession of the necessary nonrepresentational and nonmotivational skills and capacities. Someone who knows what he must do to clean and jerk the barbell that he is confronting and who is strongly motivated to perform the task may still lack the executive ability to lift the weight, for he may lack the requisite strength.

IDc may now be reformulated as follows:

> *IDd.* A *t*-desire *D* to do *A* at (during) *t* is irresistible by *S* at (during) *t* if and only if, at (during) *t*, no strategy for resisting *D* satisfies all of the following conditions: (a) it is representationally open to *S;* (b) it is motivationally open to *S;* and (c) *S* has the physical and psychological skills and capacities necessary to execute it in such a way that in executing it, he intentionally brings it about that *D* does not move him to *A* intentionally at (during) *t*.

5. Delphine Again: Refining the Analysis

There is a demon on the scene who will thwart any attempt by Delphine to prevent her desire to do *A* from being effective. Still, Delphine can easily perform an intentional action that is an alternative to her *A*-ing— provided that she makes no attempt to resist her desire to *A*. In an important sense, therefore, as I explained in section 2, her desire to *A* is not irresistible. Yet *IDd* entails that it is irresistible. For no resistance strategy satisfying the three conditions identified is available to Delphine. To have the skills and capacities identified in condition *c* Delphine must have the skills and capacities necessary to defeat the demon; and we can safely imagine that she does not.

IDd must be abandoned or revised. I shall argue for revision. Recall the distinction between conquering and circumventing a desire. An unconquerable desire might be circumventable and hence not be irresistible. But a desire that is both unconquerable and uncircumventable is irresistible. *IDd,* I suggest, is a successful analysis of unconquerability (and of irresistibility in *that* sense). If that is right, we need only add to it a compatible, successful analysis of uncircumventability.

We may say as a first approximation that a desire *D* to *A* is circumventable in the pertinent sense of the term if and only if, *without* making an effort to resist *D,* the agent can perform an intentional action that is an alternative to a *D*-motivated intentional *A*-ing. Delphine's desire is circumventable in precisely this sense. Consequently, we get the right result in the case of Delphine simply by adding to *IDd* a clause to the effect that *D* is not circumventable in the sense just articulated.

Now, an intentional action whose performance circumvents a desire *D* to *A* need not be an alternative in the strong sense that its performance is *incompatible* with the performance of a *D*-motivated intentional *A*-ing. Consider the following case. At *t*, Dean can do *both A* and *B* then, but he prefers *B* to *A* and prefers *B* to doing both *A* and *B*. Dean can easily perform an intentional *B*-ing at *t*—while also not intentionally *A*-ing—without making any effort to resist his desire to *A*, without intending not to *A*, and without intending not to perform the complex action *A*-ing and *B*-ing. However, there is a powerful demon on the scene who will prevent Dean from successfully resisting his desire to *A* if he attempts to resist it and will cause him to *A* intentionally if Dean forms or acquires either of the intentions just mentioned. (He will cause Dean to abandon the intentions as soon as they are formed and to form at once an intention to *A*.) Plainly, Dean's desire to *A* is not irresistible (in the sense of the term that has been my concern in this chapter); for it is easily circumventable: Dean can intentionally *B* while not also intentionally *A*-ing. But—and this is the crucial point—Dean's intentionally *B*-ing is *not* incompatible with his being moved to *A* intentionally by desire *D*. Hence, circumventability does not imply incompatibility of this sort.

The approximate account of circumventability offered here may be improved. First, let us say that (prospective) intentional actions *A* and *B* are *W-alternatives* at (during) *t* for an agent if and only if the agent has a *t*-desire to *A* and a *t*-desire to *B* and will not be moved by both desires to perform their targeted intentional actions. Then we can say that a desire *D* to *A* at *t* is circumventable at *t* for an agent *S* if and only if, independently of any attempt or intention at *t* to resist *D* at *t*, *S* is able at *t* to perform at *t* an intentional action that is a *W*-alternative to a *D*-motivated intentional *A*-ing. At (during) *t* an agent is able to perform an action of the sort in question then if and only if, independently of any attempt or intention to resist *D*, he is able then both to satisfy at (during) *t* the conditions necessary for having a *W*-alternative *B* to a *D*-motivated intentional *A*-ing and to *B* intentionally while not also performing a *D*-motivated intentional *A*-ing. The requisite ability involves, of course, *B*'s being motivationally and representationally open for the agent at the time and the agent's having the necessary executive skills and capacities.

IDd may be refined to handle cases of unconquerable but circumventable desires by adding to it a condition to the effect that *D* is not circumventable in the sense just articulated. Let us call the resulting analysis *IDe*. *IDe* asserts that a desire is irresistible if and only if it is both unconquerable and uncircumventable. *IDd* may now be demoted to an analysis of unconquerability.

6. Objections and Replies

I turn now to some possible objections to *IDe*.

OBJECTION 1. Suppose that *S* is physically and psychologically capable of committing suicide and that he will succeed in resisting a relatively trivial desire (e.g., a desire to eat an entire devil's food cake) if and only if he intentionally kills himself. On *IDe, S*'s desire to eat the cake is resistible; but it seems that when an agent can fail to act on a trivial desire only by employing drastic means of resistance, the desire is, practically speaking, irresistible.

REPLY. The objection is underdescribed; further details are needed. In particular, we must be told whether *S* is psychologically capable at the time of committing suicide *in order to* prevent himself from eating the cake. If he is not and if he has no effective means of resistance at his disposal, then the desire is irresistible. (Even if *S* could bring himself to commit suicide for some purposes, it might not be within his power to kill himself in order to avoid eating the cake.) If, on the other hand, it is within *S*'s power to kill himself in order to bring it about that he does not eat the cake, his desire to eat the cake is literally resistible by him.

OBJECTION 2. Suppose that *S,* who is in the habit of brushing his teeth after his morning shower, has just finished showering and now has a desire of unremarkable strength to brush his teeth. A demon allows *S* to conceive of intentionally not brushing his teeth but renders him unable to conceive of any further alternative to brushing his teeth (e.g., shaving or dressing). Moreover, he renders *S* unable to want not to brush his teeth. Finally, the demon does all this without increasing the absolute strength of *S*'s desire to brush his teeth. *IDe* entails that *S*'s desire to brush his teeth is irresistible. But this is false. On the ordinary folk-psychological conception of irresistible desires, the desires themselves, in virtue of their strength, overpower agents; but, in the imagined example, *S*'s desire is of moderate strength and can hardly be counted as overpowering. His problem lies, not in the strength of the desire, but in the machinations of the demon.

REPLY. *S*'s desire to brush his teeth is literally irresistible by him. The demon, by constraining, as he does, what *S* can conceive and want, renders S incapable of conquering his desire and renders the desire uncircumventable as well. Even if it is true that under normal circumstances an irresistible desire is so largely in virtue of some internal feature of the desire itself, it does not follow that a desire's irresistibility *must* be internally grounded in this way. Notice, moreover, that standard intuitions about irresistible desires are based on paradigm cases, cases that do not involve demons and the like. In paradigm cases, the irresistibility of a desire *is,* in significant part, a function of the strength of that desire. But an analysis of irresistible desire designed to accommodate even highly contrived examples must be sensitive to much more than intuitions fostered by paradigms.

OBJECTION 3. Suppose that if S were to make an effort to resist acting on a desire D, his guardian angel would ensure that he did not act on D. Suppose further that any effort of S's to resist D would be unsuccessful without the guardian angel's intervention and that S is capable of attempting to resist. On *IDe, D* is resistible by S. But this seems wrong, since S is incapable of successfully resisting the desire on his own.

REPLY. This objection, like the first one, is underdescribed. The precise application of *IDe* to the case depends upon further details. Suppose that S knows about his angel and intends to enlist the angel's help by making an effort to resist D. Given the details of the case, S *can* successfully resist D in this way.

From the fact that an agent cannot successfully resist a desire on his own it does not follow that the desire is irresistible by him. We often enlist the aid of others in our attempts to exercise self-control. A troubled teenager struggling with a desire to end it all might call a suicide prevention hotline for assistance. Calm, reassuring words might enable him successfully to resist a desire that would otherwise have produced tragic consequences. In a more extreme case, someone experiencing a suicidal desire that he fears will overwhelm him might ask others to restrain him. The agent might in this way thwart the desire. If the strategy works, he has successfully resisted the desire by having himself restrained. (This is not to say, incidentally, that the agent is still resisting the desire *while* he is restrained. He might be doing nothing at all—or even be attempting to free himself, owing to the presence of a desire that has become irresistible.)

Suppose, alternatively, that the agent is ignorant of the existence of his guardian angel, so that prospective actions of the angel in no way enter into the agent's strategy for resistance. Then, even if the agent both intends to bring it about that he does not act on D and contributes to the desired outcome by making an effort to resist, he does not *intentionally* successfully resist *D*. His bringing it about that he does not act on *D* is not an intentional action; for the actual etiology of his not acting on *D* is quite remote from the planned etiology. (Compare the case of the man who intends to kill *B* by shooting him through the heart but does so instead by striking a rock with a wild shot, with the result that the rock plummets from a precipice and crushes the intended victim.) Indeed, given the details of the case, he lacks the skills and capacities necessary to execute his strategy in such a way that he intentionally brings it about that he does not act on *D*. Hence (assuming that the desire is uncircumventable), *IDe* entails that the desire is irresistible by *S*. And the objection itself urges the irresistibility of the desire.

OBJECTION 4. Suppose that seeing his young daughter flailing about in the lake twenty yards away in clear and immediate danger of drowning, *S* desires to save her. Owing to his love for his daughter and to his grasp of the situation, *S* is incapable of wanting to resist that desire and of wanting not to save his daughter. *IDe* entails that *S*'s desire to save his daughter is irresistible. But that plainly is false. Effective irresistible desires to *A compel* agents to *A;* an agent possessed of an irresistible desire is a victim of a power beyond his control, and any action generated by such a desire is accordingly unfree. However, it would be absurd to suppose that *S* is compelled to save his daughter and that he does so unfreely.

REPLY. When an agent has an effective, irresistible desire to perform an action *A* that violates his values or principles, the desire is quite naturally viewed as compelling the agent to *A*. (The desire, we say, "forces" him to do something that he would not do "of his own free will.") Supposing that irresistible desires do compel in such cases, it does not follow that all effective irresistible desires compel agents. *S*'s desire to save his daughter is literally irresistible in the case as described. But setting aside scenarios involving brainwashing or other modes of coercive value-engineering, irresistible desires for courses of action that are fully supported by one's own values are not properly counted as compelling, in the intended sense. They do not *force* behavior upon one or render one a victim. To be sure, we typically advert to the irresistibility of a desire in the context of providing an *excuse* for an agent's behavior, as constituting grounds for not holding the agent morally responsible for what he did. But an irresistible desire excuses and properly counts as something that compels only when the deed at issue is such as to call for an excuse. In *S*'s case, no excuse is called for.

OBJECTION 5. In a deterministic universe there are always causally sufficient conditions of our acting on the desires on which we act. Given the
presence of those conditions, we could not have acted otherwise. And if
we could not have acted otherwise, we could not have successfully resisted nor circumvented the desires on which we acted; for both successful resistance and circumvention of a desire entail not acting (intentionally) on that desire. Therefore, if determinism is true, *IDe* has the result
that all of the desires on which agents act are irresistible. But many
determinists want to distinguish between actions motivated by resistible
desires and actions motivated by irresistible desires. Moreover, they are
capable of making this distinction. Therefore, *IDe* must be incorrect.

REPLY. If determinists can distinguish resistible from irresistible desires, it is precisely because the presence of conditions causally sufficient
for an agent's acting on *D* is compatible with a resistance strategy's being
both representationally and motivationally open to the agent and with his
having the physical and psychological skills and capacities necessary to
execute the strategy in such a way that he intentionally brings it about that
he does not perform an intentional action on the basis of *D*. The brief that
I have made for *IDe* is itself an argument for this conditional claim.
However, readers would do well to observe two further points. First,
whether a particular deterministic theory of human behavior is capable of
distinguishing resistible from irresistible desires depends upon the details
of that theory. Second, the proper interpretation of the expression 'could
not have acted otherwise' in the formulation of the objection has long
been hotly debated; and it is by no means obvious that all deterministic
theories of human behavior are committed to endorsing a reading that
precludes there being resistance strategies with the features required,
given my analysis, for the conquerability of a desire. (In this connection
see Honderich 1988, pp. 403–9, 451–87, 491–92.)

7. Conclusion

IDe is immune to the five objections just considered and avoids the
problems identified with the analyses rejected in the course of its development. *IDe* preserves what is central to standard paradigm-inspired
intuitions about irresistible desires while circumventing the pitfalls introduced by a variety of highly contrived cases. Undoubtedly, readers have
been toying with interesting cases of their own. If convincing counterexamples to *IDe* are forthcoming, someone's reading time will have
been well spent. And if decisive counterexamples are not forthcoming,

we might now *know* what an irresistible desire is. For me, the prospect of that knowledge was irresistible. More to the point, however, a satisfactory characterization of irresistible desire is required if the theoretically and practically important truth that desires and desire-strength are often subject to an agent's control is to have a suitable conceptual anchor.

Notes

1. I owe this objection to Paul Moser.

2. Some akratic agents might simply take there to be good and sufficient reason for not *A*-ing—hence, the parenthetical clause. However, we need not concern ourselves for present purposes with a distinction between such taking and taking there to be good and sufficient reason for not acting on a desire. (My guess is that Neely had the former sort of taking in mind, anyway.)

3. I argue for the possibility of genuine, uncompelled akratic action in Mele 1987a, chs. 2, 3, and 6.

4. Both sorts of resistance are discussed at greater length in Mele 1987a, chs. 2.2 and 4. Incidentally, Gilbert Harman claims that *any* "positive" intention to *A* is formed as a means of bringing it about that one *A*-s (1976, p. 440; cf. 1986a, ch. 8). I attack this contention in chapter 11.

5. Someone who is able prior to *t* to *A* at (or by) *t* may not be able at *t* to *A* then—hence, the need for double temporal indices in statements of ability. On this point, see Goldman 1970, pp. 200–201.

6. See, in this connection, the account in chapter 3.3 of an agent's taking himself to be able to *A*.

7. In a suitably broad sense of 'able', it should be uncontroversial that we succeed in doing only those things that we are able to do.

8. Ronald de Sousa contends that not all desires are such that the agent "is conscious of some point in time . . . to which the desire applies" (1987, p. 211; cf. Baier 1976). I am not denying this. More specifically, I am not claiming that all desires encompass an *explicit* or *conscious* temporal reference.

9. The broad conception is discussed in chapter 6. For a detailed analysis of intentional action, see Brand 1984, pp. 28–29, 216–17. I identify a problem with Brand's analysis in Mele 1987c. Still, Brand's tack is promising; and suitable modifications might well be forthcoming.

10. On motivational ties, see ch. 3.5–7.

6

Effective Reasons

Garden-variety explanations of intentional actions feature reasons. The reasons for which we act—what I shall call *effective* reasons—are often construed, following Donald Davidson (1980, ch. 1), as belief/desire pairs. This construal, in its standard form, postulates a division of labor between beliefs and desires that is well suited to a common species of intentional action. However, the plausibility of dividing the labor in the standard way is undermined by attention to *intrinsically motivated actions*—roughly, actions done for their own sakes. In the present chapter, I shall argue that intrinsically motivated actions are done for reasons, show that this tells against Davidson's account of the reasons for which we act, and develop an alternative conception of effective reasons that accommodates intrinsically motivated actions. My goal in so doing is further refinement of the belief/desire model of action-explanation outlined in chapter 1.

1. Reasons: Some Preliminaries

"A primary reason for an action," Davidson asserts, "is its cause" (1980, p. 12). Obviously, items other than the reasons for which agents act contribute causally to their so acting. But this observation can be accommodated by a weaker version of Davidson's claim: a reason for which an agent A-s is a (significant) cause of his A-ing. If either claim, literally interpreted, is true, the reasons for which agents act—*effective* reasons—must in some way be located, or realized, in agents.

This is already problematic for some contributors to the enormous philosophical literature on reasons. Consider, for example, the view that reasons are *propositions*. Although agents can *accept* propositions and attitudes of acceptance are properly ascribed to agents, propositions themselves are not located or realized in agents. For my purposes, it makes little difference whether reasons are viewed as psychological states of agents or, alternatively, as abstract entities (e.g., propositions) such that an agent's *having* a reason is a matter of his standing in a certain psychological relation to an abstract item. On the former view, reasons themselves can make a causal contribution to intentional action; on the latter, the contribution is made by *havings* of reasons. There is something to be said for both construals, and I opt for neutrality on this issue. If reasons are psychological states, 'reasons' in this chapter denotes these states; if reasons are *abstracta,* 'reasons' here denotes the psychological states that constitute havings of reasons, unless otherwise indicated.

The expression '*S has* a reason to *A*', as I shall use it, attributes a psychological state to *S.* This is compatible, incidentally, with one brand of externalism about reasons. My reading of '*S* has a reason to *A*' leaves it open that *there is* a reason for *A* to be done by Fred even if it is false that Fred *has* a reason to *A* (see Mele 1989d).

2. Intrinsically Motivated Actions: A Problem

Although intrinsically motivated action has received little attention in contemporary philosophy of action, it is far from being a mere technical curiosity.[1] One variety is of great importance to some prominent moral philosophers. Aristotle made it a necessary condition of being virtuous that an agent perform virtuous actions "for the sake of the acts themselves" (*Nicomachean Ethics* 1144a18–20; cf. 1105a28–33), and Kant embraced a similar idea in the *Groundwork of the Metaphysic of Morals* (1964). The phenomenon merits scrutiny.

In his pioneering book on the philosophy of action, Alvin Goldman suggested the following:

1. An action is an intentional action if and only if it is done for a reason. (1970, p. 76)

Donald Davidson is prepared to say at least that "it is (logically) impossible to perform an intentional action without some appropriate reason" (1980, p. 264). On a natural (context-sensitive) reading, this claim implies one half of the biconditional expressed in thesis 1:

1*. An action is an intentional action only if it is done for a reason.

Several years earlier, Davidson had advanced an influential conception of the reasons for which actions are done—*effective* reasons (1963). Crudely put, the account is this:

2. Any reason for which a person does an action *A* is a want/belief pair such that the belief identifies the agent's *A*-ing as conducive to the achievement of the wanted item.

Theses *1** and *2* jointly imply

3. An action is an intentional action only if it is done for a reason consisting of a want/belief pair such that the belief identifies the agent's *A*-ing as conducive to the achievement of the wanted item.

Unfortunately, thesis *3* is false.

As I shall explain in section 6, thesis *1** is controversial. However, thesis *3,* as I shall argue, is falsified by certain intentional actions that *are* done for reasons. My target is thesis *2*. In sections 4 and 5 I advance an alternative to thesis *2* that preserves the spirit of Davidson's account of effective reasons while avoiding a problem posed by intrinsically motivated actions. Additional groundwork must first be laid.

In textbook instances of intentional action, an agent has a goal that he believes he can achieve by means of an action of a certain type. Al wishes to show Bob how much he appreciates his philosophical help over the years and he believes that an excellent way of doing this is to send Bob an autographed copy of his new book along with a letter of appreciation. So Al autographs the book, writes the letter, and mails them to Bob. The conception of reasons expressed in thesis *2* is tailor-made for such cases.

Now, suppose that Al has no ulterior motive for showing his appreciation to Bob. Suppose that showing his appreciation to Bob is, for Al, an *end* and that he does not also regard it as a means to some further end. Let us refer to such action as *wholly intrinsically motivated*. Al's showing his appreciation to Bob—his *A*-ing—is an action, and it is, moreover, an intentional action. So if thesis *3* is true, Al *A*-ed for a reason; and his reason for *A*-ing consisted of a want/belief pair such that the belief identified Al's *A*-ing as conducive to the wanted item. (Again, it is not necessary to choose among major competing methods of act-individuation. The reader is free, for example, to construe the action variable '*A*' as standing for an action under a description or for an act-token, in Gold-man's fine-grained sense.)[2]

Here we encounter a problem. Ex hypothesi, it is not because Al be-lieves his expressing his appreciation to Bob to be conducive to the achievement of a wanted item that he expresses his appreciation to Bob. To be sure, he does want to show his appreciation to Bob. But that want is linked, by a conduciveness belief, to his sending Bob the letter and auto-graphed book, not to his showing his appreciation to Bob. In short, a belief of the sort called for in thesis *3* is no part of anything that might count as the (or a) reason for which Al displayed his appreciation to Bob.

Faced with the choice of rejecting thesis *1** or thesis *2,* one may be inclined to reject the former. One might maintain that although Al *A*-s intentionally, he does not *A* for a reason and that thesis *1*,* therefore, is false. However, caution is appropriate. Suppose that we ask Al why he performed the action of showing his appreciation to Bob. He might respond as follows: "I deeply appreciate everything that Bob has done for me, and I wanted to convey that to him." Here, Al does not identify a *further* reason for which he showed his appreciation to Bob. But he does, I suggest, identify an appropriate reason. The reason for which he showed his appreciation to Bob was just that he wanted to do this—for its own sake, and not for the sake of some further end. I shall return to this suggestion later. It suffices for present purposes to mark a prima facie distinction between doing something for a *further* reason (*A*-ing in order to do, get, promote one's chances of having, etc., something further) and doing something for a reason. The former may be only a species of the latter.[3]

Consider a second case. Chris is in the habit of whistling while he works alone in his tool shed. Today, in this rustic setting, he finds himself whistling a moving Vivaldi tune; and he continues, now fully aware of what he is doing. Chris's continued whistling seems quite clearly to be intentional: He does not accidentally, inadvertently, absentmindedly, or unwittingly continue to whistle. I would not be at all inclined to with-draw this judgment if I were to discover that Chris's continued whistling is done for no *further* reason.

If Chris whistles intentionally but not for any further reason, we are again faced with a choice between rejecting thesis *1** and rejecting thesis *2.*[4] Either some intentional actions are not done for reasons or some reasons for which intentional actions are done have no belief element that identifies the intentional action (or actions of that type) as condu-cive to the achievement of some wanted item.

3. Davidson's Apparent Resolution

I mentioned that (2) is a *crude* formulation of Davidson's account of effective reasons. What Davidson actually *says* is this:

2*. *R* is a primary reason why an agent performed the action *A* under the description *d* only if *R* consists of a pro attitude of the agent toward actions with a certain property, and a belief of the agent that *A*, under description *d*, has that property. (1980, p. 5)

Let some '*A* under description *d*' be Al's wholly intrinsically motivated action of showing his appreciation to Bob. Thesis 2* yields the following description of the reason *Ra* for which Al performed this action (if there was a reason): *Ra* consists of Al's pro attitude toward actions with the property of being a showing of his appreciation to Bob and a belief that his showing his appreciation to Bob has that property.[5] Thus, we see that an account of effective reasons that is tailor-made for action done for further reasons is applicable as well to wholly intrinsically motivated action. Thesis 2* has this advantage over 2. Since 2* is Davidson's own account of effective reasons, where, the patient reader may ask, is the rub?

Here. The belief component of a Davidsonian effective reason is supposed to do important causal work. In the case of actions done for further reasons, the work is easily identified. Don wants to build a superb squirrel house, and he believes that Elizabeth has the best squirrel house blueprints in the hemisphere; so he calls Elizabeth to ask for a copy of the plans. The belief contributes to Don's action by identifying an attractive means to a wanted item. But consider the belief that Al's showing his appreciation to Bob has the property of being a showing of his appreciation to Bob. What job would we reasonably call upon it to do in the etiology of Al's showing his appreciation to Bob? None at all. To be sure, Al may need some conception or representation of his showing his appreciation to Bob in order to perform the action intentionally. But there is no need to import a belief of the sort at issue to carry the conception or representation. The requisite representation, as we shall see shortly, is a feature of Al's desire to show his appreciation to Bob.

Thesis 2* has the virtue of being applicable both to effective further reasons and to what we may call effective *intrinsic* reasons, that is, effective reasons that are not further reasons. However, the belief components that 2^* supplies for these other effective reasons (if there are any such reasons) are causally otiose.

4. Another Resolution: Plan Elements

If there are effective intrinsic reasons, the *conative* side of Davidson's account of the reasons for which we act is easily applied to them. If effective further reasons also have a *representational* element in common with effective intrinsic reasons, we may be able to produce an account of effective reasons that applies attractively to both sorts. I suggested that Al's wholly intrinsically motivated action of showing his appreciation to Bob was performed for a reason and that the reason for which he performed this action was simply that he wanted to do so. If this is right, we should examine Al's *want* in attempting to locate the representational element of his effective reason.

First, however, let us take a brief look at intentions. Intentions, as I shall argue in subsequent chapters, are plausibly regarded as having both a conative and a representational element. The function of the conative element is to motivate action, while the representational element *guides* action. The representational element incorporates what we may call an *action plan,* or simply a *plan.* Plans need not be complex, detailed, or explicitly entertained. In the limiting case, an agent's plan for acting is a simple representation of his performing a basic action of a certain type. In other cases, the agent's plan is a representation of his prospective A-ing and of the route to A-ing that he intends to take.[6]

Beliefs of the sort identified in thesis 2 also incorporate plans, or elements of plans. The content of Al's belief that an excellent way to show his appreciation to Bob is to send him a letter and an autographed copy of his book constitutes part of the plan that Al forms for showing his appreciation to Bob. More generally, when S A-s for a further reason $R,$ any linking belief involved in R will provide some part (at least) of S's action plan. Indeed, we may say that these linking beliefs contribute to the causation of intentional action (at least partly) by providing constituents of the action plans executed by agents.

Return to Al's wholly intrinsically motivated action and to the suggestion that the reason for which he performed this action was simply that he wanted to do this. If wants were brute forces wholly devoid of representational content, the project of the present section would be hopeless. But wants are not like that at all. They do have representational content; for what is wanted is wanted under some conception or other.

This point can be exploited. I suggested that in the limiting case of the plan component of an intention, the plan is a simple representation of a basic action. I suggest now that in the limiting case of the plan element of an effective reason, the plan element is just a representation of a goal. Thus, while the plan element of the reason for which Al sent the letter and book to Bob is provided by a belief that doing these things would be an excellent way of expressing his appreciation, the plan element of the reason for which Al showed his appreciation to Bob is provided by his *want* to do this—or, more precisely, by the representational content of that want.[7] The plan that Al follows in showing his appreciation to Bob in the way that he does is composed of these and other plan elements.

Myles Brand has argued that belief is not the representational component of intention (1984, ch. 6); and I shall produce additional arguments to the same effect in chapter 8. What I am suggesting now, in part, is that if there is a representational element common to all effective reasons, it is not belief. This is by no means to deny that the contents of beliefs—specifically, linking beliefs—are important elements in many effective reasons. But if there are effective, wholly intrinsic reasons, there is no place for significant connecting beliefs in them. Still, if I am right, both sorts of reason do have a representational element in common; for both include elements of action plans executed by the agent. In the case of effective further reasons, linking beliefs provide plan elements. In the case of effective intrinsic reasons, the plan elements are provided by the representational content of a pertinent want.

5. Questions and Answers

The alternative to thesis 2 that I have been proposing may be formulated as follows:

2**. Any reason for which a person acts has a conative element that motivates the pursuit of a goal or a subgoal and a representational element that constitutes a plan, or an element of a plan, for achieving the pertinent goal or subgoal.[8]

This account applies to both sorts of effective reasons I have identified, and it does so without rendering the representational aspect of effective intrinsic reasons causally insignificant.

On the assumption that wholly intrinsically motivated intentional actions are done for reasons, the points just mentioned are virtues of *2***. But *are* these actions done for reasons? Paradigm examples of actions that are *not* done for reasons are *unintentional* actions.

FRANK: "For what reason did you cut your hand?"

GIL: "No reason at all (you idiot!); I accidentally nicked it while peeling potatoes."

We sometimes speak similarly of certain intentional actions.

HECTOR: "For what reason are you now chewing gum?"

IRVING: "No reason; I just feel like it."

But here, as some philosophers have noted, the speaker is plausibly taken to have identified a reason, namely, that he feels like chewing gum (Locke 1974, p. 172). His response may be taken as elliptical for 'No *further* reason (e.g., not in order to put myself in a position to blow bubbles), but only for the reason that I want to chew gum'.

In chapter 3, following Goldman, I termed a desire of something (e.g., an action) for its own sake an *intrinsic* desire. (A desire of something for its own sake—and not also for the sake of something further— may be termed a *wholly intrinsic* desire.) Now surely, insofar as someone has an intrinsic desire to perform an action, there is something to be said, from his own point of view, for his performing it, namely, that performing it would satisfy an intrinsic desire of his. In short, an intrinsic desire gives one (or *is*) a reason for action. And if an agent acts *for* a reason of the sort in question—that is, for the reason that he desires the action as an end—we have located a reason *for which* he acted, an *effective* reason.[9]

In a sense, the reason is just the intrinsic desire or want. But this is not to say that the reason is wholly conative. There is also a representational element, inherent in the want. Again, what that representational element has in common with the representational elements of further reasons is that it is an element of an action plan.

My criticism of *2** was that the connecting beliefs that it builds into the reasons for which purely intrinsically motivated actions are performed are causally otiose. However, the representational element identified in *2*** has an important function in the etiology of actions of the sort at issue. Action plans *guide* intentional actions. And the various elements of these plans contribute to the guiding function of the plans.

Consider a relatively simple action, Judy's logging into a mainframe computer that she uses frequently. To log in, she types 'login' and her two passwords and then hits the return key. Her plan for logging in represents the steps to be taken, in the appropriate order. It also represents the goal state, her being logged in. That her plan does include this last item is indicated by what one would expect to happen if, in executing the various steps in the plan, Judy does not succeed in logging in. She might try again on the same terminal, perhaps assuming that she mistyped a password not displayed on the screen or that there was a glitch in the procedure. She might try to log in at another terminal. And so on. In any case, if her plan was to log in and not just to go through the procedures involved in logging in, she would not be satisfied. A likely explanation of her not being satisfied is that she realized that she had not succeeded in doing what she planned to do, or (as we might say) that she had not successfully executed her plan. And an attractively simple explanation here is that the plan included a goal state representation that was not, to the best of her knowledge, matched in the world.

The reason that I have belabored this point about the goal element of action plans is that I have suggested, as a way of avoiding the problem with 2*, that effective intrinsic reasons incorporate representations of the agent's goal in acting and that what this representational element has in common with the representational elements in effective further reasons is that, like them, it is part of an action plan. Now, to be sure, agents do not always know whether they have succeeded in doing what they intended to do. Not all actions are like Judy's in that respect. If Kenny plans to toss a cantaloupe over a stone wall into a basket situated at the base of the other side of the wall, he may not know whether he has succeeded until he climbs the wall to check. But this does not affect the present point. For the point is that when one plans to A or to bring about B one is not satisfied with one's efforts, other things being equal, if one knows that one has not succeeded in A-ing or in bringing about B—and that this suggests that one's A-ing or bringing about B is part of the plan.

6. Acting for Reasons and Acting Intentionally

In setting the stage for the focal problem of this chapter, I made use of the popular thesis that to act intentionally is to act for a reason—thesis 1 above. Not surprisingly, this thesis is controversial. Neither my central criticism of Davidson's conception of effective reasons nor my own account of such reasons depends upon the truth of the thesis. Nevertheless, 1 merits brief attention.

The suggestion that one who A-s for a reason A-s intentionally encounters little resistance. It is noteworthy in this connection that many cases generating controversy about whether an agent has *intentionally* A-ed introduce comparable puzzles about whether the agent has A-ed for a reason. Consider a pair of questions of a kind raised in chapter 1.2. When a basketball player, Connie, tries to sink a last-second basket from midcourt and, executing her plan for doing so, succeeds in sinking the shot, is her making the basket *intentional* even though she knew that her chances of success were slim? When, intending to kill Jack by shooting him through the heart, Jill fires a shot that kills Jack by piercing his right foot, is the killing *intentional?* (Unbeknownst to Jill, Jack was a hemophiliac.)

In both cases, something was done intentionally. Connie intentionally threw the basketball, for example; and Jill intentionally fired the gun. These indisputably intentional actions plainly were done for reasons. Where questions arise about what is done intentionally in these cases, they also arise about what was done for a reason. Presumably, Connie had a reason to make the basket, a reason that figured in the etiology of her behavior. But were the circumstances such that we can properly say that she made the basket *for a reason?* Similarly, we naturally suppose that Jill had a reason to kill Jack, one that partially explains her behavior. But is her killing Jack properly said to have been done for a reason? Or is it rather the case only that ball throwing and gun firing were done for a reason?

My guess is that readers who come down squarely on one side or the other of the questions posed in the preceding paragraph will embrace the same side of the questions about what was done intentionally. If Connie's sinking the shot and Jill's killing Jack count as actions done for a reason, what is to prevent their counting as intentional actions? The question about intentionality is raised by the agent-acknowledged improbability of Connie's success and by the remoteness of Jill's actual killing from the intended killing. But these are precisely the factors that raise questions about what was done for a reason.

Whether A-ing intentionally entails A-ing for a reason is more controversial. One problem is raised by actional parts of more extended actions. Consider someone walking to work—intentionally, and for a reason. Presumably, the various steps that she takes are intentional; but is each individual step taken for a reason? Perhaps the agent, Alice, has no reason to take just this step, a wholly routine one. As I shall argue later, it would be a mistake to insist that she *intends* to take just this step. Still, we naturally say, the step was an intentional step. The step is intentional in virtue of its being a routine actional part of an intentional action,

Alice's walking to work. The intentionality of the step is inherited from the intentionality of the "larger" action of which it is a part. Similarly, we may say that the step is, in a derivative sense, taken for a reason and that its being so taken is a matter of its being a routine actional part of the larger action, walking to work, that is performed for a reason. Readers who are uncomfortable with this suggestion may hold out for a modified version of thesis *1* that is not advanced as applying to certain actional parts of intentional actions.

Another problem is posed by some cases of double effect. If certain nonintended but foreseen actional side effects of an agent's intentional actions are properly counted as intentional actions even though they are not done for reasons, then *1* is false. Consider the following passage: "In firing his gun, [a] sniper [who is trying to kill a soldier] knowingly alerts the enemy to his presence. He does this intentionally, thinking that the gain is worth the possible cost. But he certainly does not intend to alert the enemy to his presence" (Harman 1976, p. 433). Harman's claim that the sniper *intentionally* alerts the intended victim's comrades even though he does not *intend* to do so is controversial (see ch. 8). But suppose, for the sake of argument, that he is right about this. Suppose, as well, that alerting the enemy is not something that the sniper does *for a reason*. (He *fires the gun* for a reason, of course; but the reason for which he fires the gun is not also a reason for which he alerts the enemy.) Then we have an intentional alerting that is not done for a reason.

This is an issue that I shall leave open; but more can be said. Although Harman's sniper has no reason specifically to alert the enemy to his presence, he apparently has a reason to fire at the soldier *at the expense of* alerting the enemy. Harman implies that the sniper prefers this to the alternative of refraining from firing and remaining undetected. And the sniper presumably so prefers for a reason. If so, he has, as we might say, a reason for engaging in a course of action that, as he knows, includes, in addition to his firing, his alerting the enemy to his presence—a reason for "*E*-ing" (for short). And he might well proceed to *E for* that reason. Assuming that the sniper intentionally *E*-s and given the place that alerting the enemy occupies in *E*-ing, some might happily claim he alerts the enemy intentionally. But then the intentionality of his alerting the enemy is plausibly regarded as being derivative in part from his having *E*-ed for a reason. Thus, even if one were to grant that an agent might intentionally *A* while lacking a reason specifically to *A,* one might, consistently with this concession, insist on a tight connection between acting intentionally and acting for reasons. The concession leaves open the following hypothesis, for example:

H. Any intentional action *A* that (1) is encompassed by a "larger" intentional action and (2) is not done for a reason (specific to *A*), inherits its intentionality from that of some larger intentional action that encompasses *A; and* all intentionality-conferring larger intentional actions are done for reasons (or are suitably encompassed in intentional actions done for reasons).

If the allegedly problematic cases of double effect admit of plausible interpretation along the lines just sketched in the sniper's case, *H* is promising. However, for my purposes in this book, the truth of *H* is not required.[10]

7. More Neutrality

Much of this chapter has been devoted to constructing a Davidsonian account of effective reasons that is well suited both to further reasons and to what I have called *intrinsic* reasons. The account is Davidsonian in that it preserves Davidson's fruitful idea that an effective reason is composed of a conative element and a representational element that links conation to appropriate behavior.

In section 1 I opted for neutrality on an ontological issue about reasons. My primary purpose in so doing was to fix attention on the psychological antecedents of action. The question whether certain of these antecedents are properly termed "reasons" or "havings of reasons" is, for my purposes, best greeted with indifference. If 'havings of reasons' is the appropriate label, then the Davidsonian idea that I have been at pains to preserve may be reformulated as follows: effective havings of reasons—that is, effective states of reason having—possess a conative element and a representational element that links conation to appropriate behavior.

Some prefer to identify reasons with "linking" representational states alone (or the contents of the states), while others urge an identification of reasons with conative states (or their contents).[11] However, if states of both sorts play a causal role in the production of intentional action, it is of no consequence for the model of action-explanation being developed in this book whether one elects to identify (havings of) reasons with states of one or the other kind individually or with states of both kinds jointly. States of both sorts, on the view to be advanced, jointly contribute to intentional action by contributing jointly to the formation or acquisition of *intentions.*[12]

Notes

1. On intrinsically motivated action, see Audi 1986b, pp. 542–44; Champlin 1987. Audi has claimed that "if intrinsically motivated actions are actions for reasons, then intentional action is equivalent to action for a reason" (1986b, p. 544).

2. See ch. 1.1 and Goldman 1970, ch. 1.

3. On this distinction, see Audi 1986b, p. 543; Davidson 1980, p. 6; Locke 1974, p. 172.

4. More cautiously, the choice may be between rejecting thesis 2 and rejecting a qualified version of thesis 1^* that is neutral on instances of double effect, for example (see sec. 6).

5. Compare this with Davidson's remark that when 'He just wanted to' is "given in explanation of why Sam played the piano at midnight, it implies that he wanted to make true a certain proposition, that Sam play the piano at midnight, and he believed that by acting as he did, he would make it true" (1980, p. 232). I leave it to the reader to identify a want/belief pair to be given in explanation of Sam's action of making true the proposition that Sam played the piano at midnight.

6. As I use the term 'action plan' here, action plans are purely representational. There are more robust conceptions of action plans in the literature, according to which they necessarily have a motivational element. For present purposes, readers who endorse such conceptions are free to substitute 'the representational element of an (action) plan' for each instance of '(action) plan' in the text. I defend my less robust notion of plans in chapter 8.3.

7. Notice that I do not say that the representational content of *every* intrinsic want provides the agent with a plan element that is, for example, sufficiently accessible to consciousness or coherent to permit execution.

8. I am not suggesting that reasons do all the motivating work, of course.

9. The reason need not be a *good* one, of course; and an agent's having acted for a reason of the pertinent kind need not render the action *rational*. The action may be akratic, for example. On the irrationality of akratic action, see Mele 1987a.

Rosalind Hursthouse (1991) attempts to show that Davidson's "account of actions and their explanations" is "fundamentally flawed" by appealing to a species of intrinsically motivated action—what she terms "arational actions." Examples of arational actions include striking an inanimate object in anger and gouging out the eyes in a photograph of a hated person. Licking something furry (when "seized by a sudden desire" to do so) is a close relative. Arational actions (by definition) are done for no *further* reason; and actions of the kinds just mentioned typically seem unreasonable. But it would be a mistake to conclude from this that such actions are done for no reason at all. If our reasons can be every bit as bizarre as our actions, so-called arational actions are implausibly treated as exceptions to the thesis that all intentional actions are done for reasons. A man with an irrational urge to drink a can of paint and the knowledge that drinking the paint requires removing the lid might *pry off the lid* for a reason; and he can *drink the paint* for a reason, too—a reason constituted by an intrinsic desire to drink it.

10. In a paper in progress on Gregory Kavka's (1983) toxin puzzle (Mele n.d.[a]), I argue for the possibility of intentional actions that are not done for reasons (and do not inherit their intentionality from that of larger actions that encompass them). The argument would require a chapter of its own; and the point that is establishes, given the highly contrived nature of the cases that convince me of its truth, is peripheral to my concerns in this book.

11. For example, Locke identifies "agent-reasons" with the contents of beliefs (1974, p. 169); and Audi construes "reasons for which one acts as the contents of motivating wants" (1986b, p. 513).

12. Some readers might find it puzzling, given the centrality of desire to part I of this book, that I have said nothing about second-order desires. Second-order desires are real enough and can influence behavior. However, like emotions, they are among the springs that I have chosen not to examine in this already-lengthy book. (I address the topic in Mele n.d.[b], where I argue that second-order motivational states do not play nearly as pervasive a role as some have alleged for them. See also Harman n.d.)

PART II

7

Transition: Introducing Intentions

The discussion in part I was conducted largely within the framework of a traditional approach to explaining intentional action featuring beliefs, desires, and reasons as central explanatory items. In chapter 2 I identified the central presuppositions of the commonsense idea that (often enough) what we believe, desire, intend, and the like makes a difference in what we do, and I argued that the viability of an associated intentionalistic, causal approach to the explanation of intentional action is not undermined by recent worries about the causal relevance of the mental. Chapters 3 and 4 tackled the relationship between wanting and intentional action. Chapter 3 advanced a principle relating the two; chapter 4 defended the principle against objections that, I argued, misinterpreted its status. One such objection takes as a premise what I termed the *plasticity* of motivational strength—roughly, the point (defended at length in Mele 1987a) that normal agents have considerable control over desire-strength. Unless a desire is irresistible, I claimed, it is in some sense up to the agent whether he acts on it. This observation called for a characterization of irresistible desire. The burden of chapter 5 was to produce a successful one. Finally, in chapter 6 I developed an account of the reasons for which we act—effective reasons—that applies to extrinsically and intrinsically motivated action alike.

Much remains to be done. In chapter 3.6 I suggested that an agent who makes the transition from wanting to A—even preponderantly so wanting—to intending to A makes progress toward action that cannot be articulated wholly in terms of motivational strength. This suggestion clashes with "pure" belief/desire models of action-explanation, models that either do not recognize intention as a genuine mental item at all or treat it as reducible to complexes of beliefs and desires. Part II develops a nonreductive conception of intention while examining the roles that intention plays in our lives.

121

1. Reasons-Explanations

Standard belief/desire models for the explanation of intentional behavior are designed to generate *reasons-explanations*.[1] A reasons-explanation of an intentional action A supposedly explains the agent's A-ing by identifying the reason(s) for which he A-ed.

The traditional models give the distinct impression of having been designed specifically for rational behavior. At any rate, garden-variety instances of *irrational* behavior raise serious problems for them. Consider akratic action—roughly, uncompelled, intentional action against the agent's better judgment.[2] The agent of an akratic action acts for a reason. But citing the reason for which he acts does not adequately explain his action. After all, the agent also had a reason or reasons for performing some competing action, the action judged best. What cries out for explanation is the agent's acting for the reason(s) that he did rather than for a competing reason; and typically, as I argued in *Irrationality* (Mele 1987a), there is no adequate reasons-explanation of this.

Reasons-explanations of intentional behavior are adequate, at least for some purposes, when agents lack competing motivation. When I walked home today to meet Connie for lunch, I was wholly unmotivated to perform any competing action. Given the absence of competing motivation and assuming a normal context, I may adequately explain my going home simply be citing the reason for which I did so. But what explains an agent's acting as he does when he has competing reasons for action? Some philosophers have attempted to locate the answer in better judgments: though S had reasons to A and reasons to B, a competing action, he judged it better to A and consequently did A rather than B. This is Davidson's tack in "How Is Weakness of the Will Possible?" (1970); but it is unsuccessful. The agent of an akratic action judges it best to do A and yet intentionally does B, a competing action.[3]

One might seek a resolution in a retreat to the thesis that whatever an agent's better judgment may be, he acts as he is most motivated to act. However, this strategy does not yield an *explanation* of the agent's behavior. We take it for granted that the akratic agent was most motivated to act as he did. His action has not been explained until it is explained why he was in the motivational condition in question. (This is a major theme in Mele 1987a. It also appeared in chapter 4.)

Continent action (roughly, intentional action in accordance with one's better judgment) raises the same problem.[4] Resisting temptation, Mary A-s, as she judged best. Mary's behavior cannot be explained simply by noting that she judged it best to A; for if judging A best (in conjunction with such standing conditions as having the ability to A) were sufficient for A-ing, we would never act akratically.[5] Nor is Mary's behavior explained by observing that she was most motivated to A. Again, we must explain *why* she was most motivated to A. There is, then, a *general* problem about the application of standard belief/desire models to cases of motivational conflict.

Wholesale abandonment of the traditional belief/desire approach to action-explanation would be a rash response. What must be discarded is the assumption that citing the reason(s) for which an agent A-ed is, in all cases, sufficient to explain his A-ing. However, a much more modest version of this assumption, one featured in chapter 6, is quite plausible: for the most part, at any rate, intentional actions are actions done for reasons, where an action is *done for* a reason R only if R (or the agent's having R) figures in the etiology of the action.

Explaining intentional actions might profitably be seen as falling generally into two stages. Stage 1 identifies the reason(s) for which the agent acted, while stage 2 explains his acting for *that* reason (or those reasons). At this second level, the explanation of akratic action that I advanced in *Irrationality* made considerable use of a collection of psychological states, traits, and activities that have received scant attention in the philosophy of action. For example, such items as attention, the perceived proximity of a reward and self-control occupy an important place in the account offered.

But how do *intentions* enter into the story? If we can explain an agent's intentional action by identifying the reason for which he acted and showing why he acted for that reason, what explanatory role is left for intentions? One possibility is that when an agent harbors competing reasons, the reason for which he A-s is the reason that leads to a corresponding intention. If that is right, explaining why an agent acted for a certain reason might amount to explaining why that reason issued in an intention.

Unfortunately, matters are not so simple. As I argued in *Irrationality* and shall argue again briefly in chapter 9, even an intention to do something straightaway may be defeated in an instance of akrasia; and it may be replaced by another intention. Given this point about the defeasibility of intentions, more is required of an explanation of intentional action in some cases than that it identify the reason for which the agent acted and explain why that reason issued in a pertinent intention. We want an explanation, as well, of the intention's efficacy. If intentions are effective in some cases and defeated in others, one may explain why an agent's reason to A resulted in an intention to A without yet explaining his A-ing. Why is it that this agent A-ed while another akratically failed to A, even though in both cases the agent's reason for A-ing gave rise to an intention to A straightaway?

Even if akratic action raised no problems about the connection between intentions and intentional actions, an account of that connection would be desirable. In answering questions of the form "Why did S do A?" (when A is presumed to be an intentional action), we rarely cite the agent's *intention* to A. Rather, standard answers are framed in terms of reasons. However, if, as I shall argue, proximal intentions mediate between reasons and actions done for reasons, we shall want to understand intention's mediating role and the features of intention that enable it to fill that role.

One lesson that a careful look at akratic action teaches us (or so I have argued; see Mele 1983, 1984, 1987a) is that an agent need not be most motivated to do what he intends to do, even when he intends to A *straightaway*. If that is right, accounts of intention that make preponderant motivation an essential feature of the state (Alston 1974; Audi 1973, 1986a; W. Davis 1984; Tuomela 1977) must be rejected. Once we leave such accounts behind, an interesting possibility suggests itself: perhaps even effective intentions need not incorporate preponderant motivation. And now we face a very difficult question. If an effective intention to A does not issue in an intentional A-ing in virtue of its incorporating preponderant motivation to A, then what is it about intentions that enables them to give rise to intentional actions? I shall offer an answer in chapter 10, one that gets directly at the heart of the nature of intentions and their action-producing capacity.

2. Psychological Literature on Intention

Wittgenstein once remarked that "in psychology there are experimental methods and *conceptual confusion*" (*Investigations* 2.14 [1953]). This is grossly unfair, of course; but there is an element of truth in the claim as it applies to recent psychological work on intention. As psychologists Paul Warshaw and Fred Davis have observed, "Social psychologists have extensively researched behavioral intention and its relation to future behavior, *usually within the framework of M. Fishbein and I. Ajzen's . . . theory of reasoned action*" (1985, p. 213; my italics). Given their influence on the empirical work, Fishbein and Ajzen's definition of 'intention' is worth noting. "In many respects," they claim, "intentions may be viewed as a special case of beliefs, in which the object is always the person himself and the attribute is always a behavior" (Fishbein and Ajzen 1975, p. 12). More concisely: "A behavioral intention" is "a person's subjective probability that he will perform some behavior" (p. 288).[6]

Warshaw and Davis reject the definition on grounds that Anscombe's readers could not have failed to note: '*S* intends to do *A*' and '*S* believes that he (*S*) will do *A*' are not coextensive (1963, pp. 1–7). As Warshaw and Davis put the point, we have here two "distinct constructs, easily separable in people's minds"; yet "social psychologists have unknowingly lumped them together under the intention rubric, most frequently in research on Fishbein and Ajzen's theory of reasoned action" (1985, p. 214). Interestingly, Warshaw and Davis introduce the distinction by means of a case in which an agent who allegedly intends to *A* believes that he probably will not *A*. The question whether such cases are possible is addressed in chapter 8. But it is clear that an agent who does *not* intend to *A* may nevertheless believe that he will *A*. Jane, whose relations with her mother have been strained for years, believes now, simply on inductive grounds, that she will insult her mother in the future. However, she does not intend to insult her mother; indeed, Jane has resolved to do her best to improve their relationship but is skeptical about her chances of avoiding insulting her mother.

Warshaw and Davis's own definition of 'intention' is problematic: "We define intention . . . as the degree to which a person has formulated conscious plans to perform or not perform some specified future behavior" (1985, p. 214). As I shall argue later, a person may have a plan *for A*-ing without intending to *A*. Granted, having formulated a plan *for A*-ing may differ significantly from having formulated a plan *to A*. But can we make the distinction without appealing to intention? Furthermore (setting aside the issue of 'degree'), must an agent who intends to *A* actually formulate a conscious plan to *A*? When I unlocked my office door this morning, I intended to do so. But I have no recollection of formulating a conscious plan to do so; nor, since the behavior is quite routine for me, is there any evident need to suppose that I must have performed the mental action of *forming* a conscious plan then. Perhaps the executed plan is stored in memory and simply accessed, rather than formulated, when needed.

Arie Kruglanski and Yechiel Klar offer another alternative to Fishbein and Ajzen's conception of intention: "When we say that a person *p* intends to execute action *a* we mean that *p* knows or is aware that *a* is what he or she wishes at the moment" (1985, p. 46). Again, there are problems. Suppose that at a time *t* an agent knows or is aware that he wishes to perform each of two mutually exclusive actions—say, accompanying his mother to midnight mass and escorting his daughter to a midnight dance. Does he intend to perform each action? Perhaps 'wishes' is to be understood as 'wishes (or wants) *most*'; but as I shall argue in chapter 9, we do not always intend to do what we want most to do (even when we know what we want most). Further, even when what we intend to do, *A*, is what we want most to do, must we know or be aware that *A* is what we want most? Are we aware of this when we routinely answer the phone, unlock the office door, or start the car?

Each of the questions raised in this section will be addressed, directly or indirectly, in subsequent chapters. At the very least, this brief review of some of the concepts of intention guiding empirical work indicates that there is a need in social psychology for some good, old-fashioned conceptual spadework. Portions of the following chapters are devoted to that task.

3. Preview

Causal accounts of intentional action have enjoyed a long and distinguished history. It is a commonplace in the literature that important causal antecedents of intentional action include items describable in the language of intentionalist psychology, that is, a psychology that gives intentional states (e.g., beliefs, desires, and intentions) a central place in the explanation of human behavior. In recent years, some of the most exciting work in the area has addressed the roles of *intention* in the etiology of intentional action.[7] On one promising view (adumbrated in chapters 3.6–7 and 6.4), the causal contribution to intention is traceable both to motivational aspects of intention and to representational features. Intentions, on this view, *move* us to act in virtue of their motivational properties and *guide* our intentional behavior in virtue of their representational qualities (see, e.g., Brand 1984, p. IV).

The chief burden of part II is to discover what intentions are and how they function. *Proximal* intention (intention for action in the specious present), as I shall argue, plays an important mediating role in the production of intentional behavior. But intentions, as I shall explain in chapter 8, are not *just* intermediaries between reasons and intentional actions. Michael Bratman (1987) and others have forcefully argued that intentions also have distinct coordinative roles. Moreover, by prompting practical reasoning, intentions may figure in the production of reasons for action.

Two general approaches that students of intention may take to their topic are worth distinguishing (see Bratman 1987, pp. 3–8). One might begin with intentional behavior and ask what intention must be if it is to figure in the production or explanation of such behavior. Alternatively, one might start by inquiring about the state of mind itself, independently of the behavior that it generates or explains. My own approach is a hybrid. In chapter 8, I note a serious tension in ordinary usage of 'intention' as it applies to intention's relation to intentional action and to belief. To the extent to which ordinary usage captures the commonsense conception of intention, that conception has conflicting implications. Chapter 8 offers a resolution based on an examination of the functions attributed to intention in the literature; and in the process, it presents a general sketch of the functional roles of intentions and of the features of intention in virtue of which it is capable of filling these roles.

Subsequent chapters fill in a host of details and argumentative lacunae. Chapter 9 examines the relationship between intention and decision and defends a pair of theses: (1) like decision, intention is an executive state; and (2) standard analyses of intention in terms of belief and desire do not capture the state's executive dimension. Chapter 10 develops an account of the executive aspect of *proximal* intentions in particular, while chapter 11 investigates the representational side of intentions. In chapter 11, I attack the increasingly popular view that the content of any intention makes essential reference to the intention whose content it is; and I advance an alternative position on the contents of intentions. Chapter 12 identifies various modes of intention acquisition, focusing primarily on the production of intentions by practical evaluative inference. Finally, chapter 13 disarms a recent attack on intentionalistic, causal theories of action-explanation.

Notes

1. Important recent versions of the belief/desire view are advanced in Audi 1979, 1980; Davidson 1963, 1970; Goldman 1970. See also Dretske 1988.

2. For a more precise account, see Mele 1987a, pp. 3–8.

3. For criticism of Davidson 1970, see Mele 1987a, ch. 3. I address Davidson's (1982b) later effort to illuminate akratic action in Mele 1987a, ch. 6.

4. For a distinction among different grades of continent action, see Mele 1987a, ch. 7.2

5. Here I am ignoring distinctions among different types of akratic action. See Mele 1987a, pp. 6–8, 18–19, 30, 42.

6. See also Ajzen 1985; Ajzen and Fishbein 1980; Fishbein 1980.

7. See, e.g., Alston 1986; Brand 1984; Bratman 1987; Castañeda 1975; O'Shaughnessy 1980; Searle 1983; and Sellars 1973.

8

Intention, Belief, and Intentional Action

Ordinary usage supports both a relatively strong belief requirement on intention and a tight conceptual connection between intention and intentional action. More specifically, it speaks in favor both of the view that '*S* intends to *A*' entails '*S* believes that he (probably) will *A*' and of the thesis that '*S* intentionally *A*-ed' entails '*S* intended to *A*'. So, at least, proponents of these ideas often claim or assume—and with appreciable justification.

The *conjunction* of these two ideas, however, has some highly counterintuitive implications. This suggests that a certain skepticism about the coherence of ordinary usage of 'intention' may be salutary. Fortunately, the skeptic need not abandon the quest for understanding. Much can be gleaned from a careful investigation of the *functions* attributed to intention in the literature.

In this chapter I argue that the capacity of intention to do the work that the literature assigns it does not depend upon intentional *A*-ing's entailing intending to *A*, nor does it depend upon there being a strong belief constraint on intention or even relatively weak counterpart belief constraints. In addition, I present a sketch of the features of intention in virtue of which it is capable of doing this work. This sketch provides the core of a proper conception of intention, a conception developed in subsequent chapters. Toward the end of the present chapter, I briefly motivate acceptance of a modest belief requirement (for "normal" intentions) on nonfunctional grounds.

1. Ordinary Usage: A Problem

Consider the following pair of theses, each of which has been advanced in the literature:[1]

1. S intends to A only if S believes that he (probably) will A.

2. S intentionally A-ed only if S intended to A.

The expression 'believes that he (probably) will A' in thesis *1* is short-hand for 'believes that he will A or believes that he probably will A'. The first disjunct circumvents the problem posed for a seemingly weaker, strictly probabilistic belief condition by cases in which an agent who intends to A has no concept of probability (e.g., a very young child). 'Probably' here is used in the sense of "more probable than not."

Thesis *1* derives support from the connection, in ordinary usage, between intention and *confidence*. An agent who is not confident that he will A (e.g., someone who thinks that his chances of A-ing are less than even) may *hope*, but cannot *intend*, to A—or so it has been argued (Audi 1973, 1986a). To appreciate the tightness of the connection in common parlance and thought between the antecedent and consequent of thesis *2*, readers need only try the following question on their friends: Can someone do something intentionally without intending to do it? The initial response typically reveals that one's auditors (even some philo-sophical auditors) treat '*intentional* action performed by S' as *synony-mous* with 'intended action performed by S'. The rehearsal of striking cases of causal waywardness generally prompts the recognition that an intended action performed by S need not be an intentional action and that the expressions therefore are not synonymous.[2] But in the absence of further Socratic cross-examination, people seem unwilling to counte-nance the idea that an intentional action might not be intended.

Theses *1* and *2* jointly entail

3. S intentionally A-ed only if S believed that he (probably) would A.

However, *3* is incompatible with another pronouncement of common sense and ordinary usage. Unfortunately, even a crude formulation would be very complex.[3] I shall identify one of its implications by example.

Al is a 45-percent shooter from the foul line, and he knows this. He sets himself for a free throw, believing that there is a less-than-even chance that he will make the basket. The attempt is successful. Surely, barring causal deviance, the great majority of English speakers would count Al's making the basket as an intentional action. Yet *3* entails that that action was not intentional.

Some weaker replacements for *3* have the same result. Consider the following less-demanding alternative to *1:*

1*. *S* intends to *A* only if *S* does not believe (at the pertinent time) that he (probably) will not *A*.

This is what we might call a *negative* belief constraint on intention. (Notice that not believing that *p* does not entail believing that not-*p*. One might have no belief at all on the matter.) Conjoined with *2, 1** yields

3*. *S* intentionally *A*-ed only if *S* did not believe (at the pertinent time) that he (probably) would not *A*.

And *3** entails that Al's making the basket was not an intentional action.

Theses *1, 1**, and *2* individually derive appreciable support from ordinary usage, as does the statement that Al's making the basket is an intentional action. Yet they cannot all be true. What is to be done?

2. The Functions of Intention

It is natural at this point to turn to theory. In the present section I identify the functions attributed to intention in the literature and show that the capacity of intention to perform them does not depend upon the truth of any of the numbered statements above.

Intentions as Initiating and Sustaining Motivators of Intentional Action

There is widespread agreement among philosophers of action that intention is a motivating cause of intentional actions. Now, intentions do not cause intentional actions in the way that pulling a trigger causes a gun to fire. In addition to any triggering or *initiating* function that intentions may have in the etiology of intentional action, they also have a *sustaining* function. This is indicated by what we would quite properly expect to happen if, in the midst of *A*-ing, an agent were to cease intending to *A*, namely that he would cease *A*-ing (provided that the *A*-ing has not proceeded so far that it cannot be stopped). Even if the purely representational or nonconative aspect of the former intention were to remain intact (more on this later), we would expect the cessation of intention to bring a halt to the *A*-ing. This indicates that the sustaining function of intentions, as they are commonly conceived, is at least partly conative or *motivational*.

Suppose for a moment that the alleged belief requirements *1* and *1** are true. Let us use '*S*'s *intention* to A*' for whatever is left of *S*'s intention to *A* when we substitute for his belief that he probably will *A* a belief that he probably will not *A*.[4] (*S*'s *intention** to *A* will not include anything whose absence is necessitated by the belief substitution, of course.) Can *S*'s intention* to *A* initiate and sustain an intentional *A*-ing in the way that intentions are supposed to do this?

Consider the following case. When Connie approaches the foul line with the intention of sinking a foul shot, she believes both that she has an 85-percent success rate on foul shots and that she will probably sink this shot. As she begins to take aim, we show her a sheet of statistics indicating that her success rate is only 45-percent. Connie, owing to her doxastic habits, no longer believes that she probably will make the basket; in fact, she believes that she probably will miss it. She proceeds to make a successful attempt to sink the shot; and absolutely everything pertinent to the etiology of the attempt and its success is precisely what it would have been in the absence of belief substitution. She tries no harder (or less hard) than she would otherwise have done, there is no increase (or decrease) in concentration, and so on.

By hypothesis, *nothing* relevant to the causation of Connie's sinking the shot changes with the belief substitution. Thus, if Connie's sinking the shot is an intentional *A*-ing, an intention* to *A* can cause an intentional *A*-ing in whatever manner intentions to *A* do. The moral is that the presence or absence of beliefs of the sort identified in *1* and *1** does not play an essential role in the causation of intentional *A*-ings by intentions to *A*. (This is not to say, of course, that they *never* play a role. Occasionally, one's confidence that one will succeed in *A*-ing causally contributes to one's success.)

Does an adequate account of the causal connection between intentions and the intentional actions in which they issue depend upon the truth of *2*, the contention that *S* intentionally *A*-ed only if *S* intended to *A*? Certainly, the account of intentional *A*-ing as *A*-ing brought about in "the right way" by an intention to *A* has the virtue of relative simplicity. But more than that has been claimed for the view. The denial of *2* entails the occurrence of nonintended intentional actions; and some contend that such alleged actions cannot be distinguished from nonintentional actions (Adams 1986; McCann 1986b).

Various positions on the conceptual connection between intention and intentional action have been advanced in the literature. Thesis *2* is expressive of what has aptly been termed the *simple view.*[5] Near the other extreme is the view that an agent may intentionally *A* without intending to do anything at all.[6] I shall suggest that an intermediate position preserves a distinction between intentional and nonintentional action while accommodating the belief requirements on intention specified in *1* and *1**. On the view to be sketched, an agent's intentionally *A*-ing depends upon his having some pertinent intention, though not necessarily an intention to *A*.

Distinguishing between intentional and nonintentional action is a formidable project. Hurdles include causal deviance and conflicting intuitions about cases. My strategy in what follows is to relax the simple view just enough to accommodate *1* and *1**. Even if the result is overly restrictive for some philosophers' tastes, we shall see that distinguishing intentional from nonintentional actions does not require that we embrace the simple view. It is this last point that I want to establish. The following is not an endorsement of *1* or *1**.

Suppose that intending to *A* entails believing that one (probably) will *A* and recall Connie's condition just before and after she absorbs the information handed her. Now imagine that before the statistics are brought out, an exact duplicate of Connie, Connie*, is created at the other end of the court and that the statistics are handed only to the latter, with the result that Connie* believes that she will probably miss the shot.[7] Both Connies successfully attempt a free throw. Presumably, each *intentionally* sinks her shot.

Connie intends to sink the shot while Connie*, given the present supposition that *1* is true, does not.[8] But we may suppose that both have the same *plan* for sinking the shot. The plan may be described (thinly) as follows:

GOAL: Sink this free throw.

STRATEGY: Shoot this shot in manner *W*.

We may assume as well that in each case this plan is a component of an intention. In Connie's case, the pertinent intention is an intention to sink the shot. In Connie*'s, it is an intention to *try* to sink the shot—or so I shall suppose.

If intentions can incorporate plans for nonintended *A*-ings, we may attempt to tie the intentionality of an A-ing to the existence of an appropriate intention without restricting the domain of appropriate intentions to intentions to A. Thus, for example, if one intends to *try* to A by B-ing, the plan component of one's intention may be such that (barring causal deviance), in successfully executing it, one intentionally A-s.[9]

Consider the following protoaccount of nonintended intentional action:

> *PA1.* S's nonintended A-ing (an action) is an intentional action if and only if (a) S A-s and S's A-ing is not intended; (b) S performs some action B that is caused in the right way by an intention whose plan component represents S's A-ing as a goal relative to S's intended B-ing; and (c) S's B-ing appropriately generates S's A-ing.

A protoanalysis of intentional action (hence a protodistinction between intentional and nonintentional action) may be achieved by means of a synthesis of the simple view and *PA1:*

> *PA2.* S intentionally A-s if and only if S A-s and either (a) S's A-ing is caused in the right way by an intention to A or (b) S performs some action B that is caused in the right way by an intention whose plan component represents S's A-ing as a goal relative to S's intended B-ing and S's B-ing appropriately generates S's A-ing.[10]

To be sure, the "right way" clause in *PA1b* and the notion of appropriate generation in *PA1c* would require expansion in a rigorous account. But the developments needed are not peculiar to an analysis of *nonintended* intentional action. The "right way" clause refers to the etiology of an *intended* action; and an analysis of the generation mentioned in *PA1c* may be modeled after an account of the generational connection between B-ings and A-ings in the instances in which agents who intend to A by B-ing successfully execute that intention. The causal work accomplished by intentions to A by B-ing can be performed, in other cases, by intentions whose plan components identify *nonintended A-ings* as goals (or subgoals) relative to intended B-ings.

The appropriate generation clause merits further attention. Readers will have conflicting intuitions about what is done intentionally in certain cases of successful trying. According to Christopher Peacocke, it is "undisputed" that one who makes a successful attempt "to hit a croquet ball through a distant hoop while believing that one's chances of success are tiny" *intentionally* hits the ball through the hoop (1985, p. 69). But

Gilbert Harman informs us that "it is quite controversial" whether someone who successfully tries to sink a difficult putt "is properly said to have
intentionally sunk the putt" (1986a, p. 92). Even if I had intuitions about
the matter, I would not have much faith in them, since one's ear for this
sort of thing is quickly trained by one's favorite theory. Fortunately,
however, one is free to develop an account of the notion of appropriate
generation in *PA1c* that fits one's intuitions about cases. One who disagrees with Peacocke may hold, for example, that an agent's *B*-ing
appropriately generates his *A*-ing only if there is (under specified conditions) a reliable connection between his performing actions of type *B*
and his performing actions of type *A*. And one may attempt to carve out
a suitable account of reliability. A characterization of reliability may also
figure in an explication of the "right way" condition in *PA2a*.

Cases of the sort at issue also raise a problem for the simple view, of
course. Donna has never fired a gun, but she believes that hitting distant
bull's-eyes is easy: one simply aims at the bull's-eye and pulls the trigger.
She intends now to hit a certain remote bull's-eye that even experts
normally miss. She aims, fires, and strikes it dead center. Did Donna
intentionally hit the bull's-eye? (Perhaps she has a natural talent for this
sort of thing. But perhaps not. Suppose that using the same method, she
proceeds to fire two hundred additional rounds and does not even come
close.) If she is properly said to have intentionally hit the bull's-eye, a
companion case in which she intends only to *try* to hit the bull's-eye and
succeeds in hitting it poses no problem for the protoaccounts. But if her
hitting the bull's-eye is correctly deemed nonintentional in either case,
proponents of the simple view and advocates of the protoaccounts are
faced with the same task, namely, to distinguish nonintentional actions
of this sort from intentional actions. Again, in the case in which Donna
intends to try to hit the bull's-eye, advocates of the protoaccounts may
attempt to handle the example by means of a detailed version of the
appropriate generation condition. And if, intending to hit the bull's-eye,
Donna hits it but not intentionally, the explanatory resources available
to the simple view are available as well to the alternative position under
consideration.

The bottom line is that it is doubtful that distinguishing intentional
from nonintentional action depends upon all intentional actions being
intended actions. Intentions whose plan components identify nonintended *A*-ings as goals seem capable of doing the work of intentions to *A*
by *B*-ing. One might reply that any goals identified as such in plan
components of intentions are themselves intended, so that the intentions
that I have described are in fact intentions to *A*. But the premise here is

false. When Lydia purchases a lottery ticket with the goal of winning a million dollars and the knowledge that her chances of winning are less than one in a million, surely she does not *intend* to win. Although we may plausibly suppose that Lydia intends to try to win the prize, to insist that even given what she knows, she intends to win it is to bite an intolerably large bullet.

I conclude this section by eliminating a possible source of confusion. Elsewhere (Mele 1989c) I made the point that an agent might intent to try to *A* without also intending to *A* partly by means of an example in which someone, Betty, who tried to sink a basket from midcourt sincerely replied to the query, "Do you intend to make a basket from *here?*" with "No. But I do intend to try." Hugh McCann counters with what he takes to be a "parallel" example:

> The characters and setting are the same, but now we have: Alice: "Do you plan to make a basket from *here?*" Betty: "No. But I do plan to try." Now if Mele's example shows that Betty does not *intend* to make a basket, then this one shows that she does not *plan* to make one, either. Furthermore, the argument can be generalized. For Alice might instead have asked Betty if it were her goal, or purpose, or objective to make a basket from midcourt, and Betty might still have replied, "No. But it is my goal (purpose, objective) to try." Obviously, something has gone very wrong here. (1989, p. 109; cf. McCann 1991, pp. 33–34)

Two observations are in order. First, we must distinguish between '*S* plans to *A*' and '*S* has a plan for *A*-ing'. The former expression, on one natural reading, is synonymous with '*S* intends to *A*'. But the latter plainly does not entail intending. I am now mentally reviewing a plan for making paper airplanes that I once committed to memory. Consequently, it is true that I now *have* such a plan. (On having a plan, see sec. 3.) But I do not now plan to make a paper airplane. Even if Betty (or Connie*, in a parallel case) sincerely and truly reports that she does not plan to make the basket, this is perfectly compatible with her having a plan for making the basket. Second, in the original example, Betty—like Connie* and Connie—has the desired goal (purpose, objective) of making the basket. The supposition that her desired goal is merely to *try* to make the basket changes the subject: it yields an example that is *not* "parallel" to mine, an example of the sort discussed toward the end of chapter 3.3 (the mate-in-two case). Moreover, the conceivability of cases in which an agent has her trying to *A* as a desired goal—not her *A*-ing—in no way blocks the possibility that someone whose desired goal is to *A* does not intend to *A*.

Intentions as Guides and Monitors

Intentions have been assigned a *guiding* function in the production of intentional action (Bishop 1989, pp. 167–72; Brand 1984, p. IV; Heckhausen and Beckmann 1990; Thalberg 1984, pp. 257–59). Consider my intention to make myself a cup of tea. The intention incorporates a plan for making tea: first, fill the pot with water; then place the pot on the hot plate; then turn the hot plate on; and so on. In executing the intention, I am guided by the plan. This guidance is dependent upon the *monitoring* of progress toward my goal. The information (or misinformation) that I have placed the pot on the hot plate, for example, plays a causal role in the continued execution of the plan. The monitoring function has also been ascribed to intention.[11]

The guiding function of intention rests in its plan component. Again, we must distinguish between *following* a plan and merely *acting in accordance with* one (see ch. 2.2). An agent may act in accordance with a plan that he has and yet not have followed the plan. His behavior's fitting the plan may be purely coincidental. One follows a certain plan in A-ing only if that plan figures appropriately in the etiology of one's A-ing. A detailed specification of the required causal connection between plan and behavior will include an account of guidance.

In many cases, the plan component of an intention is provided by beliefs. If I intend to A and then discover (come to believe) that my B-ing would most probably result in my A-ing, I may intend to A by B-ing. This intention will incorporate a plan that identifies my B-ing as a means to my A-ing. In some cases, however, an action plan does not derive in this way from beliefs. Suppose that I intend to A now, that A-ing is a basic action for me, and that I am not aiming in A-ing at doing anything further: it is for the sake of my A-ing alone that I intend to A. Here, my plan for A-ing is simply a representation of my A-ing. This plan is not supplied by a belief.[12]

In any event, the earlier example of the two Connies shows that an agent who believes that she probably will not A may have and success-fully execute a plan for A-ing. If either 1 or 1^* is true, Connie* does not intend to sink the foul shot. Rather, she intends* to sink it. But she is guided no less by her plan for sinking the shot than Connie is by hers. Given that the plans are identical in all relevant respects, the behavior-guiding capacity of the plan component of Connie's intention does not rest on her being in either of the doxastic states required by 1 and 1^*. Other things being equal, she would have been guided by the plan (as Connie* was by hers) even if she had been in neither of these doxastic states. By the same reasoning, the alleged monitoring function of intention is independent of the truth of *1* and *1**.

Since claim *2,* that one intentionally *A*-ed only if one intended to *A,* is plainly irrelevant for present purposes, we may turn to another function of intention.

Intentions as Elements in Coordinative Plans

Intention, it is claimed, has a *coordinative* function (Bratman 1987; Harman 1976, 1986a). Among intentions there are intentions for the specious present and intentions for the nonimmediate future, or what I shall call, respectively, *proximal* and *distal* intentions. Distal intentions, Michael Bratman has argued, "are typically elements in larger plans," plans that "help me to coordinate my activities over time, and my activities with yours" (1984, p. 379; cf. 1987). For Bratman, the coordinative roles of distal intentions rest on several features of these intentions: they have the capacity to control behavior; they "resist (to some extent) revision and reconsideration"; and they involve dispositions to reason with a view to intention satisfaction and "to constrain one's intentions in the direction of consistency" (1987, pp. 108–9).

The question before us is whether the capacity of intention to perform its coordinative function rests on *1* or *1**. (Once again, *2* may be set aside as irrelevant.) Here at least, one might think, *1* or *1** is required. How, one might ask, can an agent form plans for later action based on his intentions for the less distant future if he does not believe that the earlier intentions will (probably) be successfully executed—or, more precisely, if he does not believe that he will (probably) perform the actions in question? And can there be any point in intending to do *A* in the near future if what motivates that intention is an intention to do *B* in the more distant future and one believes that one probably will not do *B?* Moreover, unless one is confident about one's prospects of executing one's intentions, how can those intentions serve as a basis for the coordination of one's behavior with the activity of others?

Consider the following case. There are three seconds left in the basketball game. The Pistons are behind by four points, and Dumars has just drawn a foul. The players have a standing plan for just this situation. Dumars will sink the first free throw. He will throw the second one hard off the front rim so that a teammate may get the rebound while Dumars runs to the three-point line. Finally, if a teammate does get the ball, he will quickly pass it to Dumars, who will sink a three-point shot.

Dumars and his teammates believe that their chances of executing this plan beyond his sinking the initial foul shot are slim. Nevertheless, it is the best strategy open to them; and the plan has been sufficiently rehearsed to coordinate some fairly complicated behavior. Its coordinative success need in no way depend upon their believing that the plan will (probably) be successful or upon their not believing that it will (probably) fail.

Nothing has been said thus far about the Pistons' *intentions*. Philosophers who deny that there is any belief condition on intending or who accept only weak conditions, such as that the agent believes that he is *able* to *A*, may quite happily say that Dumars intends to execute the portions of the plan that directly concern him. Proponents of *1* or *1** will deny this. The point to notice is that the issue between them cannot be settled by attending to the coordinative function of intentions. If Dumars does intend to execute his portion of the plan, his intention can help to coordinate his activities, including his interaction with his teammates. If, alternatively, he only intends* to execute that segment of the plan, the same is true of his intention*. There is nothing about coordinative capacity itself that calls for these belief constraints on intention. Coordination may often be *facilitated* by beliefs of the sort at issue and *hampered* by a belief that one will probably fail to execute a plan. Occasionally, coordination may even be rendered (psychologically) *possible* by a belief of the former kind, and *impossible* by a belief of the latter variety. But none of this implies that intention's having the capacity to coordinate behavior requires that *1* or *1** be true.

Notice also that some of Dumars's plans for the nonimmediate future may rest on his intention or intention* to execute his portion of the plan, even though he believes that the odds are against him. For example, Dumars's intention or intention* may figure in the etiology of an intention (formed on his way to the foul line) to explain the strategy later, in a postgame interview.

Intentions as Prompters and Appropriate Terminators of Practical Reasoning

Finally, intentions are plausibly regarded both as providing motivation to engage in practical reasoning with a view to their execution (where such reasoning is called for) and as being well suited to put a proper end to practical reasoning. Some intentions, we may say, *prompt* practical reasoning, while others *appropriately terminate* it. More precisely, the *formation* or *acquisition* of some intentions prompts or appropriately terminates practical reasoning. Not every intention issues in practical reasoning of course: Sometimes there is nothing to reason about; and an intender may be killed before he has time to start reasoning. Nor am I suggesting that just any instance of intention formation generated by practical reasoning terminates that reasoning. A lengthy string of intentions may be produced in the course of an agent's practical reasoning about a certain issue. The acquisition of the earlier intentions terminates only a *stage* in the reasoning.

The capacity of intention to prompt practical reasoning plainly does not rest on either of the two belief conditions identified above. Even if we suppose that *S*'s intending to force a draw in a chess match entails *S*'s believing that he probably will force a draw or his not believing that he probably will not, the doxastic states in question play no necessary causal role in the intention's initiating practical reasoning about tactics. The intention* that remains when we subtract these states from the original intention is capable of motivating careful and detailed practical reasoning about means of forcing a draw even though *S* believes that he probably will not succeed.

Now, practical reasoning, in one familiar sense of the term, is reasoning with a view to settling upon a course of action. (This is compatible with the reasoning's beginning with an intention, of course. An agent who intends to *A* and who therefore is settled upon *A*-ing or upon trying to *A* may need to reason about means of *A*-ing or even constituents of *A*-ing.) Intentions are appropriate terminators of practical reasoning; for (as I shall argue in chapter 9) intention acquisition settles for agents the question what they will attempt, and in some cases the content of the intention formed identifies the agent's resolution of the practical problem about which he is reasoning in such a way that no further reasoning is required—at least *then*. In forming an intention to *A*, an agent settles upon *A*-ing or, in some cases, settles upon trying to *A*. Some intentions, as I shall argue later, are not *formed* if forming an intention is construed as an action. But even in passively acquiring an intention to *A*, an agent enters a condition of being settled upon *A*-ing or upon trying to *A*. (The connection between intending and being settled, as I shall explain in chapter 9, is compatible with the revocability and revisability of intentions.)

Proponents of strong belief requirements on intention may object to the clauses about trying, on the grounds that being settled merely upon *trying* to *A* involves a lack of confidence not found in agents who intend to *A*. However, this objection may safely be ignored for present purposes; for even granting the belief requirements, the doxastic states at issue do not play a necessary functional role in the appropriate termination of practical reasoning by intention. Suppose that Clark's reasoning about how to save the life of his cherished wife leads to the judgment that he must begin at once to lift the log that has her pinned and is terminated by an intention to lift the log. Surely, the pertinent belief and nonbelief about the probability of his lifting the log make no necessary causal contribution to the intention's terminating the reasoning. Clark would have stopped reasoning and started acting on the basis of his reasoning (other things being equal) even if he had believed that he probably would not succeed in lifting the log. In short, intention's capacity appropriately to terminate practical reasoning does not depend upon the truth of *1* nor *1**.

A word is in order, finally, about claim *2,* that we intentionally do only what we intend to do. To be sure, practical reasoning is geared to *intentional* action. But this point can be used to show that intention's being an appropriate terminator depends upon the truth of *2* only if a necessary condition of a terminator's appropriately producing an intentional *A*-ing is that the terminator be an intention to *A*. The underlying claim about the causation of intentional action was challenged earlier (pp. 130–35).

None of the functions identified in this section is properly attributed to *all* intentions. Obviously, there are intentions that do not trigger, sustain, guide, nor monitor action—for example, some intentions for future actions that one does not live to perform.[13] Many simple proximal intentions are not coordinative. Some intentions do not prompt practical reasoning, and some are not products of practical reasoning (Audi 1982a, pp. 34–37; Mele 1984). The suggestion, rather, is that these are important functions that intention is capable of performing and that many intentions do perform. I have shown that the capacity of intention to perform these functions does not depend upon the truth of *1, 1*,* nor *2.*

3. *Intention*

Let us suppose that there is a psychological item (-type), tokens of which initiate and motivationally sustain intentional actions, guide and monitor behavior, help coordinate agents' behavior over time and their interaction with other agents, prompt practical reasoning, and appropriately terminate such reasoning. It is perhaps tempting to *stipulate* that this item is intention and that an account of the constitution or structure of intention is to be gleaned from a list of properties that must be possessed by a psychological item that plays each of the roles identified. But this would be overly hasty. One might miss, in the process, an important feature of intention, namely, its *broad range.*

Decisions plainly have much in common with intentions. Like intentions, they can prompt and appropriately terminate practical reasoning. Moreover, they can serve a coordinative function; and they certainly seem capable of initiating action. However, even if decisions (augmented for monitoring by a capacity to receive information about the agent's actional progress) can perform all the functions attributed to intention, there is an important difference.

In deciding to *A* one forms an intention to *A.* (So, at least, it is typically and plausibly assumed.) But not all intentions are arrived at via decision. 'Decision', of course, refers both to the act of deciding and to its immediate issue. In the former sense, a decision is a deed; in the latter, it is the product of a deed. Intentions, however, are not deeds, and it is doubtful that all intentions are products of acts of intention formation. Under ordinary circumstances, when I hear a knock at my office door I intend to answer it; but I do not consciously decide to answer it, nor do I consciously perform any other action of intention formation.[14] Nor can I think of any decisive theoretical reason to postulate the occurrence of an underlying *unconscious* mental action for each such intention. Generally, these intentions are products not of a present decision but of habit. (Indeed, if every intention were a product of an act of intention formation and if these acts are themselves intended, we would be faced with a vicious regress.)[15] Moreover, as far as I can see, there is no compelling reason to deny that an intention to *A* can be implanted in an agent by one of the many demons or devices of philosophical folklore independently of any *decision* (in the mental action sense) on the agent's part to *A.* The devil can give Denise an intention to *A* without having to get her to decide to *A*—or so it seems (and notice that mental actions, unlike states, are not themselves implantable—even by demons). In short, the range of intention is broader than that of decision. This broadness must be captured in any account of intention.[16]

In the remainder of this section, I shall assume that there is a psychological item that performs all of the functions I have identified and that has the broadness or generality just mentioned. I shall use the term '*intention*' for this item. My guiding question is this: How is a psychological item that performs these functions and has the generality in question likely to be constituted? For stylistic reasons, the asterisks will generally be omitted in what follows.

Since the initiating and sustaining functions of intention are at least partly motivational, intention is safely assigned a motivational aspect or component. Effective intentions motivate intentional actions. Now, an intention is not raw motivation. Intentions have representational content, as is indicated by the close link between intentions and plans in dictionary definitions of 'intention'. The content of an intention is at least partially constituted by a representation of what is intended.

Compare an intention to A with a desire (or want) to A. Both incorporate motivation to A; and the representational content of each is or includes a representation of one's (prospective) A-ing. So how are the intention and the desire different?[17] Notice that one can have a desire to A without being at all *settled* upon A-ing (or upon trying to A). I now have a very strong desire to smoke a cigarette. But I am not settled upon smoking one—partly because I have resolved to kick the habit. Intending to A, on the other hand (as I shall argue in chapter 9), is partially constituted by the agent's being settled upon A-ing or, in some cases, by his being settled upon trying to A. This feature of intention explains why it is an appropriate terminator of practical reasoning; and it helps to explain, as well, why intentions can play a coordinative role in behavior.

One may be inclined to identify a person's being settled upon A-ing with his being *preponderantly* motivated to A, perhaps in conjunction with his believing that he probably will A or with his believing that his motivation (desire) to A probably will result in his A-ing.[18] But this inclination must be resisted. An agoraphobic woman's fear of open spaces may be so strong that she is presently more motivated to avoid traveling than she is to attend her son's upcoming wedding; and she may believe, on the basis of experience, that her desire to avoid open spaces will probably motivate her to remain at home and miss the wedding. However, if she has sought professional help and is doing everything in her power to reduce her fear or otherwise enable herself to brave the dangers of the outside world and attend the wedding, then—her skepticism about her chances of success notwithstanding—we would find the suggestion preposterous that she is settled upon missing the wedding (or upon staying home on the day of the wedding).

A person's state of being settled upon A-ing undoubtedly has motivational force. But preponderant motivational force is not distinctive of the condition of someone who is settled upon A-ing. We have just seen that a person who is preponderantly motivated to A need not be settled upon A-ing. It is also worth noting that someone who is settled upon A-ing need not be preponderantly motivated to A. S may be settled upon petting a snake but find himself (psychologically) unable to do so, owing to fears whose power he finds quite surprising. In some cases of this sort, S may be most motivated to pet the snake at the moment at which he settles upon doing so, and his motivational condition may change as he approaches the snake or as the time for petting it draws nearer. But it is surely imaginable that at the very time at which he becomes settled upon petting the snake, *S* is preponderantly motivated not to do so. Because the strength of our desires and fears is not under our control to the same degree that what we decide and intend is, we may settle upon doing one thing and be more motivated to do another (Mele 1987a, chs. 3 and 6). I return to this point in chapter 9.4.

It is natural to suppose, in light of the preceding discussion, that there is *some* motivational difference between someone's being settled upon *A*-ing and, say, someone's preponderantly wanting to *A* while believing that his want will motivate him to *A*. Here one might wish to introduce *volitions* to *A* and build them into the state of being settled upon *A*-ing. But if—as standard dictionary definitions indicate and as a number of volitionists insist (e.g., Ginet 1990; McCann 1986a)—volitions are *actions*, this will not do. Intending to *A* is conceptually sufficient for being settled upon a pertinent course of action. And intending is not, even in part, an action; nor, as we have seen, need it issue from an action.

The popular idea that intentional action is causally dependent upon intention provides a clue that can be instructively pursued in locating the central motivational feature of being settled upon *A*-ing. Suppose that every intentional action is a product (in part) of a pertinent intention; that wanting, as some have claimed, is properly understood as encompassing a disposition to form or acquire a corresponding intention; and that the causal route from wants to intentional actions, accordingly, is mediated by intentions.[19] Wants, on these suppositions, dispose us to act by disposing us to form or acquire appropriate intentions.[20]

If this is right, a central motivational difference between wants and intentions lies in the *access* that they have to the mechanisms of intentional action. This difference coheres with the claim that intending to *A* entails being settled upon *A*-ing while wanting to *A* (even in conjunction with beliefs of the sort discussed) does not. Whereas our becoming settled upon *A*-ing straightaway is normally sufficient to initiate an *A*-ing at once, this is false of the acquisition of desires to *A* straightaway. To be sure, someone's being settled at t upon *A*-ing at some later time t^* normally will not initiate an *A*-ing at t. But if the intention is still present at t^* and the agent recognizes that the designated time has arrived, an attempt at *A*-ing will normally be immediately forthcoming. On the other hand, someone who still has a desire at t^* to *A* at t^* may simply choose not to *A* and behave accordingly.

If intentions initiate actions, it is *proximal* intentions that do so—

intentions for the specious present. I address the motivational dimension of intention in chapters 9 and 10. I want now to ask why proximal intentions initiate and sustain the actions that they do. Why, for example, does an intention to walk to work tend to initiate and sustain one's walking to work rather than one's cycling to work or one's walking to a friend's house?

Here we turn from the motivational to the representational side of intentions. Which action(s) an intention generates is a partial function of the *plan* component of the intention. An intention to *A* incorporates a plan for *A*-ing (in the limiting case, a simple representation of one's *A*-ing); and one who successfully executes this intention is guided by the plan.

Plans for *A*-ing, as I conceive of them, need have no motivational component. Marvin has on a computer disk a plan for building a doll house. While looking through the disk's files, he notices the plan. Though he is not the least bit motivated to build a doll house, he memorizes the plan—simply to test his powers of memory. The plan on the disk obviously has no motivational component. Nor does the plan in Marvin's head. He is still devoid of motivation to build a doll house.

To avoid confusion, it is worth mentioning two different tendencies in the literature on the connection between plans and intentions. The contrast is nicely illustrated by Myles Brand's claim that "the cognitive component of prospective [i.e., distal] intention is a plan" (1984, p. 153) and Michael Bratman's assertion that "we form future-directed [i.e., distal] intentions as parts of larger plans" (1987, p. 8). The difference here is partly one of emphasis and partly a matter of convention. Though I am focusing on plans as representational elements of intentions, I have no quarrel with the idea that distal intentions are sometimes formed with a view to the execution of larger plans. However, I have not adopted Bratman's convention that plans involve "an appropriate sort of commitment to action: I have a plan to *A* only if it is true of me that I plan to *A*" (1987, p. 29). Marvin has a plan to *A*, but he has no such commitment—he does not plan to *A*.

How are the motivational and representational features of intentions related? We can say, as a first approximation, that a proximal intention is, in part, a propensity to execute a plan for immediate action, which plan is itself embedded in the intention. Similarly, a distal intention is, in part, a propensity to execute an intention-embedded plan for action in the nonimmediate future. But this does not fully capture the differences between intentions and wants identified above. The point about settling must also be included. The intender's propensity to *A* lies in his being

settled upon *A*-ing or, in some cases, in his being settled upon trying to
A. To have a proximal intention is, in part, to be settled on a course of
action for the immediate future. The central difference between distal
and proximal intentions is a temporal one. If and when distal intentions
become proximal, they obviously acquire any previously absent defining
properties of proximal intentions.

We are now very close to a characterization of *intention* that can
accommodate all of the functions of intention identified in section 2. The
functions, again, are these. Intention initiates and motivationally sustains intentional action; it guides and monitors behavior; it coordinates
one's activities, including one's interaction with others; and it can both
prompt and suitably terminate practical reasoning.

Proximal intention—or, more precisely, the *acquisition* of such an
intention (see ch. 10)—initiates intentional action in virtue of a proximal
intention's encompassing a propensity to act that involves the agent's
being settled upon a course of immediate action. The motivational sustaining function of proximal intention is also accomplished in virtue of
its settling feature: the agent is settled upon *A*-ing or upon making a full-
blown attempt to *A* and not just upon *starting* to *A*. *Which* intentional
actions an intention initiates and sustains depends upon the plan component of the intention.

The guiding function of intention rests on its plan component. An
intention-embedded plan provides action directions, as it were. If a
monitoring function is properly attributed to intentions, the state of
intention must include, in addition to a plan component, a capacity for
detecting progress toward a goal. I have not argued that monitoring is a
function of intention; but if it is, a monitoring capacity can be added to
the features of intention I have identified.[21] (This addition would yield a
characterization of *intention* that *fully* accommodates the functions
specified.)

Intention's coordinative capacities lie both in its settling aspect and in
its plan component. Comprehensive plans for extended activity can be
constructed out of plans embedded in less inclusive intentions; and developments in plans will be influenced and constrained by what one is
already settled upon doing. (This is not to deny the possibility of revising
earlier intentions.) Moreover, knowledge of what others have settled
upon doing will assist one in forming intentions and plans for cooperative
ventures. Notice also that to the extent to which coordination depends
upon practical reasoning, intention promotes coordination by providing
motivation for required reasoning—motivation deriving from the settling
aspect of intention. The tendency of intentions to resist reconsideration is

also tied to this settling aspect. Bratman attempts to explicate this resistance by noting that one who intends to A "will normally see (or, anyway, be disposed to see) the question of whether to [A] as settled and continue so to intend until the time of action" (1987, p. 16). But—again normally—an important part of what explains the agent's *seeing* (or being disposed to see) the issue as settled is that he *is settled* upon A-ing.

As I have already suggested, intention is an appropriate terminator of practical reasoning precisely because in forming or acquiring an intention one becomes settled upon a course of action. Practical reasoning is aimed at action. And if all goes well, one will do what one has settled upon doing on the basis of one's practical reasoning. Intention's capacity to prompt such reasoning, as just noted, also derives from its settling aspect.

Finally, intention has the broadness I have identified because its settling feature does not depend upon deciding or any comparable mental *action*. In deciding to A, one forms an intention to A. But some intentions are nonactionally acquired.

4. Belief Requirements Again

Even though the capacity of intention to do the work attributed to it in the literature does not depend upon the truth of 1, 1^* or 2, one cannot infer from this alone that these theses are false or insignificant. Of course, it is very unlikely that they are all true, since the conjunction of 1 or 1^* with 2 has some strikingly counterintuitive consequences. In the present section I briefly motivate acceptance of a version of 1^*.

Standard alleged counterexamples to 1, the claim that S intends to A only if S believes that he (probably) will A, are inconclusive. Consider the following cases, presented by Myles Brand:

> Hilary has gotten himself into a precarious situation by climbing, the only way to safety being to leap across a wide chasm. He might have serious doubts about his ability to leap the distance successfully, but he nonetheless intends to jump it.

> Richard is absolutely convinced that, no matter the strength of his current resolve, he will succumb to weakness and not exercise. He has . . . observed that whenever he intends to undertake a program of exercise, he changes his mind before he can complete the program. He is as confident about the continuation of this pattern as he is about any behavior pattern of anyone. Thus, although he now intends to jog every day next week, he does not believe that he will do so. Richard . . . knows on the basis of

overwhelming evidence that this resolve will dissipate prior to the week's end. At the present time he *does* intend to jog every day next week; but he does *not* believe that there is a chance that he will keep his resolve. (1984, pp. 149–50)

In neither case is it clear that the agent has the intention that Brand attributes to him. Indeed, the commonsense response, unless I miss my guess, is that Hilary and Richard do *not* have the intentions in question, though they may intend, respectively, to *try* to leap across the chasm and (perhaps) to *try* to jog every day next week.[22]

There is, however, a seemingly counterintuitive consequence of *1*. In numerous instances of intentional *A*-ing, the question whether we will succeed in *A*-ing would appear to be the furthest thing from our minds. Yet in many such cases, the claim that we intend to *A* is unproblematic. A few minutes ago, while I was typing, I heard a knock at my office door. As is my habit, I answered the knock. I answered it intentionally, and the suggestion that I intended to answer it would encounter little resistance. Yet I do not remember having a belief at the time to the effect that I (probably) would answer the knock. Indeed, I seem to recall that I had no such conscious belief. Moreover, given that my intention (or my **intention**) can do its work without the assistance of a belief—conscious or *unconscious*—that I (probably) would answer the door, there is no apparent need to postulate the existence of this belief.

A predictable response is that I had at the time a *tacit* belief that I (probably) would answer the door. After all, one might observe, if in the split second between my acquiring the intention to answer the knock and my answering it, a speedy spirit had forced me to estimate the likelihood of my doing so, I would explicitly have given it a high probability. On the notion of tacit belief under consideration, a sufficient condition of *S*'s having a tacit belief that *p* is that *S*'s mere entertaining of *p* would prompt an *explicit* belief that *p*. On this account, we have a great many tacit beliefs, of course, including the beliefs that the president of the United States is not an aardvark and that there are more than 326 stars in the universe.[23]

Another way around the present problem is to substitute *1** for *1*. Since the postulation of tacit beliefs raises more questions than I can answer here, I turn my attention to *1**, the contention that *S* intends (at *t*) to *A* (at *t'*) only if he does *not* believe (at *t*) that he (probably) will not *A* (at *t'*).[24] (Again, not believing that *p* must be distinguished from believing that not-*p*. An agent might simply have no belief on the matter.)

Ordinary speakers of English are disinclined to attribute intentions to *A* to agents who estimate their chances of succeeding in *A*-ing as less than even. What accounts for this, I suspect, is not just that there is something very odd about such *assertions* as 'I intend to *A* but I believe that I probably will not *A*' but also that the ordinary concept of intention incorporates a confidence condition—perhaps only a negative one. If this is right and if *1** generates no significant theoretical problems, then *1** ought to be accepted. Of course, *1** does raise problems for accounts of intentional *A*-ing that require the agent to intend to *A;* but we have already seen that the theoretical grounds offered for such accounts are weak.

One might attempt to counter the case just sketched for *1** with a parallel case for *2*. I have already noted that there is a strong connection in ordinary language and thought between '*S A*-ed intentionally' and '*S* intended to *A*'. People tend to treat 'intentional action performed by *S*' as synonymous with 'intended action performed by *S*'—*until they are pressed*. The issue can be effectively pressed by means of vignettes. Consider the following. Sam has been lifting weights for several years. Though he has tried on numerous occasions recently to bench press 300 pounds, he has never succeeded in lifting more than 290. Sally, a philosophy student who works out regularly with Sam and is writing a paper on ordinary usage of 'intention', has noticed both his failures and his successes. Seeing that Sam is about to make another attempt at 300 pounds, she asks, "Do you intend to bench press that?" Sam replies, "No, but I do intend to try." Now, suppose that Sam has accurately reported his intention. And suppose that he makes a successful attempt. To forestall any doubts that might rest on the thought that Sam's success was a fluke, let us suppose as well that Sam attempts the 300-pound lift four additional times at half-hour intervals later that day and that he is successful each time. The first time Sam bench pressed 300 pounds, was his doing so an intentional action?

Undoubtedly, the most popular answer by far is *yes*. If asked how Sam can have lifted the weight intentionally given that he did not *intend* to lift it, the ordinary speaker of English has little trouble finding a suitable response: "Well, he did intend to *try*." The response can be filled out in accordance with *PA1* or a more rigorous version thereof.

Another worry merits consideration. In section 2, I said that the view to be sketched here would be compatible with the idea that an agent's intentionally *A*-ing depends upon his having some pertinent intention, though not necessarily an intention to *A*. Does accepting *1** commit one to rejecting this idea about the connection between intention and intentional action? If I am right, an intention to try to *A* can often stand in for an intention to *A* when the agent believes that his prospects of *A*-ing are slight. But are there possible cases of intentional action in which even the possession of an intention to try is precluded by the truth of *I*?* If so, would we then be saddled with a case of intentional action in which nothing at all is intended?

Suppose that Jane, standing at the free-throw line, wants very much to sink a foul shot but believes that her chances of doing so are slim. Jane has no reservations about her free-throw prowess; her success rate, as she knows, is close to 90 percent. However, she is convinced that there is a mind-reading demon on the scene who will probably prevent her even from *trying* to sink the shot. He has, Jane believes, absolute power to "freeze" her brain (temporarily and harmlessly) before a trying can be initiated; and she is convinced both that there is an 80-percent likelihood that he will exercise this power and freeze her brain if he sees that she is about to try and that he is certain to know whether she is about to try.[25]

Now supposing that Jane is right about all this, it is still possible, apparently, for her to try to sink the free throw. There is, after all, the 20-percent window of opportunity. And if she not only tries but also succeeds in sinking the shot in the normal way, we might happily say not only that she intentionally tried to sink the shot but also that her sinking the shot was an intentional action. However, *I** implies that Jane lacks an intention to try to sink the shot if she believes that she probably will not try. Supposing that she does believe this and that she tries to sink the free throw (and even intentionally sinks it), does *I** imply that an agent can intentionally *A* in the absence of an intention?

For reasons to be set out in chapter 10, I find it difficult to believe that an agent can intentionally *A* without intending to do anything at all. But if Jane cannot even intend to *try* to sink the foul shot, what can she intend? The suggestion that she might intend to try to try gets us no-where. If the demon can prevent trying, he can prevent trying to try as well (whatever that might be). So what might Jane intend if she wanted very much to sink the shot and did not mind running the 80-percent risk of having her brain temporarily and harmlessly frozen by the demon? A natural answer is that she would have a *conditional* intention of the following sort—an intention to sink the shot (or to try to sink it) *if permitted to try.* (Conditional intentions are intentions with conditional contents.) Jane's so intending is compatible with the truth of *I*:* presumably, she does not believe that it is probably false that she will sink the shot (or try to sink it) if permitted to try. And such an intention can play an important role in the etiology of an intentional action. Other things being equal, Jane, armed with the conditional intention, will try to sink the shot if the demon does not freeze her brain; and her attempt might well be successful.

One final worry. I have argued that an intention* to A can do the work of an intention to A: the absence of a belief that one (probably) will not A is not functionally required. If I^* is endorsed as a constraint on intentions to A, it will be endorsed as a concession to ordinary usage, considered as reflective of the commonsense concept of intention. However, that concept might presuppose a conception of intending agents that does not fit some possible cases. If it is possible for an agent to be confident that he will A while also believing that he (probably) will not A, then cases of intending to A that do not satisfy I^* might also be possible. An agent's believing p at t might not preclude his also believing not-p at t if beliefs with contradictory contents can be lodged in distinct mental partitions in such a way as not to come into contact with one another, as it were. This is not the place, however, for an examination of mental partitioning (see Davidson 1982b; Pears 1984; Mele 1987a, ch. 6). To the extent to which I^* is encompassed in the ordinary conception of intention, that conception presupposes an integrated agent. Viewed as restricted to such agents—"normal" agents—thesis I^* is a theoretically innocuous constraint on "normal" intentions driven by a sensitivity to ordinary usage. And it coheres with a commonsense distinction between intending to A and—when considerably less confident about one's chances of A-ing—intending to try to A.

If, as I shall urge in chapter 11, the representational content of an intention is a plan, the confidence requirement on intentions will not be satisfied by their representational content. That leaves the intending *attitude* toward that content. We might say that that attitude, in the case of "normal" intentions to A, is characterized in part by the absence of a belief that one (probably) will not A. Thus, we may distinguish the intending-to-try attitude toward a plan for A-ing from the intending (without qualification) attitude. The intending* attitude is an attitude of the former kind. (I shall return to these matters in ch. 11.)

My chief aim in this chapter has been to sketch, in fairly broad strokes, a plausible account of the features of intention in virtue of which it is capable of doing the work (and having the range) that we properly assign it; for the functional features of intention constitute its core. The settling and plan aspects discussed in sections 2 and 3 are of central importance, and they will receive more detailed treatment in subsequent chapters. None of the functions of intention identified here depends upon the truth of the belief requirements laid down in *1* and *1** or upon the truth of *2*. However, I have suggested that *1** captures a truth about "normal" intentions.

Notes

1. Proponents of *1* include Audi 1973, 1986a; Beardsley 1978; W. Davis 1984; Harman 1976 (cf. 1986a, p. 82); Honderich 1988, p. 220; and Velleman 1989. For alternative belief conditions, see Davidson 1980, ch. 5; Davidson 1985a, pp. 211–17; Grice 1971; and Pears 1985. Recent proponents of *2* are Adams 1986 and McCann 1986b, 1991.

2. For example, *S* intends to phone his mother. He plans to do this by dialing her phone number, but he mistakenly dials his brother's number. As luck would have it, his mother is visiting his brother; and she answers the phone. *S* intended to phone his mother, and he did precisely that; but his phoning her was too coincidental to be intentional.

3. For some central ingredients of a rough formulation, see Bratman 1987, ch. 8.

4. Later, I shall use '*S*'s *intention** to *A*' to include states that *would be* intentions if *S* believed that he (probably) would *A*.

5. Recent defenses of the simple view (Adams 1986; McCann 1986b, 1991) are motivated by Bratman's much-discussed attack on that thesis (1984; 1987, ch. 8). I shall not rehearse Bratman's arguments, but the replies will receive due attention.

6. Audi 1986a, pp. 27–28. The middle ground is occupied by a range of positions. See Brand 1984, pp. 28–30, 215–17; Bratman 1987; Harman 1976; and Harman 1986a, chs. 8 and 9.

7. Readers need not concern themselves about the manner in which beliefs, desires, and the like are broadly preserved in the duplication process. I have created Connie* for illustrative purposes only. A little science fiction can save a lot of ink.

8. The reader who thinks that Connie's confidence about her chances of success does not reach the level required for intention is free to boost her imagined free-throw percentage.

9. Grounds for the parenthetical qualification emerge in ch. 11.2.

10. I mentioned earlier that this protoanalysis might be deemed overly restrictive by some opponents of the simple view. It is sometimes claimed that in cases of double effect an agent may intentionally perform an action that is no part of his plan (see ch. 6.6 and the final paragraph of ch. 10.1). For present purposes, the issue may be left open.

11. See Brand 1984, p. IV; Thalberg 1984, pp. 257–59. Compare with Searle 1983, ch. 3 on the presentational nature of "intentions in action."

12. On simple plans of this sort, see ch. 6.

13. Notice that some intentions for unperformed future actions may motivate present *preparatory* action.

14. Sometimes, of course, I might decide to answer a knock at my door. If I am especially busy or trying to hide, I might consider whether to answer the knock or to remain silent. And I might decide in favor of the former. Typically, however, I do not consider the matter at all, it being my habit to answer knocks at my office door.

15. On the problem of infinite regress, see ch. 11.4.

16. What I have said about decision, I am also inclined to say about choice. Bratman (1987, ch. 10) rejects the assumption that choosing to *A* entails intending to *A*: we choose practical packages but intend only the elements of the packages that we (1) are disposed to engage in means–end reasoning about (if such reasoning is called for), (2) will endeavor to do if we have the opportunity, and (3) are disposed to count as constraints on other intentions (p. 142). For example, a strategic bomber may choose to bomb the enemy's munitions dump and to kill the children in the school next door but not *intend* to do both, if he lacks the dispositions in question concerning the children and would not make a special attempt to kill them. However, I am not convinced that 'choice' is the appropriate term for the agent's attitude toward the compound action. I am inclined to say that he both chooses and intends to bomb the dump and that he is *willing* to kill the children as a by-product of the bombing of the dump.

17. For useful discussions of the difference between intentions and desires, see Brand 1984, pp. 121–27; Bratman 1987, pp. 18–20; Harman 1986a, p. 83; and McCann 1986b, pp. 193–94.

18. For representative belief/desire analyses of intention, see Audi 1973, 1986a; Beardsley 1978; and W. Davis 1984.

19. On wants as intention formers, see ch. 10.2; Brand 1984, p. 127; Castañeda 1975, p. 284. On the mediating role of intentions, see Davidson 1985a, p. 221; Harman 1976, p. 441.

20. On a broader conception of wanting than the one presently at work, intentions incorporate wants (see ch. 3.7); and perhaps some intention-incorporated wants (in the sense of 'wants' in question) do not encompass dispositions to intend. Concerning the broader conception and its bearing on the present issue, see ch. 9.5 and ch. 10, n. 9.

21. I suggest in chapter 11.7 that monitoring is not a proper function of intention.

22. Some have distinguished between acting *with* the intention of *A*-ing and acting while intending to *A* (Bratman 1987, ch. 9; Harman 1986a, pp. 93–94). It might be suggested that when Hilary jumps, he does so with the intention of leaping across the chasm even though it is false of him that he intends to leap across the chasm. If acting with the intention of *A*-ing amounts to acting with *A*-ing as a goal (even a goal that is not intended), I have no objection to the suggestion.

23. For a related conception of tacit or implicit belief, see Harman 1986a, pp.

13–14. Interesting problems about tacit belief are raised in Audi 1982b and Lycan 1988, ch. 3.

24. The times t and t' may or may not be identical. Thesis I^* can be refined further to avoid problems posed by cases in which S does not realize that he is S or in which he believes that someone else is S.

25. I am grateful to Brendan O'Sullivan for convincing me to address a case of this sort.

9

Executive States: Settling Things

There is, in the literature on intention, a significant division over whether the state is reducible to combinations of belief and desire.[1] On the reductionist view, intention may figure in the etiology of intentional action; but its contribution is just that of belief/desire complexes. The attraction of belief/desire reductionism about intention is explained in part by the popular assumption that belief and desire are the most fundamental intentional states.[2] But this is not the whole story. It is generally recognized that intention has a motivational dimension; and 'desire' (like 'want') is often used in the literature as an umbrella term for motivation. Moreover, although I have noted that this point is controversial, intention is commonly regarded as involving a "confidence" condition, a condition naturally explicated in terms of belief. Few people are inclined to maintain that a sprinter who believes that his chances of winning a certain race are about one in ten *intends* to win the race, no matter how strongly motivated he is to win.

The present chapter performs a dual function. It displays the shortcomings of familiar brands of belief/desire reductionism about intention and helps to prepare the way for the account in chapter 10 of the executive nature of intention. I argue here that intention has an executive dimension that goes well beyond belief/desire complexes, standardly conceived. This dimension, I shall urge, is something that intention shares with decision. Since the executive character of decision is more readily apparent, I begin there—or rather, I begin with a question upon which attention to decision will shed considerable light.

1. Two Angry Men

CASE 1. Earlier today, Carl insulted Alan at a faculty meeting. Alan now wants to humiliate Carl at the dean's party tomorrow more than he wants to do anything that he takes to be incompatible with his doing this;

154

that is, his *preponderant motivation* falls on the side of his humiliating Carl at the party, and he realizes that this is so. However, largely because Alan thinks that it would be morally wrong to humiliate Carl at the party, he has decided to resist his desire to do so. Though he feels that he must go to the party, he plans to do everything in his power to avoid humiliating Carl there. (He plans, for example, to refrain from initiating conversations with Carl and to abstain from alcohol at the party, since drinking strengthens his combative tendencies.) Now, Alan has an excellent memory, a lengthy history of trading insults, and a fondness for statistical calculations. He believes that his past attempts to resist strong desires to humiliate colleagues at parties were successful only 25 percent of the time; and in light of this and other pertinent considerations, he believes that owing to his desire to humiliate Carl at the dean's party, he probably will humiliate him there.[3]

CASE 2. Bob, a friend of Alan's, was also insulted by Carl at the meeting. Like Alan, he is preponderantly motivated to humiliate Carl at the dean's party but has moral qualms about doing so. He considers the possibility of resisting his desire to humiliate Carl but decides against resistance. Bob decides to humiliate Carl, and he begins to plot a strategy for doing so. Like Alan, Bob believes that his desire to humiliate Carl will probably motivate his doing so.

It certainly looks as though Bob intends to humiliate Carl and Alan does *not*. Bob decided to humiliate Carl, therein forming an intention to do so. Alan did not. Indeed, Alan decided to do his best to bring it about that he does not humiliate Carl at the party. Even if intending to *A* does not depend upon one's having decided to *A*, we are strongly disinclined to believe that someone like Alan, who is resolved upon resisting his desire to *A*, *intends* to *A*. Agents who are more strongly motivated to *A* than not to *A* sometimes actively resist their motivation to *A*. They deliberate carefully about means of resistance and intentionally take measures to counter the pull of unruly desires—even when they think that their chances of success are slim. In such cases—or so people not already in the grip of a theory are strongly inclined to believe—the agents do *not* intend to *A*.

Nevertheless, on familiar belief/desire analyses of intention, Alan, like Bob, does intend to humiliate Carl.[4] These analyses typically make *preponderant motivation* an essential feature of intending. *S* intends at *t* to *A* at *t**, it is claimed, only if *S* is *more motivated* at *t* to *A* at *t** than he is to do anything that he takes to be incompatible with his *A*-ing at *t**— only if his desire to *A* is motivationally stronger than his competing desires (t^* may or may not be identical with t). It is often claimed as well that combining preponderant motivation with a suitable *belief* yields sufficient conditions for intending. Candidates include the belief that one (probably) will A and the belief that one's desire to A will effectively motivate one to A.[5]

Both Alan and Bob are preponderantly motivated to humiliate Carl at the dean's party, and each believes both that he probably will humiliate Carl and that his doing so will be motivated by the pertinent desire. Therefore, on the view just sketched, both men *intend* to humiliate Carl. This result is, at best, highly counterintuitive.

If, as I shall argue, familiar belief/desire analyses of intention give us the wrong result in Alan's case, where, precisely, does this reductionism go wrong? And if Bob intends to humiliate Carl but Alan does not, where does the crucial difference in the two cases lie? There are several noteworthy differences. One is motivational. Though both Alan and Bob are more motivated to humiliate Carl than not to do so, we may suppose that Alan, unlike Bob, is more motivated to try to master his desire to humiliate Carl than he is to make no such attempt. A second likely difference concerns their beliefs. Though both men believe that they will probably humiliate Carl, their beliefs probably do not rest on the same grounds. Bob's belief, we may suppose, rests significantly upon his decision to humiliate Carl or upon some aspect of that decision, while Alan's derives from his estimation of the relative force of his motivation to humiliate Carl and his information about pertinent past behavior of his.[6] (Bob's confidence that he will humiliate Carl might also be greater than Alan's confidence about what he will do.) There is also the more fundamental difference to which I just alluded. Bob has *decided* to humiliate Carl but Alan has not.

2. Decision

Deciding is commonly and plausibly understood to encompass intending: in deciding to A one forms an intention to A. If deciding to A were also a necessary condition of intending to A, one might try to develop an account of intending on the basis of a prior account of deciding. But even if (as I have argued in chapter 8.3) not all intentions depend upon corresponding decisions, attention to deciding will prove illuminating in revealing problems with belief/desire reductionism.

I begin with two points about decision. I motivate them briefly in the present section and develop the initial defense in subsequent sections in connection with parallel claims about intention.

First, one can be preponderantly motivated to *A*—and even believe that this motivation will effectively motivate an *A*-ing—without simultaneously being decided upon *A*-ing. Alan is in this motivation/belief condition with respect to his humiliating Carl; but he is not decided upon humiliating him.

Second, one may decide to do something without being preponderantly motivated to do it. Decisions about what to do are often based, in significant part, on the agent's evaluative assessment of pertinent attractive or aversive items. And an agent's assessment of an item can be out of line with the motivational force of his desire or aversion for that item. Thus, for example, a cigarette smoker may judge that his reasons to quit smoking are better than his reasons for continuing to smoke and yet be more strongly motivated by the latter. On the basis (in part) of his evaluative reasoning, such a smoker may decide to quit smoking while also being preponderantly motivated to continue: even though he has decided to quit smoking, the smoker's motivational condition may be such that unless it changes, he will akratically continue to smoke. If deciding is sufficient for intending, it is false as well that intending to *A* entails being preponderantly motivated to *A,* a point to which I shall return in section 4.

Now, if the smoker realizes that he is preponderantly motivated to continue smoking and believes that owing to this fact about his motivational condition, he will probably continue to smoke, we may well be disinclined to suppose that he has decided to quit smoking. Indeed, we *should* be so disinclined if the belief condition that I urged in chapter 8 for intention is a condition for decision as well.[7] But nothing prevents our supposing that the smoker does not see where his preponderant motivation lies or that realizing that he is most motivated to continue smoking, he believes it probable that he will suitably alter the strength of his motivation provided that he decides to quit.

My central claim about the possibility of one's not being preponderantly motivated to do what one is decided upon doing admits of succinct expression. Because our assessments of attractive and aversive items have a firmer grip on decision making than on the motivational force of our desires, we can decide to *A* and yet not be preponderantly motivated to *A*. I have argued at length in *Irrationality* (Mele 1987a) that assessment and motivation are not always aligned with one another (a thesis for which there is considerable empirical support); and I shall produce some pertinent arguments later.[8] However, skeptics about my contention that decision does not essentially incorporate preponderant motivation are more likely to dig in their heels at another juncture. Can something actually count as a *decision* to A if it does not incorporate preponderant motivation to A? One might argue for a negative answer on causal/explanatory grounds, perhaps contending that decision cannot play its explanatory role vis-à-vis intentional action unless it incorporates preponderant motivation. Or one might advert to alleged meaning conventions about 'decision'.

We shall see later that the functional connection between decision and intentional action does not rest on decision's essentially incorporating preponderant motivation. As for the appeal to ordinary usage, it seems to me plain that assent to the alleged connection between decision and preponderant motivation rests on theoretical considerations— specifically, considerations about how decisions must be constituted if they are to issue in corresponding intentional actions. In fact, one who is willing to let matters rest on pretheoretical intuitions (e.g., about the aforementioned akratic smoker) will probably have to concede that what we decide to do is not always what we are most motivated to do.

'Decision' has multiple referents. It refers (1) to the act of deciding; (2) to the immediate issue of the act, a decision *state,* a state of being decided upon something; and (3) to *what* we decide, as in 'Her decision was to A.' Where disambiguation is important, I shall generally rely upon the context to accomplish it. Now, some decisions are for the specious present while others are for the nonimmediate future. I shall call them, respectively, *proximal* and *distal* decisions. A proximal decision is naturally regarded as involving a disposition or propensity to make an appropriate attempt at once. However, being disposed to A is not sufficient for being in a decision state. Presumably, a desire to A now—even a nonpreponderant one—disposes one to some degree to A (or attempt to A) now; but desiring to A plainly is not sufficient for being decided upon A-ing, or for having decided to A. Even if a decision state incorporates a desire, the desire does not exhaust the state.

The connection between deciding to A and A-ing is much tighter than that between desiring to A and A-ing. We have fleeting desires, relatively weak desires, and even some very strong desires, to do any number of things that we do not do, largely because we decide or intend to do something else. Here, the notion of *settling* upon a course of action is useful. In deciding to A, one *settles* upon A-ing (or upon trying to A), and one enters a state—a decision state—of *being settled upon A*-ing (or upon trying to *A*). But one may desire to *A*—even preponderantly—without being settled upon *A*-ing (or upon trying to *A*).[9]

These claims about the connection between decision and settling are compatible with an obvious pair of points about decision. Decisions are typically revocable; and some decisions are *firmer* than others, in the sense that they are less open to revocation and revision. The same is true of the condition of being settled upon *A*-ing. Though I am now settled upon meeting a friend for dinner this evening, I would cancel the arrangements if a pressing problem were to arise at home: one may be settled upon *A*-ing without being *irrevocably* settled. And I am now more firmly settled upon meeting my friend for dinner than upon executing some plans of mine for the more distant future.

Although we most naturally speak of being settled upon doing something in the nonimmediate future, we plainly do settle upon some immediate actions as well; and in so settling we become *settled upon* an immediate action. As I shall use the expression, to say that *S* is settled at *t* upon *A*-ing at once is not necessarily to say that *S* has a notable resolve or determination to do *A* (at once). Rather, I use the expression (at this point) only to mark what I shall call the *executive* aspect of proximal decisions, an aspect best fleshed out gradually.

In moving from beliefs and desires (or reasons) to proximal decisions, agents make important progress toward action. They enter a state whose function includes the immediate initiation of an appropriate intentional action—a state whose immediate goal is the *execution* of the decision. In contributing to the formation of proximal decisions, beliefs and desires make an indirect contribution to the etiology of intentional actions initiated by these decisions.

Making decisions for the nonimmediate future—*distal* decision making—also constitutes practical progress. In deciding today to *A* tomorrow, we settle upon *A*-ing tomorrow; and our condition of *being* settled incorporates (or perhaps supports) a collection of dispositions conducive to our *A*-ing. Examples are the disposition to regard the question whether to *A* as closed (if only tentatively and temporarily), the disposition to coordinate present and future plans with our *A*-ing, and the disposition to reason about means to *A*-ing (if necessary).[10] Moreover, distal decisions share at least one executive function with their proximal counterparts: under favorable conditions, they will persist until the targeted time and figure in the initiation of appropriate action then (see Bratman 1987, p. 108 on future-directed intentions). In such cases, a distal decision state might perhaps "evolve" into a proximal one or, alternatively, play a part in producing a proximal decision state. This issue can be left open for present purposes.

The idea that moving from beliefs and desires to decisions involves significant progress toward action merits further attention. Ethel is inclined to buy Fran's house. Though it is not the house of her dreams, she deems it satisfactory and believes that all things considered, it would be better to purchase this house than any of the others that she has seen in two years of careful house hunting. Moreover, she thinks that it would be best to buy a house soon; and Fran has agreed to sell her the house provided that she signs a contract within one week. Still, Ethel has not decided to buy the house. She is procrastinating. In the end, however, she decides to buy it.

One can well imagine that when Ethel finally makes her decision she is no more strongly motivated to buy the house than she was a day earlier. Indeed, her motivation to buy it might have weakened. Faced with the reality of the financial commitment, the paperwork, and the like, her former enthusiasm about home ownership may be dampened, with an attendant decrease in motivation to buy the house. Nevertheless, in deciding to buy the house, Ethel certainly makes (internal or psychological) progress toward buying it—progress that evidently cannot be articulated wholly in terms of motivational strength (see ch. 3.6).

3. Intention: An Executive State

Decision, in the product sense, is simply the immediate issue of deciding. Some might hold that being settled upon A-ing similarly requires one's *having* settled upon A-ing. Though I do not share the linguistic intuitions that I suspect partially underlie the latter idea, I shall try to avoid lexical quarrels. In the present section, I develop the idea that intention—*including* intentions not arrived at by decision, or any other mental act of intention formation—shares an important characteristic with decision. Both, I think, involve a feature that can be marked by the expression 'being settled upon'; but I shall eventually shift to a term whose linguistic associations are less rich.

The common intuition that in my opening pair of cases, only Bob intends to humiliate Carl rests, I believe, on the idea that intending entails being settled.[11] Though Bob is settled upon humiliating Carl, Alan is not. Indeed, Alan is settled upon doing his best to bring it about that he does not humiliate Carl.

Now, one might object that intuitions to the contrary notwithstanding, Alan *is settled* upon humiliating Carl. One might claim that being settled upon *A*-ing simply consists in being preponderantly motivated to *A* or in being in this motivational condition while also having a belief of a certain type—a belief that one (probably) will *A* or a belief that one's desire to *A* will effectively motivate one to *A*. However, this will not do (as I argued in chapter 8.3). Consider someone who is deliberating about whether to quit smoking. He realizes that he is preponderantly motivated to continue to smoke; and he believes that this motivation will probably win out, partly on the grounds that his numerous past attempts to kick the habit have been unsuccessful. Still, he regards the issue as open. He believes—truly and justifiably, we may suppose—that there is some chance that his next attempt will be successful. And he is trying to decide whether to make the effort. Plainly, this person is not consciously settled upon continuing to smoke even though he satisfies the conditions just suggested for being settled upon this. Nor is there any evident need to suppose that he is unconsciously settled upon continuing his smoking.

Belief/desire reductionists about intention need not cave in at this point, of course. They might contend that intending to *A* does *not* entail being settled upon *A*-ing and that Alan intends to humiliate Carl even though he is not settled upon this.

I have encountered two objections (Audi 1988) to the claim that intending entails being settled. First, we *irresolutely* intend to do some things, and this is incompatible with our being settled upon doing them. Second, we are not settled upon doing some of our *sudden* intended actions (e.g., swerving in order to avoid hitting a dog that is darting in front of one's car).

The first objection rests on the assumption (1) that being settled upon something implies unwavering firmness. The second may rest on either or both of two assumptions: (2) that the state of being settled upon something must have considerable duration; and (3) that being settled upon something entails *having* settled upon it. Section 2 does something to deflect the force of these suppositions; but there is no need to insist upon the aptness of the *expression* 'being settled upon'. Intending to *A* does not entail being settled upon *A*-ing, if assumptions 1–3 identify essential characteristics of the latter state. But when we subtract what assumptions 1–3 imply about being settled upon *A*-ing from that state (so conceived), we are left with *something*. That something is crucial to intention and is not captured by familiar belief/desire analyses. So, at least, I shall argue.

First, subtract firmness. Other things being equal, the resulting state will be more easily revoked or revised than the initial one; but we are still left with an executive state, something having the function of producing intentional action (either now or later). Presumably, the state still is of such a kind that if it is *not* revoked or revised, it will initiate appropriate action under favorable conditions.

Next, shorten the duration of the state. Suppose that even someone who makes a proximal *decision* to A does not enter a state describable as "being settled upon A-ing." Here, again, a state having the function of initiating action remains; for this is unquestionably a function of proximal decisions to A.

Finally, subtract the supposed etiology of being settled upon A-ing, namely, the state's being caused by a mental act of settling upon A-ing. Just as we often acquire beliefs and desires without actively forming them, so may we enter executive states without actively forming those states (see ch. 8.3). Suppose that in a case like that of the darting dog, a driver may acquire an intention to swerve without *forming* one. Then, quite independently of any act of settling, the sight of a dog running into the path of one's car in conjunction with a pertinent standing aversion, one's awareness of traffic conditions, and the like may result in an executive state that represents avoidance of the dog as a goal and swerving as a means.

Intentions, like many psychological states, have both a representational and an attitudinal component. I have termed the former component a *plan*. Obviously, we have any number of attitudes toward plans, in my purely representational sense (see ch. 8.3). We might believe that a plan is elegant, admire it, hope that it is never executed, and so on. Intention, like decision, incorporates an *executive* attitude toward plans. Intentions are executive states whose primary function is to bring the world into conformity with intention-embedded plans.

Return to Alan. Even if intending to A does not entail being settled upon A-ing, on a restrictive reading of the expression, it does entail being in an executive state having one's A-ing as its goal. Alan does not intend to humiliate Carl, precisely because he is not in the requisite executive state with respect to his humiliating Carl. To be sure, he is motivated to humiliate Carl, even preponderantly motivated. And he may be in possession of a plan for this, a representation of his humiliating Carl by X-ing. But his attitude favoring his doing so is not an executive one. He has not made the progress toward action that intention involves. Our recognition of this last point, I think, accounts for the common intuition that Alan does not intend to humiliate his colleague.

4. Intention and Preponderant Motivation

Several sources of the attractiveness of belief/desire reductionism about intention were identified at the outset of this chapter. This reductionism might also be partially motivated by the popular thesis—very roughly framed, that whenever we act intentionally we do what we want most strongly to do—that I have termed the *motivational strength thesis* (MST). Partly for reasons of simplicity, a proponent of the MST who also holds that intention plays an important motivational role in the etiology of intentional behavior may be inclined to locate the basis of the role in intention's being partly reducible to the alleged prerequisite of intentional action, namely, preponderant wanting.

It is worth asking, then, whether intending to *A* entails being preponderantly motivated to *A*. I have argued at length elsewhere that it does not (Mele 1987a); and in chapter 10 I will show that intention's motivational role in intentional action does not rest upon intention's essentially incorporating preponderant motivation. But something should be said here.

I start with an observation that—in general outline at least—is by now familiar. Many intentions rest partially on agents' evaluations or assessments of attractive or aversive items; and our evaluation of a given item is not always in line with the motivational strength of our desire or aversion for that item. An agent who judges that he has better reasons to quit smoking cigarettes than to continue may nevertheless be more motivated to continue smoking than to quit. (This simple point goes a long way toward explaining how incontinent behavior is possible.) Suppose that a smoker weighs up the considerations for and against his continuing to smoke and judges that all things considered, it would be best to quit smoking now and forever. Suppose further that (partly) on the basis of his assessment, he *intends* to do this. Must we also suppose that he is now more motivated to quit smoking now and forever than he is not to do so? No. Our intentions can be at odds with our preponderant motivation for the simple reason that what we are most motivated to do is not under our control to the same extent to which what we intend (or decide) to do is. Evaluation does not have the same grip in both spheres.

This last claim rests partially on two more fundamental theses:

1. The motivational force of our wants (broadly construed) is not always in line with our assessment or evaluation of the "objects" of our wants, that is, the wanted items.

2. Many intentions are formed, in significant part, on the basis of our *assessment* of the objects of our wants.

Now, as I explain in *Irrationality,* there is considerable empirical support for *1* (1987a, ch. 6). To make a very long story very short, studies of delay of gratification provide excellent evidence both that representations of wanted items have two important functional dimensions—an informational and a motivational one—and that they are not always aligned.

Walter Mischel and his colleagues, in a series of ingenious studies, kept one feature of the experimental design constant: children who ranked one snack higher than another were told that they could have the lower-ranked snack upon request but must wait for the experimenter to return before they could have the preferred one. The length of time that they waited for the preferred treat varied markedly, depending upon whether and how the children attended to the snacks during the waiting period. Children who attended to the very features of the snacks on the basis of which they ranked them requested the lower-ranked treat much earlier than did other children under a variety of different attentional conditions. To put the experimenters' conclusion simply, attention to the consummatory features of the snacks increased the children's motivation to request the lower-ranked snack, even though these very features were the basis for the children's ranking of the snacks. More simply yet, even when one's evaluative ranking of a collection of items and one's desires for those items are sensitive to the same features of the items, evaluation and motivational strength are not always responsive to those features in just the same ways or with matching results. Real human beings are more complicated than that.[12]

Thesis *2* is a central element in a standard conception of practical reasoning. Practical reasoning, commonly construed, often proceeds to a considerable extent on the basis of our *assessment* of considerations. Accordingly, many intentions formed on the basis of practical reasoning are formed, in significant part, on the basis of these assessments (see Mele 1987a, pp. 36–45).

Now, if the motivational force of considerations can be out of line with agents' pertinent assessments and if intentions issue in significant part from assessments, why should anyone doubt that in some cases, an agent may intend to *A* and yet not be most motivated to *A?*

One might worry that if intention does not essentially incorporate preponderant motivation, it cannot do its motivational work. A central thesis of chapter 10 is that this worry rests on a mistake.

Another worry derives from a particular interpretation of ordinary usage. It might be claimed that meaning conventions dictate that intention essentially incorporates preponderant motivation. The cases to be examined shortly challenge the pertinent linguistic intuitions. And there is even a story to be told about how intentions and preponderant motivational force can diverge, a story involving theses *1* and *2* above. If intentions are sensitive to assessments in the way that standard conceptions of practical reasoning presuppose, and assessments can be out of line with the motivational force of assessed items, we can understand how someone who, as it happens, is not most motivated to *A* may nevertheless intend to *A*.[13]

Of course, someone can stipulate that intention, as he chooses to use the term, essentially incorporates preponderant motivation. But in so doing, he will not have located what it is about intention in virtue of which it plays its motivational role in intentional action if (as I shall argue in chapter 10) the motivational work of intention depends upon its having a certain executive dimension—a dimension not reducible to preponderant motivation.

The intuitively most powerful real-life illustrations of the point that intending to *A* does not essentially incorporate being preponderantly motivated to *A* pit an intention against a strong aversion. A boy, Alex, deliberates about whether to accept his friend's proposal that they become blood brothers—a ceremony that involves his cutting his own right hand with a knife. He judges that it would be best to do so and decides accordingly to cut his hand straightaway. But as he moves the knife toward his hand *with the intention of cutting it,* he stops, 'defeated' by an aversion whose force he finds surprising. The process that resulted in his intending to cut his hand did not also result in a preponderance of motivation to cut it.[14] A man standing on a third-story porch of a burning apartment building intends to jump (immediately). He is shocked to find that (at least for a time) he cannot bring himself to do it. He is frozen with fear—fear whose motivational force exceeds that of his motivation to jump.

One might suggest that in the former example, Alex is preponderantly motivated to cut his hand while he intends to do so and that the balance of his motivation shifts only when he ceases to intend to cut it. This might be true in some version of the case. For example, the bulk of Alex's motivation might fall on the side of his cutting his hand when he forms the intention to do so; and as he moves the knife toward his hand, his desire not to cut himself might grow stronger—so strong indeed, that when the knife touches his hand he is preponderantly motivated to refrain from cutting it. However, there is another possibility.

It is in *deciding* to cut his hand at once that Alex forms the intention to do so. But his decision was based, in significant part, on his *evaluation* of his reasons for and against cutting his hand; and his evaluation of these reasons need not be in line with their *motivational force*. Alex may judge that his reasons for cutting his hand are better, on the whole, than his contrary reasons, even though, at the very time at which the judgment is made, the latter set of reasons is motivationally stronger. Although, he might, for example, give his aversion to drawing blood from himself a relatively low evaluative ranking, this aversion may have a disproportionate motivational force. Still, on the basis in part of that judgment, he may *decide* to cut his hand. When we decide what to do we do not, in general, ask ourselves what we are *most motivated* to do; but we often do ask what it would *best* to do. And what we judge best need not be what we are most motivated to do.[15]

I willingly grant, incidentally, that when Alex intentionally stops moving the knife toward his palm he no longer intends to cut his hand.[16] At that point, the intention is absent. My contention is that even when the intention is in place, Alex might not be preponderantly motivated to perform the action. It is quite possible, for example, that at the very time at which Alex decides to cut his hand—thereby forming the intention to cut it—he is less motivated to cut his hand than to refrain from doing so. Again, that this is possible should be evident when we notice that Alex's decision about what to do rests significantly on his evaluation of his reasons for acting and that this evaluation need not be in line with the motivational force of the evaluated items.

The difference in question between evaluation and motivation helps to explain, among other things, interesting cases of incontinent action, such as the case of Alex. Perhaps in an ideally rational agent the motivational force of competing reasons for action is always in line with the agent's evaluative ranking. But this is not true of the rest of us. Intending to A and recognizing our A-ing to be precluded by our doing a B, we may nevertheless be more motivated to do the latter.

5. Motivational States: Desires and Intentions

If every motivational state either is or incorporates a desire or want in the broadest (technical) sense of these terms, then every *intention* is or incorporates a desire or want. Here, again, terminological disputes can be avoided. But a word of warning is in order: the supposition that intentions are a species of desire is naturally associated with the further supposition that the motivational role of an intention to *A* in the production of an intentional *A*-ing is just that of any desire to *A*. As desires are typically understood, their tendency to result in action leading to their satisfaction is a function of their *motivational strength:* stronger desires have more action-causing clout than weaker ones. And one might infer from this that it is precisely in virtue of their motivational strength that intentions give rise to intentional actions.

This would be a mistake; for (as will become evident in chapter 10) it does not do justice to the executive dimension of intention. As in Alan's case (one of our angry men), an agent may be preponderantly motivated to *A* and yet not intend to *A* even if he believes that he probably will *A* and that his desire to *A* will probably effectively motivate his *A*-ing. In such cases, agents satisfy conditions sufficient for intending to *A* on representative belief/desire analyses of intention; yet they have not made the progress toward action that intention involves. If intentions are a species of desire in a very broad sense of 'desire', they are a very special species, a species whose distinctive role in the motivation of action depends upon their having an executive feature that is not reducible to relative motivational strength.

In the case of the executive dimension of *proximal* intentions in particular, we can profitably borrow a page from the computer scientist's book. The immediate triggering of appropriate actional mechanisms can be construed as a *default condition* of the acquisition of a proximal intention to *A*. The idea is roughly this: the mental and physical architecture of any being capable of intentional action is such that when such a being acquires a proximal intention to *A,* an immediate effect is the triggering of appropriate actional mechanisms, unless something prevents this.[17] (As in default procedures generally, the proposed default assignment for intention acquisition can be preempted. I shall return to this point shortly.) *What* is triggered when the default procedure is effective is a function, in significant part, of the plan component of the pertinent intention. The triggering itself is due (again in significant part) to the settledness aspect of proximal intentions—or at least (for those who wish to understand 'being settled' restrictively) to a "thinner" feature of proximal intention identifiable as what is left of full-blown settledness when its special firmness, duration, and etiology are subtracted. This latter condition may be termed *thin settledness*.

The points just made apply indirectly to *distal* intentions as well. Under favorable conditions, as I have noted, distal *decisions* will persist until the targeted time and figure in the initiation of appropriate actions then. The same is true of distal *intentions*. It is the distal states' becoming proximal or, alternatively, the acquisition of corresponding proximal intentions—intentions whose acquisition is a partial consequence of associated distal intentions—that initiates action.[18] And it is partly in virtue of the settledness encompassed in distal intentions that they contribute as they do to intentional action.

Turning now to the MST, it should be observed that accommodation of the thesis does not require supposing that preponderant motivation is an essential feature of intentions. For example, one may treat S's preponderantly wanting to A as a required *background* condition for an intentional A-ing to issue from his intention to A; and this in no way presupposes that preponderant wanting is a defining feature of intentions themselves.[19]

This last suggestion oversimplifies matters in a way that demands attention. Perhaps, in a very broad sense of 'want', an intention to A is, or incorporates, a want to A; and in many cases what we intend to do we preponderantly want to do. Moreover, a preponderant proximal want to A can figure in the *production* of a corresponding intention. Indeed, acquiring a proximal intention to A is plausibly regarded as being a restricted default condition of one's acquiring a preponderant proximal want to A: if an agent acquires a preponderant want to A straightaway and does not yet proximally intend to A (the restrictive condition), he immediately acquires a proximal intention to A if nothing prevents this. And again, in the absence of prevention, an immediate effect of the acquisition of the intention is the triggering of appropriate actional mechanisms. To be sure, on this account, acquisition of a preponderant proximal want to A does not immediately trigger appropriate actional mechanisms; and the move from want acquisition to triggering will take some time. But the time is hardly so great as to force us to deny that we can ever satisfy our proximal wants on the view suggested.

If preponderant proximal wanting to A is sometimes incorporated in proximal intentions and sometimes figures in the production of these intentions, it is not *merely* a background, or enabling, condition of the initiation of intentional A-ings by proximal intentions to A. But we may acknowledge these points about proximal wanting without having to accommodate the MST by making preponderant motivation to A an essential feature of proximal intentions to A. We can grant that in some cases, an agent who proximally intends to A does not have a preponderant proximal desire to A.

This last observation raises an interesting question: What happens when, proximally intending to A, S is more motivated (wants more) to do some competing action B (e.g., to refrain from A-ing)? One consequence, I suggest, is that the default procedure linking intention to intentional action is preempted. But this leaves a number of possibilities open. For example, S might successfully exercise self-control in support of his acting as he intends, with the result that the balance of his motivation changes. Or S might make an *aborted* attempt to A. (The motivational condition of an agent who intends to hack off his arm with an ax in order to free himself from a trap may permit the initiation of the project even if it blocks the project's completion.)[20] Or S's intention to A might be replaced by an intention to B. In any case, one can suppose that an intention—even a proximal one—can be at odds with what an agent is most motivated to do at the time without having to despair of finding an explanation of the agent's intentional behavior. If the MST is true, an agent's intending to A cannot result in an intentional A-ing as long as he is preponderantly motivated to do something else instead. But this does not force a practical stalemate; it need not paralyze the agent. In general, motivational conditions and intentions are not immutable.

How are intentions different from desires generally? An important difference has already emerged. Intending entails being settled, or at least being thinly settled. However, one can desire to A—even preponderantly and while holding beliefs of the sort identified in belief/desire analyses of intention—without being even thinly settled upon A-ing. Moreover, owing significantly to the settledness feature of intentions, agents who intend to A are disposed to see the practical question "Shall I A?" as closed, at least tentatively; but we desire to do many things without being at all disposed to see the pertinent practical questions as closed.[21] And for this reason, distal intentions facilitate planning in a way that distal desires, as a class, do not. Having formed or acquired a distal intention to take Connie to lunch, I am in a better position to coordinate the day's activities than I was when, merely *desiring* to take Connie to lunch, I still regarded the matter as open.[22]

Now, if any motivational state is to be counted as a desire in a broad, technical sense of the term, asking how intentions differ from desires generally is rather like asking how sailboats differ from boats generally. Of course, the latter question is a sensible one. We can identify what distinguishes sailboats from other boats. Similarly, if we define 'desire' broadly enough that states having the executive dimension characteristic of decisions and intentions count as desires, we can locate what distinguishes these desires from others. What I want to emphasize here is that the broad, technical sense of 'desire' at issue does not save traditional belief/desire reductionism about intention. For that reductionism lodges the primary functional connection between intention and the initiation of intentional action in desire strength (see ch. 3.7); and that (as we shall see in more detail) is a mistake. If intentions are to be counted as a species of desire, traditional conceptions of desire must be revised. Desire must now be understood in such a way that there is a kind of desire—namely, intention—whose contribution to intentional action rests significantly on its having an executive dimension not captured in terms of desire strength. To accept this new conception of desire is to reject familiar belief/desire reductionism about intention.

The central destructive purpose of this chapter has been to show that standard belief/desire analyses of intention are not adequate to the task. But this chapter has a constructive side as well. I have argued that intention, like decision, is intimately linked with being settled (or thinly settled) upon a course of action. The executive dimension of intention sketched here is developed further in chapter 10.

Notes

1. Reductionists include Audi (1973, 1986a), Beardsley (1978), and W. Davis (1984). Their opponents include Brand (1984), Bratman (1987), Davidson (1980, ch. 5; 1985, pp. 211–17), Harman (1976, 1986a), and McCann (1986b).

2. For resistance to this assumption, see Brand 1984 and Searle 1983.

3. This example originally appeared in Mele 1988b.

4. See Audi 1973, 1986a; Beardsley 1978; and W. Davis 1984.

5. For the first candidate, see Audi 1973, 1986a; Beardsley 1978. W. Davis (1984) proposes the second.

6. This is not to deny that there are cases in which an agent who is decided upon A-ing believes, for reasons like *Alan's,* that he will A.

7. If deciding encompasses intention and the belief condition at issue is required for intention, then it is required for deciding as well.

8. See especially Mele 1987a, chs. 3 and 6.

9. Hereafter, for stylistic reasons, I shall generally suppress the parenthetical qualifiers. See n. 11.

10. Compare with Bratman 1987 on intentions.

11. I have left it open that someone who intends to A might be settled only upon *trying* to A. In some cases, one's estimation of the likelihood that one will succeed in A-ing might be such that one cannot properly be said to be settled upon A-ing itself even though one intends to A. The "confidence condition" on being settled upon A-ing might be stronger than that on intending to A. (This, at least, is something that I shall leave open.) I shall generally use 'S is settled upon A-ing' as shorthand for 'S is settled upon A-ing or settled upon trying to A.'

12. See Mele 1987a, pp. 88–93, for further discussion. For references to the studies see, in same source, ch. 4, n. 4. The distinction just sketched between evaluative ranking and motivational strength is mirrored in Alan Gibbard's

recent distinction between "*accepting* a norm (or more precisely, *accepting* that one set of norms outweighs another in a given situation)" and "*being in the grip* of a norm" (1990, p. 60). Thus, Gibbard suggests that the compliant subjects in Stanley Milgram's (1974) famous study of obedience to authority accept "norms against inflicting pain and danger . . . as having most weight in [their] situation" but are "in the grip" of "norms of politeness and cooperativeness" (1990, pp. 60–61). In my terminology (Mele 1983, 1984, 1987a), they take their reasons for noncompliance with the experimenter evaluatively to outweigh their reasons for compliance (i.e., if their behavior is akratic, as Gibbard contends); but the motivational strength of the latter exceeds that of the former.

13. For a detailed explanation, see Mele 1987a, ch. 6.

14. This case first appeared in Mele 1984.

15. This is not to deny that one's deciding to do *A* might itself contribute to one's motivation to do *A;* but in some cases the contribution apparently is not sufficient to tip the motivational balance.

16. Notice that it does not follow from Alex's no longer intending to cut his hand that he no longer judges it best to do this. On the relationship between intentions and better judgments, see Mele 1987a, ch. 3.

17. I am not here *limiting* the action-producing role of proximal intentions to the triggering of actional mechanisms. In chapter 10 I argue that proximal intentions also have a causal sustaining function, a point raised in chapter 8.2.

18. These alternatives are addressed at the end of chapter 10.2.

19. The central idea of this paragraph is developed in chapter 10.

20. Some motivational details of aborted attempts are addressed in chapter 10.3. See also Mele 1987a, pp. 36–39.

21. On this dispositional feature of intentions and the following point about planning, see Bratman 1987.

22. For additional alleged differences, see Brand 1984, pp. 121–27; Bratman 1987, pp. 18–20; Harman 1986a, p. 83; and McCann 1986b, pp. 193–94.

10

The Executive Dimension of Proximal Intentions

The contribution of intention to intentional action, on the view that has been taking shape in the two preceding chapters, rests upon motivational and representational features of the state. In this chapter, I restrict the discussion to *overt* intentional action, intentional action that essentially involves peripheral bodily movement; and I focus on the motivational dimension of proximal intention. My guiding question is this: If there is a specific *motivational* role that intention is plausibly regarded as playing in all cases of overt intentional action, in virtue of what feature(s) of intention does it play this role?[1] I am looking for an answer that can be articulated in the terminology of intentionalist psychology, a psychology that accords intentional states (beliefs, desires, and the like) a prominent place in the explanation of intentional behavior.

A familiar answer lies in a certain synthesis of two attractive ideas about the etiology of intentional action. The first is roughly that whenever an agent acts intentionally, he is *more motivated* to perform the intentional action(s) that he performs than he is to perform any competing action that he takes to be open to him at the time.[2] This is an approximate expression of what I have termed the motivational strength thesis (MST). (As a convenient bit of shorthand, I shall use the expression 'preponderant motivation' for the motivational condition in question.) The second idea is that whenever we act intentionally, we are *moved* to act as we do, at least in part, by an appropriate intention. This is the *intention thesis* (IT).

Some philosophers have attempted to combine the MST and IT by maintaining that preponderant motivation is built into intention as an essential feature and that intentions move us to act in virtue of their incorporating preponderant motivation. For example, William Alston contends that "a present intention to do *S* can be construed as . . . an 'executive' desire for *S,* a desire that has come out victorious [in respect

172

of strength] over any immediate competitors and that will therefore trigger off mechanisms leading to overt movement provided that the relevant mechanisms are working normally" (1974, p. 95).[3]

Unfortunately, this tidy synthesis is unacceptable, as chapter 9 demonstrated. Someone who intends, even proximally, to *A* need not be most motivated to *A*. The present chapter advances an alternative to this synthesis.

Again, some intentions are for the specious present while others are for the nonimmediate future. I have called them, respectively, *proximal* and *distal* intentions. (Although the temporal content of proximal intentions typically ranges into the future, part of any proximal intender's plan, as I conceive of proximal intentions, is to begin acting appropriately at once.) On the view to be developed here, proximal intention plays roughly the triggering role identified by Alston even though it does not essentially incorporate preponderant motivation. My task is to locate a feature of proximal intention that enables it to perform the triggering work at issue. Or, more precisely, since I shall argue that the moving role of proximal intention extends beyond triggering to the causal sustaining of the functioning of actional mechanisms, my task is to identify what it is about proximal intention that enables it to play this *compound* role.

1. Background

Fred, who is deliberating about whether to have a second helping of pie, is more motivated to have a second helping than to refrain from doing so. On the basis of our knowledge of this motivational feature of the case alone (presuming the continued availability of a second helping, Fred's ability to eat it, and the like), we cannot be sure whether Fred will eat the pie; for he might decide *not* to eat it, and his decision might result in a corresponding shift in the balance of his motivation. *While* Fred is deliberating, the question whether he will eat the dessert is unsettled both in our minds (given our limited information) and in his. In forming an intention, Fred settles the question for himself.

Fred's story illustrates an important point. We are not always at the mercy of our preponderant motivation. An agent who is most motivated to *A* can decide not to *A;* and the decision, either directly or by prompting a special effort of self-control, can have the consequence that the agent's balance of motivation falls on the side of his not *A*-ing.[4] Unless the agent's preponderant motivation to *A* is irresistible, it is up to him, as we say, whether he A-s (or, at least, makes a full-blown attempt to A: our environment is not always conducive to the execution of our intentions). This is not to reject the MST. It is only to acknowledge cases in which agents can effect a shift in the balance of their motivation.

Furthermore, in some cases (at least), intentions play a motivational role that preponderant motivation does not. Fred's motivational condition while he is considering eating the dessert does not at that time *settle* for him the question, "What shall I do?" But his decision does settle the question. (Recall that in deciding to A one forms an *intention* to A.) And settling of this sort certainly seems capable of playing an important role in moving an agent to act. When one acts as one is settled upon acting, one typically does so *because* (in part) one is settled upon so acting.

I am not suggesting, of course, that an agent's being settled upon A-ing is *sufficient* for his A-ing or even for his being most motivated to A. The agent may, for example, be unable to A; and, as I have argued elsewhere (Mele 1987a, ch. 3), the balance of an agent's motivation in some instances of incontinent action is not in line with a pertinent proximal decision or intention. An agent's settling *his* question, "Shall I A?" does not necessarily settle *our* question, "Will he A?"—even when his question is about immediate action. And, once again, the claim that intentions *settle* something for agents is compatible with the revocability and revisability of intentions. Just as intentions can be more or less firm, one can be more or less firmly settled upon an action. (Similarly, just as an intention to A may persist for only a few moments, someone's being settled upon A-ing may be a short-lived state.)

A distinction noted in chapter 8 between a stronger and a weaker thesis about the conceptual connection between intention and intentional action should be recalled here. The stronger thesis asserts that every intentional action is an intended action—that for any action A, if S A-ed intentionally, S intended to A. The attractive simplicity of this thesis notwithstanding, critics urge that certain actional consequences of intentional actions may themselves be intentional actions even if they are not intended. Thus, for example, Gilbert Harman holds that a sniper who intentionally fires his gun, knowing that in doing so he will alert the enemy, intentionally alerts the enemy even if he does not intend to do so (1976, p. 434).[5] For present purposes, it suffices to notice that a weaker thesis relating intentions to intentional actions is open to one who agrees with Harman. It is that no one acts intentionally at t unless, at t, he has some relevant intention or other.[6] On this view, every *case* of intentional action involves an intention, though there may be *particular* intentional actions that are not intended. (Harman's sniper intends at least to fire his gun, or to shoot at *X*.) I shall assume for now that at least the weaker thesis is correct. An objection to the thesis is discussed in section 3.

2. A First Approximation

According to what I have termed the *intention thesis* (IT), intentions perform a motivational function in all cases of overt intentional action. As I argued in the preceding chapter, intending to *A* does not entail being preponderantly motivated to *A;* incorporating preponderant motivation to *A* is not an essential feature of intentions to *A*. But perhaps intentions move us to act in virtue of some feature that they do possess essentially. I shall argue that they do. (Even though, for reasons identified in chapter 3, I do not endorse the MST, it is worth mentioning that the view to be defended is consistent with the MST.)

One may attempt to make some elbow room for the IT by advancing what I shall call the *strong intention-centered model* (the strong ICM). This view, as I shall explain shortly, is *too* strong. But brief consideration will prove instructive.

On the strong ICM, the explanatory role of preponderant motivation vis-à-vis overt intentional action is analogous to that of ability. In a suitably broad sense of 'able', an agent cannot intentionally *A* at *t* unless, at *t*, he is able to *A* intentionally at *t*. Ability is a necessary condition of intentional action; but it is not (in general) an explanatorily central condition. Similarly, on the strong ICM, a necessary condition of an agent's intentionally *A*-ing at *t* is (perhaps) that at *t*, he be more motivated to *A* at *t* than he is to take any competing course of action at *t;* but an agent's having preponderant motivation to *A* is not explanatorily central to his intentionally *A*-ing. What is central is his *intending* to *A* (or his intending to do some other action *B* that is appropriately related to his *A*-ing) and perhaps certain features of the etiology of that intention.

Explanatory centrality, is, of course, relative to an interrogative context. When we ask why Caesar crossed the Rubicon, our primary concern may be with the *reason(s)* for which he did so (or, depending upon our interests, with general features of Caesar's personality). When we ask how (or why) the beliefs and desires that constituted Caesar's reasons for crossing the Rubicon led to his crossing the river or how (or why) anyone's reasons result in an appropriate intentional action, the explanatory focus shifts. What becomes central now, on an ICM, are intentions. Intentions provide the primary link between agents' reasons and the actions that they perform for reasons.[7]

The strong ICM, as I said, is too strong; for it underestimates the role of preponderant motivation in the generation of many intentional actions. Intentions are often partial products of an agent's preponderant motivation (see ch. 9). In some cases, the motivational force of certain of one's wants may influence one's practical judgments, and consequently have an indirect effect upon one's judgment-based intentions. But the connection between preponderant motivation and intention often seems much more direct. For example, Barney's proximal intention to take a drink at the drinking fountain that he is approaching may have resulted simply from his possessing an uncontested—and hence (by default) preponderant—desire for a drink of water (and from his having some appropriate representation of the fountain as a suitable source of water). In treating preponderant motivation as analogous to ability, the strong ICM does not do justice to these points.

What is crucial for a proponent of the IT is that intention function as a motivator in all cases of intentional action. To defend this point about intention it is not necessary to restrict preponderant motivation wholly to the background. It is sufficient that preponderant motivation not usurp the motivational role accorded to intention.

On a weaker intention-centered model, preponderant motivation is allowed greater latitude in the etiology of intentional action. However, as on the strong ICM, a fundamental motivational role is reserved for intention. What is crucial for the weak ICM that I shall advance is that a particular motivational role be played by *proximal* intentions in all cases of overt intentional action.

The activation or triggering of appropriate actional mechanisms, I have suggested (see ch. 9.5), is part of the *default condition* of the acquisition of a proximal intention. When a proximal intention to A is acquired by an agent whose actional mechanisms are, in Alston's words, "working normally," appropriate actional mechanisms are triggered at once, provided that nothing blocks the triggering. Of course, this suggestion about the architecture of the mind is not fully evaluable in the absence of further details. How, for example, can the triggering be blocked? How can the default procedure be preempted, as it were? Pertinent details will emerge gradually.

Proximal intentions, on the view to be developed here, are *executive* states. A proximal intention to do an A incorporates a propensity of the agent to *execute* a certain representational component of the intention, what I have called a *plan*.

Executive states, as I conceive of them, incorporate propensities to act (intentionally). Wants, like intentions, incorporate propensities of the latter sort. But, as I have observed (ch. 9.5), whereas an agent can want to do something—even *preponderantly* want to do it—and yet not be (thinly) settled upon doing it (or even upon trying to do it), intending to *A* entails being (thinly) settled upon *A*-ing, or at least upon trying to *A*.[8] Thus, there is a tighter connection between intending and doing than between wanting and doing. On the ICM that I am urging, wants lead to intentional actions only indirectly, by leading to proximal intentions. Wants encompass *second-order* propensities to act intentionally. They encompass propensities to form or acquire first-order propensities that partially constitute intentions (see Brand 1984, p. 127; Castañeda 1975, p. 284). Proximal intentions occupy a mediating role between wants and intentional actions, and this point about the causal route is reflected in the divergent causal natures of wants and proximal intentions.[9]

What is the central motivational task that proximal intentions perform according to the ICM that I am suggesting? Here is a first approximation:

> *Approx.* In all cases of overt intentional action, the acquisition of a proximal intention settles for the agent the practical question "What shall I do now?"—thereby triggering appropriate actional mechanisms.

Approx requires considerable elaboration. First, I am not suggesting that proximal intentions always come into being as a response to an explicitly formulated or entertained practical question. When the phone on my office desk rings, I typically do not ask, "What shall I do now?" If I have nothing more pressing to do, I simply pick up the receiver and say *hello*. Nevertheless, my answering the phone seems typically to be an intentional action; and overt intentional actions, on an ICM, are generated by some relevant intention.

Now, even if when the phone rings I do not literally ask myself (aloud or otherwise) what I shall do, this practical question does, in a very real sense, arise for me. The ringing phone is a stimulus that opens up new possibilities for action. And my responses to ringings of my office phone are varied in a way that mere "reflex" actions are not: when I am in the midst of typing a sentence or speaking to a student, I often complete the sentence or the thought before answering the phone. My forming or acquiring the intention to answer the phone in a particular case settles the question that the new stimulus introduces for me. Of course, it might not settle the question "What will this philosopher do?" of some prescient, intention-reading spirit in my office. If I am shot to death before I have time to make a move, I will not even reach for the receiver.

To say that the acquisition of a proximal intention settles a practical issue for the agent is not to say that it settles all the details. Wilma, standing at a bus stop, sees a baby leaning out of a fourth-story window and feels certain that he will fall. We may suppose that Wilma proximally intends to save the baby and that she immediately begins running toward him with that intention, though her plan for saving the baby is not yet fully determinate. As Wilma runs, the details fall into place: she must make a diving catch. Here, Wilma's acquiring a proximal intention to save the baby does settle in her mind what she will do, namely, save the baby, or at least try. But there was a time, however brief, during which she was settled upon saving the child without yet being settled upon the precise manner in which she would save him.[10]

I suggested that by settling first-person practical questions about what is to be done, acquisitions of proximal intentions trigger actional mechanisms (provided, of course, that the latter are, in Alston's words, "working normally"). In cases of overt action what is triggered is obviously a *physical* process; and the triggering intentions, consequently, are realized in *physical* states—or so, at least, someone with my philosophical prejudices would contend. For this reason, a fully detailed answer to the question how, in a particular human being, the acquisition of a particular proximal intention triggers a particular set of actional mechanisms capable of issuing in overt action will properly be cast (at least partly) in the language of neurophysiology (or perhaps physics). I do not know how to construct such an answer in detail; nor does anyone else. The best that I can do is to offer a psychological answer: to acquire a proximal intention to A is, in part, to acquire an executive propensity with respect to the plan component of that intention. This propensity (in ordinary human beings) is realized in some physical state of the agent—a state involved in the triggering of appropriate actional mechanisms if they are in proper working order.[11]

Notice that *Approx* does *not* assert that when actional mechanisms are working normally, the acquisition of a proximal intention will always result in the intended action or even that it will issue in the completion of the pertinent bodily movement under these conditions. A golfer whose physical condition is quite normal may accidentally miss a two-foot putt that he proximally intends to make. And executions of proximal intentions are cut short for a variety of reasons having nothing to do with physical malfunctions. If I hear a piercing scream while lifting a cup of coffee to my lips, I might stop the upward movement of my arm at once and rush to locate the source of the trouble. *Approx* is consistent with these points.

Should a provision be made in *Approx* for the possibility that some *motivational* state of an agent may prevent the acquisition of a proximal intention from triggering appropriate actional mechanisms that are in proper working order? For example, can someone's fear be so great that when he forms a proximal intention to jump from the third story of a burning building, his forming that intention has no effect whatever on appropriate actional mechanisms that are working normally? This is a difficult question. If the intention acquisition is wholly without effect, the explanation may be that the agent's fear caused pertinent actional mechanisms not to work normally. But in that event, the case does not constitute a problem for *Approx*.

We can safely leave the question open and say that a necessary condition of the acquisition of a proximal intention's having an appropriate triggering effect is that its having such an effect is compatible with the agent's motivational state at the time.[12] However, it would be a mistake to maintain that a proximal intention to *A* must be supported by concurrent preponderant motivation to *A* if the agent's acquiring that intention is to trigger appropriate actional mechanisms. An agent can *begin* to act as he proximally intends, even if his intention is at odds with his preponderant motivation. The motivational condition of a man who proximally intends to cut off his arm with a machete in order to free himself from a trap may permit the initiation of a downward stroke of the machete toward his ensnared arm while blocking completion of the gruesome project. (Incidentally, this does not require that the agent have distinct desires to initiate the action and to complete it. Rather, the motivational opposition to his desire or intention to cut off his arm may be such that although it permits the initiation, it blocks the completion.)

I have suggested that the *acquisition* of a proximal intention triggers actional mechanisms under certain conditions. Contrast two cases: (1) Fred, having formed at 8:30 P.M. an intention to turn his television on at 9:00 P.M., has at 9:00 P.M. a proximal intention to turn his television on; (2) Barney, who had no distal intention to watch television (or to turn the television on) this evening, forms at 9:00 P.M. a proximal intention to switch his television on. Barney's acquiring a proximal intention to *A* is partly a matter of his coming to have an intention that he did not have previously. But what about Fred? *Must* Fred's proximal intention to turn the television on be a distinct intention from his distal intention? Or might the latter in some way evolve into the former? Might Fred's distal intention have *become,* as we might say, a proximal one? For my purposes it is not necessary to take a stand. If distal intentions cannot become proximal intentions, the acquisition of the proximal intention in case 1, as in case 2, is partly a matter of the agent's coming to have an intention that he did not previously possess. If, alternatively, Fred's distal intention in some way evolved into his proximal intention, his *acquisition* of the proximal intention consists in a change of another sort—his distal intention's having become a proximal one. On either view of the relation between counterpart distal and proximal intentions, it is true of the agent at one time and false of him at another that he proximally intends to A. As I am using 'intention acquisition' here, the preceding is sufficient for the acquisition of a proximal intention. If distal intentions can evolve into proximal ones, acquiring a proximal intention need not involve acquiring a *new* intention.

3. A Second Approximation

Although I have been focusing on triggering, this is only part of the moving role attributed to proximal intentions in chapter 8. Suppose that someone proximally intends to sign a check. Interrupted by a knock at his office door, he stops in the middle of his first name and invites his visitor to enter, intending to finish signing the check later. His acquiring a proximal intention to sign the check initiated a process that would have constituted his signing the check if it had been completed. But obviously, that is not sufficient for the production of a continuous intentional check signing. Now, one might try to explain the cessation of the check signing by adverting to the knock at the door. Suppose, however, that the agent's intention had not been altered by this interruption. Other things being equal, he would have completed the check signing. This indicates that intentions may play a causal *sustaining* role in the production of intentional action. The execution of a proximal intention takes time; and the moving work of a proximal intention might not cease with the initiation of an actional process. That proximal intentions do have a sustaining role is precisely what we should expect, if proximal intentions incorporate propensities of an agent to execute the plan components of the intentions and not simply propensities to *initiate* execution.[13]

In light of what I have said thus far about proximal intentions, a second approximation of the core of the ICM that I am advancing may be offered.

1. In all cases of overt intentional action, the acquisition of a proximal intention triggers appropriate actional mechanisms and the intention causally sustains their functioning.[14] This triggering-cum-sustaining is the most

fundamental *motivational* role of proximal intentions in overt intentional action.

2. The acquisition of a proximal intention N triggers appropriate actional mechanisms—and N sustains the functioning of these mechanisms—in virtue of N's encompassing an executive propensity with regard to the plan component of N.

3. The acquisition of a proximal intention that remains present throughout t will trigger appropriate actional mechanisms, and the intention will causally sustain their functioning, provided that the mechanisms are in proper working order and the agent's motivational condition during t permits such triggering and sustaining.

This approximation does not, of course, provide an *exhaustive* account of the causal contribution of proximal intentions to overt intentional action. The approximation says little about the distinctly *representational* functions of proximal intentions; and, as I have mentioned, proximal intentions can play motivational roles that are not specified in claims 1–3. The purpose of claims 1–3 is to identify the most basic *motivational* role of proximal intentions in overt intentional action—a role that is played in all cases of such action—and to specify, in the language of intentionalist psychology, the features of proximal intention in virtue of which it plays this role. (The representational functions of proximal intentions are addressed in chapter 11.)

CLAIM 1. Thus far, I have simply *assumed* that proximal intention is involved in all cases of overt intentional action. This popular assumption, which enters into claim 1, is controversial; and the major criticisms should be addressed.

John Searle (1983) has argued for what purports to be a species of intention that is distinct from proximal and distal intentions—something he calls *intention in action*.[15] At the heart of his distinction between intentions in action and "prior" intentions (both distal and proximal) is the idea that only the former are *parts* of actions. Effective prior intentions cause *actions*. Effective intentions in action "present" and cause *bodily movements;* and together with bodily movements that they cause, intentions in action *constitute* actions (pp. 93–94).[16] My target in much of this subsection is *Searle's contention* (SC) that "all intentional actions have intentions in action but not all intentional actions have prior intentions" (p. 85). If Searle is right, claim 1 is false: In some cases of overt intentional action, no proximal intention is involved.[17]

Searle's brief for SC addresses four issues: (1) problems posed by deviant causal chains; (2) the intimacy of the connection between actions and intentions; (3) the status of subsidiary intentional actions such as shifting into third gear while driving to work; and (4) the etiology of sudden or impulsive actions. I shall treat each issue in turn.

Consider an instance of what Myles Brand has termed "antecedential" waywardness (1984, p. 18). A philosopher intends to knock over his glass of water in order to distract his commentator. However, his intention so upsets him that his hand shakes uncontrollably, striking the glass and knocking it to the floor. Plainly, he does not *intentionally* knock over the glass, even though his intention results in the glass's crashing to the floor. *Why* is this not an instance of intentional action? Searle's answer is that the agent's prior intention to knock over the glass did not cause an appropriate *intention in action* (1983, p. 94).

There are, however, other plausible answers. One is that the philosopher's "prior" intention to knock over the glass did not *guide* the movements involved in his hand's striking the glass. Searle supposes that in instances of intentional action involving prior intentions, the prior intention's work is finished when it causes an intention in action. But one may maintain instead, as I have done, that the causal role of the prior intention extends through the completion of the bodily movement.[18] Very roughly speaking, what Searle calls an intention in action might be part of an intention that appears on the scene before the action begins and remains as long as the pertinent bodily movements continue. (To say that an intention N is a *prior* intention relative to an action A is to say that it is present before A begins; but, at least as I shall use the term, it is not to say that N is no longer present while A is occurring.)

I turn to issue 2, the intimacy of the connection between intentions and actions. Searle claims that "the reason there is a more intimate connection between actions and intentions than there is between, say, beliefs and states of affairs is that actions contain intentions in action as one of their components" (1983, p. 107). The data that Searle is trying to explain are these:

D1. "Whereas there are lots of states of affairs which are not believed to obtain or desired to obtain, there are no actions without intentions." (p. 82)

D2. "My belief will be satisfied [i.e., true] iff the state of affairs I believe to obtain really does obtain and my desire will be satisfied iff the state of affairs I desire to obtain does obtain . . ."; but I may do something that I intend to do without satisfying my intention. (pp. 81–82)

Searle attempts to account for D1 by means of what might be termed a *constitutive* explanation—specifically, by building intentions into actions. But alternative *causal* explanations of this point have been offered (Brand 1984, pp. 37–39, 15–31). If there are no actions without intentions, the explanation, for all that Searle says, may be that action is *causally dependent* upon prior intention.

D2, of course, rests upon the problem(s) of causal deviance. I have already suggested that on this matter one can accomplish with extended proximal intentions what Searle attempts to accomplish with intentions in action. In chapter 11.1 I shall explain in some detail how this can be done.

This brings us to issue 3, the status of subsidiary actions. Searle states that "even in cases where I have a prior intention to do some action there will normally be a whole lot of subsidiary actions which are not represented in the prior intention but which are nonetheless performed intentionally" (1983, p. 84). In virtue of what are the subsidiary actions intentional? Searle's answer, of course, is that they are partially constituted by appropriate effective intentions in action (p. 85).

Searle does not commit himself to the implausible view that there is a distinct intention in action for each subsidiary intentional action (e.g., for each step I take in walking to work). Intentions in action can be quite complex. For instance, a child's intention in action may be "to break the vase by means of hitting it with a hard object, by means of moving the hard object, by means of moving the hand holding the hard object" (1983, p. 129). Similarly, I suppose, a man walking to work may, in Searle's view, have a single intention in action that is somehow associated with each of his steps.

Given that even unintentional actions "have" intentions in action, for Searle (1983, p. 107), we must ask how intentional subsidiary actions are supposed to be rendered intentional by intentions in action. My guess is that intentions in action are, for Searle, a species of trying:[19] an intention in action is effective—results in movements partly constitutive of a pertinent intentional action—when an agent succeeds in doing what he is trying to do, *because* he is trying to do it.[20]

Why, then, are the various steps that Barney takes in walking to work intentional? They are intentional because he is successfully trying to take these steps, because he is making an effective effort, however minimal that effort may be, to take these steps. So far, so good. Notice, however, that this answer does not remove prior intention from the picture. Why is Barney trying to take these steps? Perhaps because of a prior intention to walk to work. And this prior intention may continue to play a causal role in his walking even after the action begins—a role that may involve motivation and guidance. Once again, Searle has not shown that we can act intentionally without prior intentions. The trying associated with what he calls an intention in action may be initiated and sustained by a prior intention that continues to be present and causally active through the completion of the bodily movement.

We are left with issue 4, the etiology of sudden or impulsive intentional actions. Searle contends that we perform many intentional actions "quite spontaneously, without forming, consciously or unconsciously, any prior intention to do those things" (1983, p. 84). In these cases, he claims, there is an intention in action but no prior intention. For example, when, angered by a remark that Richard just made, John suddenly slaps Richard in the face, there is no prior intention to strike Richard. But John's slapping Richard is partially constituted by an appropriate intention in action.

Does the impulsiveness of John's behavior make it likely that no intention of his issued in the slap? Perhaps John's violent reaction is sufficiently sudden that we would be disinclined to say that he did anything that could properly be counted as *forming* an appropriate prior intention. But even if he does not form such an intention, he may *acquire* one. Notice that if forming an intention is itself an action, it does not follow from the fact that no prior intention is *formed* in a particular case that the agent *had* no prior intention in that case. Some intentions may be *passively* acquired, as is the case with many of our beliefs, desires, thoughts, and so on. So suppose that 'S formed an intention to A', as Searle uses these words, means only 'S acquired an intention to A, actively or otherwise'. (Notice that 'S formed a belief that p' and 'S formed a desire for x' are often used in a correspondingly loose sense.) Then the claim that John did not form an intention to hit Richard has less intuitive appeal. The idea seems to be that sudden or impulsive action leaves insufficient time for intention formation. But how much time does it take to acquire an intention? John's hearing the remark, in conjunction with other pertinent features of the case, may produce an intention whose acquisition initiates action, without his having to perform the mental action of forming that or any other intention. Impulsive intentional actions may well be products of impulsively acquired intentions.

On Searle's view, the agent of any intentional action has an appropriate intention. Therefore, the agent of any intentional action must *acquire* an appropriate intention. But if this is right, the issue between Searle and those who wish to give prior intentions a more comprehensive role cannot be whether there is time for a suitable intention to be acquired. It is agreed on both sides that there is sufficient time for this. The dispute must be, at least in significant part, about how to answer the question "When does an intentional action *begin?*" Are the intentions most intimately associated with intentional actions *causes of those actions,* so that the actions begin just *after* the intentions are acquired? Or are the intentions at issue *constituents* of those actions, constituents that cause other constituents?[21]

Consider again the case of the impulsive slap. John makes a successful effort to slap Richard, and the slap is intentional. Searle claims that there is an intention in action but that John did not intend to slap Richard prior to the beginning of the action. How is this issue to be decided?

My own inclination is to opt for theoretical simplicity. For Searle, the only intentional actions that are not caused by a prior intention are intentional sudden or impulsive actions and certain intentional subsidiary actions. Since his case for treating these actions differently from the rest is far from persuasive and since strategies for explaining them by means of prior intentions are available, simplicity suggests that they, too, ought to be treated as products of prior intentions. This is not to say, of course, that each intentional action has its own distinct prior intention. The various steps that I take in walking to work do not depend for their being intentional upon a long series of discrete and rapidly acquired prior intentions. Rather, the walk in which they occur is initiated and sustained by a prior intention.

The story does not end here. I have suggested that for Searle, intentions in action are a species of trying. But standard, commonsense conceptions of trying and intention do not permit intentions to be tryings. Tryings are actions; but intentions are not actions, not even partly. An intention to *A* may be, in part, a *disposition* to try to *A*. But this is not to say that to have an intention is, in part, to be trying to *A*. Indeed, the dispositional claim suggests that there is something about intentions that figures *causally* in the production of trying under certain conditions.

It is clear where the argument is heading. One may attempt to halt its progress by maintaining that intentional actions start not with (the beginning of) a trying but rather with whatever causes trying. However, adequate support for this suggestion must go well beyond what Searle provides; for his defense of his account of the constitution of actions is precisely his defense of SC. An interesting alternative is the suggestion that '*intention* in action' is simply a poor tag for the notion that Searle has in mind—the notion, namely, of a kind of trying. One could preserve the spirit of SC by holding that all intentional actions involve such a *trying* but that some intentional actions—sudden actions and certain subsidiary actions—are not initiated by prior intentions. Moreover, one might maintain, with Hugh McCann (1986a), that trying is intrinsically intentional and hold, accordingly, that tryings and certain actions partially composed of tryings are intentional even in the absence of a prior intention.[22]

This is, to be sure, an intriguing idea. With a little tinkering, it can even be used by proponents of an appropriately modified version of SC to dissolve a commitment that I have been able to exploit, namely, SC's commitment to the view that there is always time in cases of intentional action for the acquisition of a suitable intention. But we are still owed a convincing argument for the claim that there is no pertinent prior intention in some cases of intentional action. McCann (1986a) emphasizes sudden actions in an effort to circumscribe the influence of prior intentions (see L. Davis 1979, pp. 59–60; Malcolm 1968, p. 61; Wilson 1989, pp. 238–39). However, if, as I should think, intention acquisition may occur at something approaching the speed of thought, McCann's and Searle's opponents have little to fear on this score.[23]

Can an agent intentionally A without intending to do anything at all at the time? Robert Audi answers in the affirmative. He maintains that S intends at t to A only if, "at t, . . . S believes that he will (or that he probably will) A" (1986a, p. 18). In some cases of intentional action, Audi claims, this belief condition on intending is not satisfied. For example, someone who "very much doubts that she can move" her arm, may respond to a doctor's request by moving it—intentionally (p. 27).

Although I have already rejected Audi's controversial belief constraint on intention (ch. 8), let us suppose for the sake of argument that it is correct; and let us suppose as well that the woman *intentionally* moves her arm.[24] Audi's agent, Sally, does not intend to move her arm. The suggestion that she intends to *try* to move it preserves the IT. But, Audi asks, "What has she done, or formed an intention to do, that is plausibly called trying? And if there is such an action, why must she have formed an intention (or even a want) to perform it, in order to have moved her arm intentionally?" (1986a, p. 28).

The answer to Audi's first question, I suggest, is that Sally's *trying* to raise her arm is her *making an effort* to move her arm, however slight that effort may be. Sally's making an effort *to move her arm* is roughly a matter of her expending energy with that end in view, her moving her arm. (The "end" here, of course, need not be a terminal one; it may be sought by Sally as a means to something else.) Perhaps we typically reserve attributions of 'trying' for instances in which an agent makes a considerable effort; but, as others have observed, this is a matter of conversational implicature and does not mark a conceptual truth about trying.[25] The blindfolded, anesthetized man who reports that he has raised his arm as requested, quite properly responds to the information that his arm is strapped to his side by observing that in any case, he *tried* to move it—even though, encountering no felt resistance, he made no *special* effort to move it.

A plausible answer to Audi's second question runs, in outline, as follows. There is no need for Sally to have *formed* an intention (or a want); she may simply have acquired one. More important, in the absence of any pertinent intention or want, we are at a loss to identify what motivated Sally's intentional behavior; and that every case of intentional behavior involves some motivated behavior may well be a conceptual truth. Finally, nothing about this example suggests that Sally's merely *wanting* to move her arm (or, alternatively, her merely wanting to *try* to move it, or to comply with the doctor's request, or to try to do the latter, or something of the sort) is sufficient to initiate an attempt independently of a suitable intention.

CLAIM 2. Some readers will feel uneasy about claim 2 in my second approximation (see pp. 180–81). Is the claim any more informative than the seemingly empty assertion that cheese makes good mouse bait in virtue of its possessing mouse-attracting properties? Two observations are in order. First, I have tried to put some flesh on the skeleton that claim 2 expresses. Most important, acquisitions of proximal intentions *settle* for agents the question what they will do (or attempt); and on my intention-centered view, proximal intentions have a kind of access—direct access—to pertinent actional mechanisms that other psychological motivators do not have. (Recall that their having this access does not depend upon their incorporating preponderant motivational strength.) Second, while claim 2 does bear some similarity to dispositional claims like "Sugar dissolves in water because it is water-soluble," such claims are not wholly uninformative. As Davidson observes: "Explaining why something dissolved by reference to its solubility is not high science, but it isn't empty either, for solubility implies not only a generalization, but also the existence of a causal factor which accounts for the disposition: there is something about a soluble cube of sugar that causes it to dissolve under certain conditions" (1980, p. 274; cf. Lewis 1986, p. 221). Similarly, if I am right, there is something about proximal intentions in virtue of which their acquisition triggers actional mechanisms and their continued presence causally sustains the functioning of appropriate mechanisms. In ordinary human beings, this something is neurophysiologically grounded.

CLAIM 3. Given the proviso about motivation in claim 3, have I really separated myself from my opponents? My aim has been to preserve the thesis that intention performs an important function in the causation of overt intentional action while rejecting the untenable idea that we are always most motivated to do what we intend to do. However, some readers might doubt that the position advanced here is in fact separable from the latter idea. It might be objected that on my own view, one who proximally intends to *A* is preponderantly motivated to *begin* to *A* or to *try* to *A* and that my putative opponents are not claiming anything more than this. After all, the objection continues, no one in his right mind would hold that the presence of a proximal intention to *A,* even in conjunction with possession of the requisite abilities, is sufficient for one's intentionally *A*-ing. We have here a causally sufficient condition only for an *attempt* to *A;* and one who builds preponderant motivation into intention is (or should be) contending only that intention involves preponderant motivation to attempt the intended action. Or so the objection goes.

Several observations are in order. The first is that I have left open the possibility that someone who proximally intends to *A* lacks a motivational prerequisite even for beginning or trying to *A*. I do say, in the case of the ensnared arm, that a motivational condition that blocks an agent's *A*-ing may nevertheless permit his beginning to *A*. But this is quite compatible with its sometimes happening that an intender's motivational condition blocks even a beginning or an attempt. Perhaps, in some cases, motivation that competes with one's proximal intention preempts the default procedure for the triggering of actional mechanisms.

Though this undercuts the present objection, as formulated above, more remains to be said. Suppose, for the sake of argument, that the motivational element in proximal intentions is such that no acquisition of the state can be prevented by contrary motivation from resulting in the agent's beginning to act as he intends and that provisions for this point are made in my account of proximal intention. Does this commit me to joining the ranks of my opponents? No. There is a difference between an intentional beginning and an attempt, and attempts themselves may be either aborted or unaborted. According to the view that I wish to reject (view "*V*"), one who proximally intends to *A* has, at the time, preponderant motivation to make a complete or unaborted attempt to *A*. On my own view, even as modified to accommodate the aforementioned hypothetical fact, one may proximally intend *A* even while one is preponderantly motivated *not* to make an unaborted attempt. The agent who proximally intends to cut off his arm may concurrently be preponderantly motivated to stop short.

Furthermore, whereas proponents of *V* locate the basis of the fundamental motivating function of proximal intention in the (relative) *quantity* of motivation allegedly involved in intention, I have been suggesting that this motivating work rests instead on a *qualitative* point about proximal intention. A proximal intention is suited to its motivational work in virtue of its being a certain sort of executive state—a state partially characterized by the fact that intending to *A* (unlike wanting—even preponderantly—to *A*) entails being *settled* upon *A*-ing (or upon trying to *A*). Although a particular proximal intention and want might have the same representational content, they involve distinct *attitudes* toward that content.[26] In virtue of the attitudinal component of intention and the settledness that it involves, intentions can play a more direct role in the etiology of action. The attitudinal difference is a *qualitative* difference: it is not a matter of intentions having greater motivational strength than corresponding wants (see chs. 3.7 and 9.5). Rather, owing to the differences in the attitudinal qualities of intentions and desires, the states are fit for different functional roles in the etiology of intentional action.

I see no reason to reject a properly cautious version of the thesis that our intentional actions—including beginnings and complete and partial attempts—are the actions that we are most motivated to perform at the time. But again, this thesis (the MST) does not entail that only a quantitative conception of the motivational element in proximal intention is adequate to the fundamental motivating function of proximal intentions. Nor does it entail that we are always most motivated to do (or to make a complete attempt to do) what we intend (proximally or otherwise) to do. Nor does it follow from the MST that preponderant motivation, *rather than* proximal intending, plays the fundamental triggering-cum-sustaining role at issue. The MST is compatible with preponderant motivation's being a member of the supporting cast.

If, as I have been urging, proximal intentions do the fundamental, triggering-cum-sustaining work, this cannot be because proximally intending to *A* entails being preponderantly motivated to *A*. For there is no such entailment. One might suggest that in the cases in which agents *are* most motivated to do (or to make a complete attempt to do) what they proximally intend to do, the proximal intentions in some way incorporate the preponderant motivation and trigger and sustain appropriate operational actional mechanisms in virtue of this. However, if, as I have indicated, agents are not universally at the mercy of their preponderant motivation, then preponderant motivation alone is not sufficient to turn the trick. Someone who is preponderantly motivated to A straightaway might form the intention to refrain from A-ing; and this event might have the results that his preponderant motivation shifts in favor of not A-ing and that he intentionally refrains from A-ing. If this is right, the preponderant motivation allegedly incorporated into effective proximal intentions cannot be all there is to the motivational element in proximal intending. I have suggested that the psychological story involves an executive quality of proximal intentions and that this quality has a leading role.

Sometimes, as I have suggested, preponderant proximal motivation to A issues in a proximal intention to A. I have suggested, as well, that proximally intending to A (or to try to A) is a *default condition* of being preponderantly motivated to A straightaway: if one is in the latter condition and nothing preempts the immediate acquisition of a corresponding proximal intention, the intention is formed or acquired at once (ch. 9.5). If the connection between preponderant motivation and overt intentional action were ever direct, we could easily imagine cases in which an overt intentional action is performed in the absence of any pertinent intention. Postulation of such a direct link, then, is incompatible with acceptance of the IT.

In addition to issuing *from* preponderant motivation, intention acquisition can issue *in* such motivation. Indeed, being preponderantly motivated to A straightaway is plausibly regarded as a restricted default condition of the acquisition of a proximal intention to A: if one acquires a proximal intention to A and one is not *already* preponderantly motivated to A at once (the restrictive condition), one immediately becomes preponderantly so motivated, provided that nothing preempts this change. This is not to say, however, that in a case of this sort preponderant motivation somehow intervenes between proximal intention and intentional action. Rather, intention acquisition, in such a case, results in the presence of an enabling or background causal condition of the proximal intention's generating appropriate intentional action.

What place in the etiology of overt intentional action have I left for preponderant motivation? First, assuming the truth of the MST (preferably, a version compatible with the results of my investigation of motivational ties in ch. 3), being preponderantly motivated to A (or, more precisely, *not* being preponderantly motivated to perform a competing action) is an enabling condition of the effectiveness of proximal intentions to A. Second, the motivational strength of wants (broadly conceived) has an influence on what human agents intend. Third, an agent's preponderant motivation can "defeat" an intention of his—even a proximal intention—as in some incontinent actions.

Consider again, in connection with this last point, the case of the ensnared arm. Suppose that the man judges it best to cut off his arm at once with the machete and that he intends to do so and in fact begins to execute his intention but that because he is preponderantly motivated not to cut off his arm, he intentionally stops the downward motion of his arm in midstroke (however, without changing his mind about what it is best to do). Does his preponderant motivation usurp the role of proximal intention in generating his intentional halting of the amputation? Not at all. The case is so constituted that if he *intentionally* stopped short, we would have every reason to believe that he intended to do so. This does not commit us to supposing that the agent simultaneously intended to cut off his arm and intended to refrain from doing so. Indeed, radical partitioning aside, I doubt that it is possible for an agent simultaneously to have intentions that are opposed in this way. Rather, what happens is that his proximal intention to cut off his arm is replaced by a proximal intention to halt the activity. This latter intention is a product of his motivational condition, and it arises independently of any all-things-considered value judgment.

The moral is that wants (broadly construed to include fears and the like) can give rise to intentions independently of intervening all-things-considered value judgments. The lesson is *not* that preponderant motivation can initiate intentional actions directly, independently of proximal intentions. A "strong" MST entails that the acquisition of a proximal intention to A at t will result in one's intentionally A-ing at t only if one is simultaneously preponderantly motivated to A at t. But even a strong MST neither makes preponderant motivation an unmediated cause of intentional action nor requires that preponderant motivation somehow be built into proximal intentions.

Occasionally, for stylistic reasons, I have written as though proximal intentions themselves trigger actional mechanisms. Strictly speaking, it is the *acquisition* of a proximal intention—that event—that does the triggering. Of course, *what* is acquired—*a proximal intention to A*—is crucial to the triggering, on the view advanced. Owing in part to the content of the intention, the event triggers, in normal cases of intentional action, actional mechanisms appropriate to an A-ing. And if the state acquired were not to incorporate the executive attitude toward its representational content that is partially constitutive of proximal intentions, the agent's acquisition of the state would not, other things being equal, trigger actional mechanisms at all.

4. The Final Account

Bob intends to run from *A* to *C*, a distance of ten miles, and he has the following plan: "Either I will stop to rest at *B*, the half-way point, or, if I am still feeling strong when I reach *B*, I will run straight through to *C*." As it happens, when Bob reaches *B*, he decides to run to *C* without stopping and he succeeds. Now, in so deciding, Bob forms an intention to continue running; and that intention presumably figures in an explanation of his continuing to run. But does his acquisition of this new intention *trigger* actional mechanisms involved in his continued running? I see no reason to suppose that it must. Rather, Bob's intention may simply sustain the functioning of actional mechanisms that are already in operation.[27] If this is what happens, claims 1 and 3 of the second approximation (pp. 180–81) are in need of revision.

Fortunately, the required modifications are easily made. Claim 1 becomes

1'. In all cases of overt intentional action, the acquisition of a proximal intention triggers appropriate actional mechanisms—unless
they are already operating—and the intention causally sustains
their functioning.

Claim 3 may be modified accordingly. Notice that on the revised ac-
count, it is the sustaining role of proximal intentions that is performed in all cases of overt intentional action. However, there is often nothing for a proximal intention to sustain unless its acquisition first *triggers* pertinent actional mechanisms.

A second modification is also required. When proximal intentions issue in overt intentional action, how long does the sustaining of actional mechanisms continue? An attractive (if overly simplified) answer is that it continues through the completion of the bodily movement(s) involved in executing the intention.[28] The extent of these movements depends upon the content of the proximal intention, and there are restrictions on the latter. The student who realizes that he cannot read the entire *Meno* at once will not (other things being equal) have a *proximal* intention to read the entire dialogue. To be sure, even actions performed straightaway take some time; but they take less time than ordinary, knowledge-
able readers set aside for reading the *Meno*.

It is plausible that the movements and other actional processes involved in some hypothetical instance of my reading the *Meno* at one sitting are sustained by a single intention. If this sustaining intention is not a *proxi-*

mal intention, what role do proximal intentions have here? The supposed sustaining intention may, of course, help to produce pertinent proximal intentions—for example, a proximal intention to turn a page. But my reading the *Meno* need not *begin* with a proximal intention that is distinct from the sustaining intention. I may have an intention to read the *Meno* at one sitting, *beginning now,* and not have a distinct intention to begin reading the *Meno* now. If this is right, intentions cannot be neatly and exhaustively sorted into proximal and distal. Rather, some intentions will have both proximal and distal *aspects.* We may refer to them as *temporally mixed* intentions. A temporally mixed intention is an intention whose plan component identifies both behavior to be engaged in now and behavior to be engaged in later. When one *executes* such an intention, the proximal aspect (typically) figures in the triggering of pertinent actional mechanisms, and the distal aspect sustains whatever portion of the actional process falls outside the scope of the proximal aspect. For example, the proximal aspect of my intention to read the *Meno* at one sitting, beginning now, may figure in the triggering and sustaining of the actional mechanisms involved in my beginning to read the dialogue, while the distal aspect sustains my continued reading.

Here again, the required modifications of the earlier account are not difficult to state. The proximal aspect of a temporally mixed intention includes a propensity of the agent to execute the proximal aspect or portion of the plan component of the mixed intention—for example, a propensity to begin reading the *Meno* at once or to continue running.

Are proximal intentions, as I have characterized them, *volitions?* This question is less straightforward than it may seem, since 'volition' is a technical term and there are many competing accounts of volition in the literature. One point, however, is clear. Proximal intentions, on my account, are not actions; consequently, they are not volitions if, as some have insisted (e.g., McCann 1986a; Ginet 1990), volition is a species of action. If what I have been calling proximal intentions are properly counted as volitions in some well-defined nonactional sense of the term, so be it.

Must proximal intentions be *supplemented* by volitions, construed as actions, in order to issue in overt intentional action? Hugh McCann recently suggested that the agent of an overt intentional action must be "continuously engaged in the activity of producing" bodily changes required by the action. Were a golfer "to cease this activity in the middle of his swing, the swing would cease as well" (1986a, p. 262). The "activity of producing" bodily movements to which McCann refers is, for him, volitional: "Volition *is* action. It is precisely by engaging in the activity of willing that we bring about the bodily and other changes overt action requires" (p. 262; cf. Ginet 1990, ch. 2).

In giving proximal intention a sustaining function in the generation of intentional action, I side with McCann in rejecting ballistic conceptions of the production of intentional action. On my view, as on McCann's, the golfer who, in midswing, loses his proximal intention to swing will not complete the swing (other things being equal). However, I see no need to suppose that an agent must be continuously engaged in the activity of willing bodily movements in order to execute the pertinent proximal intention. McCann is right to reject views that limit the moving role of intentions to triggering. But he offers no compelling reason to think that the story must be supplemented by importing volition, construed as action, rather than by *extending* the moving role of proximal intentions as I have done.

My primary goal in this chapter has been to preserve a very attractive thesis about the role of intention in the etiology of intentional action—a thesis that may seem to lose its intuitive plausibility when a popular assumption about the connection between intention and preponderant motivation is rejected. The thesis is that intention has an important motivational part to play in all cases of overt intentional action. Though we can perhaps get over the oddness of assertions like 'S intentionally A-ed but he did not intend to A', the idea that someone may intentionally A without intending to do anything at all seems more intractably paradoxical. Furthermore, we are disinclined to view the role of intention in the etiology of intentional action as purely representational. Intentions, as commonly conceived, have a motivational function. Intentions are capable of *moving* us to act. On the intention-centered view articulated in this chapter, proximal intentions play a crucial motivational role in overt intentional action. And their playing the role identified here does not depend upon the mistaken idea that we are always most motivated to do (or to attempt to do) what we intend to do.

Notes

1. Brand raises this question in a seminal article (1979) and again in a ground-breaking book (1984, pp. 45–46). But he does not answer it. Although he develops a detailed model for the transmission of motivation from scripts to motor schemata and sketches an account of the source of motivation (1984, ch. 9), he does not identify the feature(s) of "immediate" intentions (roughly, what I have termed *proximal* intentions) in virtue of which they move us to act.

2. Let us say, again, that *S*'s intentionally *A*-ing at *t competes* with *S*'s intentionally *B*-ing at *t* if and only if either he believes that he cannot do both *A* and *B* or his doing either would make his doing the other sufficiently unattractive that he would not intentionally do, or try to do, each.

3. For other analyses of intention that involve essential reference to preponderant motivation, see Audi 1973, 1986a; W. Davis 1984, p. 50; and Tuomela 1977, pp. 132–33.

4. On self-control, see Mele 1987a, chs. 4 and 5; Mele 1990e.

5. Cf. Bratman 1984; Bratman 1987, ch. 8; Harman 1986a, p. 89. For an instructive rebuttal, see O'Shaughnessy 1980, vol. 2, pp. 328–29. See my discussion of double effect in ch. 6.6.

6. See Bratman 1984, pp. 378, 394–405; Bratman 1987, pp. 119–22. Arguments for the stronger thesis are offered by Adams (1986) and McCann (1986b).

7. Cf. Davidson 1985a, p. 231; Harman 1976, p. 441.

8. For stylistic reasons, I will generally omit the qualifier 'thinly' in what follows.

9. In a very broad sense of 'want', as I noted in chapter 9.5, intention may be treated as a species of want. Obviously, wants that constitute the second-order propensities identified here are what I earlier termed *mere* wants, wants that are not themselves intentions and are not encompassed by intentions. In the broader sense, some "wants" have a more direct bearing on intentional action—but they do so precisely in virtue of being intentions or being encompassed by intentions, on the view being advanced. (Recall that accepting the legitimacy of the broad sense of 'want' at issue is entirely compatible with rejecting familiar belief/desire reductionism about intention. See ch. 9.5.)

10. I suggest in section 3 that proximal intentions, in addition to triggering actional mechanisms, causally sustain their functioning. Notice that Wilma's proximal intention to save the child gets her moving and sustains the moving. At some point, she may acquire the proximal intention to dive, which intention triggers and sustains the actional mechanisms involved in her diving. But her intention to save the child continues to sustain her intentional behavior. Other things being equal, if she ceased to have that intention, she would not dive to save the child; she would halt her attempt to save him.

11. I am not suggesting that there is some unique physical state–type in which all proximal intentions are realized in ordinary human beings.

12. O'Shaughnessy commits himself to the view that no motivational condition of an agent can render a proximal intention incapable of triggering appropriate actional mechanisms that are in proper working order (1980, vol. 2, pp. 336–38). About fear in particular, he maintains that it can prevent one from attempting to execute an intention only by destroying the intention (p. 337). I am unconvinced.

13. Cf. Alston 1986, p. 284. The motivational work of proximal intentions need not always be *limited* to triggering and sustaining. For example, I have suggested elsewhere (Mele 1987a, ch. 2.2) that when an agent fears that he will

succumb to temptation, a proximal intention to A might help to motivate an act of resistance in support of his A-ing.

14. Again, I am assuming *not* that each intentional action is intended but only that in any case of intentional action something relevant is intended. For example, if Harman's sniper intentionally alerts the enemy without intending to do so, it is true, at least, that he intended to fire his gun.

15. Searle 1983, ch. 3; Searle 1979; see also Malcolm 1968, pp. 61–62.

16. I follow Searle in focusing on behavior that involves bodily movement. Searle defends a parallel account of other sorts of action (1983, pp. 102–3).

17. Divorced from its context, the sentence of Searle's just quoted is compatible with the truth of claim 1. But as will become evident shortly, the view that he intends it to express is, in part, that in some *cases* of intentional action there is no prior intention.

18. Compare this with Brand's contention that "immediate intention," which he identifies as the proximate cause of action, "continues as long as the guidance and monitoring continues" (1984, p. 175).

19. Searle has little to say about trying; but see Searle 1983, pp. 88–90.

20. This is an approximation. It must be qualified to circumvent problems posed by causal waywardness. See ch. 11.1.

21. Fans of simultaneous causation would formulate the question differently.

22. McCann, like Searle, wants to "bring intention into the actual sequence of events that is constitutive of action" (1986a, p. 260).

23. For more extensive exposition and criticism of Searle's view, see Adams and Mele 1989.

24. Some readers might be inclined to regard the woman's moving her arm as unintentional. Ginet says of a structurally similar case that the agent "unintentionally exerts her arm" (1990, p. 9).

25. See Armstrong 1980, p. 71; McCann 1975, pp. 425–27; and McGinn 1982, pp. 86–87.

26. Donagan (1987), Harman (1986a, 1976), and Searle (1983) have argued that intentions, unlike most wants, are self-referring—that the content of an intention makes reference to the intention itself. For criticism of their arguments and for arguments to the contrary, see ch. 11.

27. This is compatible with Bob's intention's being a cause of his continuing to run. (The case is such, we may suppose, that if Bob had not decided to continue running, he would not have done so.) Bob's intention may be a cause of his continued running without *triggering* actional mechanisms.

28. A more refined answer would accommodate *ballistic* movements. When a person kicks a ball, for example, the leg is "flung" by the quadriceps muscle, which ceases its activity before the leg stops moving and before the foot comes into contact with the ball (Sheridan 1984, p. 54). Once the leg is flung, its movement in the kicking is no longer guided. For present purposes, this need not concern us.

11

Intention's Content

What is it, precisely, that an agent intends when he intends, as we might say, to clean his stove today? What is the *content* of his intention? According to some, all intentions are self-referential—that is, an adequate expression of the content of any intention makes essential reference to the intention whose content is being expressed. I shall call this the *self-referentiality thesis* (SRT). A leading proponent of the thesis, Gilbert Harman, provides a succinct formulation: "The intention to do *A* is the intention that, because of that very intention, one will do *A*" (1976, p. 441; cf. 1986a, ch. 8).[1] John Searle contends, similarly, that the "Intentional content" of an agent's "prior intention" to *A* identifies that very intention as a cause of the agent's (prospective) *A*-ing (1983, pp. 85–87, 92–95).[2] Alan Donagan accepts the SRT at least for the "determinate intentions" or "choices" that causally explain action (1987, chs. 5, 7, 9).[3]

Originally, I had planned to say little about the SRT in my investigation of the representational dimension of intention here and to refer the reader instead to my earlier criticism (Mele 1987b). But the SRT has a seductive appeal—and some very influential proponents. Furthermore, the position on the contents of intentions defended in the last few sections of this chapter can be motivated in part by criticism of the SRT. I deemed it best, consequently, to display both the deficiencies in the major arguments advanced for the view and the central problems with the thesis. An additional benefit of so doing is that some important points made by way of rebutting the SRT serve as well (as I shall explain in chapter 13) to disarm recent objections to intentionalistic, causal theories of action-explanation.

1. Deviant Causal Chains: An Unsuccessful Argument for the Self-Referentiality Thesis

According to standard causal analyses of intentional action, an action's being intentional is a function of its causation by psychological items: for example, want/belief pairs, intentions, or volitions. Such analyses must come to grips with the problem of deviant causal chains. The problem (or so it has seemed to some) is that whatever psychological causes are deemed both necessary and sufficient for a resultant action's being intentional, cases can be described in which, due to a deviant causal connection between the favored psychological antecedents and a pertinent action to which they lead, that action is not intentional.[4]

Myles Brand helpfully divides the examples of deviance that abound in the literature into two types, depending upon what portion of the causal chain is singled out for attention (1984, p. 18; cf. Davidson 1980, p. 79).[5] Some cases focus on behavioral consequences of actions that are more directly generated by antecedent mental events and on the connection between these actions and their consequences. These examples pose what Brand terms the problem of *consequential waywardness*. Other cases raise a problem about a more direct connection between mental antecedents and resultant behavior—the problem of *antecedential waywardness*. The following are representative instances of consequential and antecedential waywardness, respectively:

> A man may try to kill someone by shooting at him. Suppose the killer misses his victim by a mile, but the shot stampedes a herd of wild pigs that trample the intended victim to death. (Davidson 1980, p. 78)

> A chemist who is working with cyanide near his colleague's cup of tea may desire to kill his colleague and believe that he can do this by dropping some cyanide into the tea. . . . This desire and belief may so upset him that his hands shake, with the result that he drops some of the poisonous substance into the tea. (Mele 1983, p. 346)

Harman (1976; 1986a, p. 86) presents several examples in which behavior proceeds from a deviant causal chain. These cases, he contends, "confirm the claim that a positive intention to do something is the intention that that very intention will lead in a more or less explicitly specified way to one's doing the thing in question" (1976, p. 445). In each of his examples, Harman argues, the agent does not, in *A*-ing, "do what she intends" and therefore does not intentionally *A*. In each case, he attempts to account for the agent's failing, in *A*-ing, to do what she intends by hypothesizing that the pertinent intention is self-referential. In the present section, I argue that in none of these examples does the unintentional status of the agent's *A*-ing depend upon her having a pertinent self-referring intention.

Consider the following case, an instance of consequential waywardness. Mabel intends to drive to Ted's house, pick him up there, drop him off in her driveway, and then back her car over him. As she sets out for Ted's house, Mabel inadvertently backs over Ted: unbeknownst to her, he was lying in her driveway. Now, Mabel intended to back over Ted in her driveway; and she did so. Nevertheless, she did not *intentionally* back over Ted. Harman accounts for this point by arguing that Mabel's intention "includes a plan specifying how that intention will lead her to do what she intends to do. She does not in the example do what she intends, because what she does differs significantly from the plan that is part of her intention" (1976, p. 444).

Notice that one can agree with the second sentence in the passage just quoted without accepting the first sentence. If the plan component of Mabel's intention includes her running over Ted only *after* she drops him off in her driveway, then she does not do what she intends even if her plan makes no reference to her intention and hence does not specify how that *intention* will result in what is intended. What renders Mabel's backing over Ted unintentional may be a function of the plan component of a pertinent *non*-self-referential intention. There is no evident need to suppose that Mabel's intention incorporates a plan of hers about how that intention will result in her performing the intended actions.

Harman's remaining examples also fail to establish that intentions are self-referential. Consider the following case, one most naturally construed as an instance of antecedential waywardness. Betty, intending to kill someone (a prowler, say), aims her gun at him. Her "intention makes her nervous and nervousness causes her to pull the trigger" (Harman 1976, p. 445). If what her nervousness causes is an involuntary finger contraction that releases the hammer, one may easily account for the falsity of the assertion that she intentionally pulls the trigger without having to suppose that she has a pertinent self-referring intention. The assertion is false for the simple reason that Betty does not pull the trigger; rather, due to her nervousness, her finger contracts, with the result that the trigger moves in such a way as to release the hammer. But perhaps Betty really does *pull* the trigger, and perhaps her nervousness is a cause of her doing so. Perhaps, if Betty were not nervous, she would abandon her intention and would not pull the trigger. However, if this is the basis of the claim that "nervousness causes her to pull the trigger," why should we say that the trigger pulling (or the shooting, or the killing) is not intentional? Betty's nervousness might cause her pulling the trigger (shooting the prowler, etc.) by causing her retention of the intention to do so; and the intention may function quite normally in the etiology of her subsequent behavior.

Here is another case:

Betty intends to kill someone. She aims her gun and, at the crucial moment, a noise startles her, leading her to contract her finger so that she
shoots and kills him—but not intentionally. (Harman 1976, p. 445)

Betty does not intentionally kill the victim, Harman explains, "for her
intention to kill him is the intention that that very intention will lead her
to pull the trigger at the crucial moment; and that does not happen."
Again, there are alternative explanations. If Betty does not pull the
trigger but instead suffers an involuntary finger contraction consequent
upon her being startled, one such explanation is that Betty's behavior
does not fit the plan component of a pertinent *non-self-referring* intention of hers: Betty's plan, one may suppose, involves her *pulling the
trigger;* but she does not do that.

The suggestion that in this last case there is some *action* of trigger
pulling is highly implausible, to say the least. The upshot of Betty's
being startled, presumably, is not that she *moves* her finger, but rather
that her finger moves reflexively—and quite independently of her intention to kill the prowler (see Thalberg 1984, p. 152). This is not to deny
that one might move one's finger as a partial result of being startled. For
example, if Betty is startled by a noise behind her, she might immediately execute her intention to shoot the prowler in order that she may
safely turn to investigate the source of the noise—perhaps another
prowler. But then the trigger pulling, the shooting, and so on, are intentional. And this is not the sort of case that Harman envisages.

Let us suppose, however, for the sake of argument, that Betty does
pull the trigger in Harman's example—unintentionally and due to her
being startled. Must we then suppose, as well, that she has some pertinent self-referential intention in order to explain why her shooting the
prowler and her killing the prowler are not intentional actions? Suppose
that rather than having a self-referring intention incorporating a plan
specifying how that intention will lead to the intended behavior, Betty
has an intention that includes the following plan: "I will now both aim
this gun at this man's heart and pull the trigger with this finger, with the
result that the bullet in the chamber will pierce his heart and kill him."
Suppose further that the killing transpires as it is represented in the
plan. Does it follow from this that Betty *intentionally* kills the prowler?

Not at all. There is, again, an important difference between an agent's
following a plan and his behavior's *fitting* a plan (see ch. 8.2). It is
analogous to a familiar distinction between following a rule and acting in
accordance with a rule.[6] Someone who just happens to stop walking
when he comes to a corner at which the traffic signal is red acts in

accordance with a traffic rule, but he does not *follow* the rule. As I noted earlier, one follows a rule only if one's behavior is in some way *guided by* that rule. Similarly, in *A*-ing, one follows one's plan for *A*-ing only if one's *A*-ing is guided by that plan. This is not the place for a detailed account of plan following and of the guidance that this involves. It is sufficient for immediate purposes to notice one natural requirement: a bodily movement is guided by the plan component of the agent's pertinent intention only if that intention is a cause of the movement. Now, the bodily movement involved in Betty's supposed action of pulling the trigger is her contracting a certain finger. But (ex hypothesi) her contracting her finger is a result not of her intention to kill the prowler but, rather, of her being startled. Thus, Betty's contracting her finger and, consequently, her pulling the trigger are not guided by her plan for killing the prowler. And for all that Harman has said about deviantly caused action, the basis of the explanation of the nonintentionality of Betty's killing the prowler (and her shooting him, and her pulling the trigger) might lie here. It is arguably the case that the supposed actions at issue are not intentional because, in performing them, Betty is not guided by her plan—a plan that, ex hypothesi, does not refer to any intention of hers. There is no evident need to suppose that her pertinent intention includes an *intention-referring* plan.

Let us modify the last case slightly. Suppose, again, that Betty does contract her finger and that she does so unintentionally, because she is startled. But suppose, additionally, that her intention to kill the prowler *is* a partial cause of her contracting her finger. Imagine that if Betty had not already been agitated by her intention to kill the prowler, the noise would not have startled her or that its startling her would not have resulted in her contracting her finger. Must we then hold that Betty has a self-referential intention in order to explain why the killing, the shooting, and so on, are unintentional?

Again the answer is *no*. Plainly, what renders the supposed actions unintentional is the deviant causal connection between intention and behavior. But the deviance of this connection need not be explicated relative to some putatively self-referring intention of the agent. Instead, following a lead in some recent literature on deviant causal chains, one may maintain that a necessary condition of an overt action's being intentional is that (the acquisition of) a pertinent intention *"proximately* cause the physiological chain" that begins concurrently with, and partially constitutes, the action.[7] (Since the causal route from intention acquisition to overt bodily movement in beings like us involves a causal chain initiated in the brain, the suggestion that the acquisition of a proximal intention must proximately initiate the action requires that the action begin in the brain, too.)[8] In the present case, Betty's intention (or her acquiring it) does not proximately cause the pertinent physiological chain. Rather, it causes this chain via her agitation and her being startled. To allow that the acquisition of a proximal intention is not itself causally sufficient even for the initial stage of an action, the necessary condition at issue may be put as follows: an overt action is intentional only if a pertinent intention (or the agent's acquiring it) proximately causally initiates the action, either alone or in conjunction with other partial causes.

Consider, finally, a case of a kind not adduced by Harman. Wilma is climbing a mountain when she notices her former lover, Will, hanging from a branch over a chasm. Unfortunately for Will, Wilma spies a saw in the grass and forms the intention to kill Will by sawing deeply enough into the branch from which he is dangling that the bough will break off. While sawing, Wilma observes that if she cuts a little deeper she will send Will to his death. That thought so unnerves her that she loses control over her sawing arm. Further, her nervousness causes the arm to jerk back and forth twice, with the result that the saw cuts sufficiently deep that the bough breaks, sending Will to his death.

Although Wilma intentionally sawed for a time, she did not, it seems, intentionally break the branch (or intentionally cut into it deeply enough to break it). Here, the deviance owing to which she does not intentionally cause the bough to break occurs after she has embarked on that project. Her sawing, we may suppose, was initiated in a way appropriate for an intentional bough breaking, so must we account for her having unintentionally caused the branch to break by supposing that her intention to break the branch was self-referring? If, to use a formulation of Harman's, Wilma intended that her intention would result in her breaking the branch "in a more or less explicitly specified way" (1976, p. 445), then we might contend that since her intention did not issue in her causing the branch to break in a manner close enough to the way specified in her intention, she did not intentionally break the branch. But to obtain this result, we need not view the intention as self-referring. Again, appeal to the plan component of a non-self-referring intention will do. The "way" specified in that plan might not be closely enough approximated by what happens. (Wilma's plan includes her sawing deeply enough into the branch that it would break off; but when her arm starts jerking uncontrollably, it is no longer the case that she is sawing.)[9] Further, once Wilma loses control over her arm, the motions of that arm are no longer being guided by her intention—even if the intention is not abandoned. Indeed, the presence of the intention might even contribute to the generation and sustaining of the nervousness that issues in the fatal jerking motions of the arm.

For Harman, when an agent executes her intention to *A*, she follows a plan that is *part* of the intention and *refers* to the intention. Thus far, I have shown not that Harman is wrong about this but only that his examples of deviant causal chains do not establish the point about reference. In the next three sections, I shall argue that the self-referentiality thesis is problematic and that the other major arguments for it, including additional arguments of Harman's, are unsuccessful.

2. Execution, Content, and Self-Referentiality

Executing an intention entails success. To execute a law is to put that law into effect. To execute a deed is to legalize that deed. To execute a will is to perform or carry out what the will requires. In none of these cases is mere trying sufficient for execution. 'Execute,' in these contexts, is a success term. This is true as well of the execution of an intention. One executes one's intention to *A* only if one *A*-s.

What else is required for the truth of '*S* executed his intention to *A*'? According to what I shall call the *content/satisfaction view* (CSV), the conditions required for the truth of this sentence, whatever they may be, are identified by a proper expression of the content of *S*'s intention to *A*. John Searle (1983) advances the CSV. He maintains that in the case of belief, desire, and intention, "the *specification* of the content is already a *specification* of the conditions of satisfaction" (p. 13). The "satisfaction" of an intention consists in its being carried out or executed (p. 11). Thus, a proper expression of the content of an intention specifies the conditions under which it is true that that intention is executed. In the present section, I comment briefly on the relationship of the CSV to the SRT, identify some problems with these theses, and sketch an account of intention satisfaction that avoids these problems.

Suppose that I intend, as we might say, *to raise my left arm*. Searle claims that "the Intentional content of my intention must be at least (that I perform the action of raising my [left] arm by way of carrying out [i.e., executing] *this intention*)" (1983, p. 85). If, as Searle maintains, a proper specification of the content of an intention is a specification of the conditions of satisfaction of that intention (i.e., if the CSV is true), his claim about the content of my intention is correct, or at least very close to correct. For I "satisfy" my intention (in his sense) only if I execute it; and my raising my arm is not sufficient for my having executed the intention of mine at issue—*that intention* must also figure appropriately in the explanation of my raising my arm. (Suppose that I forget my intention *N* to raise my left arm at *t,* and that at *t,* I raise my left arm by way of executing another intention.) A proper expression of the conditions of satisfaction (execution) of an intention makes essential reference to that intention; and, on the CSV, this expression is also an expression or specification of the content of the intention. Thus, the CSV has the result that a proper expression of the content of any intention makes essential reference to the intention whose content is being expressed—that is, the CSV entails the *SRT.*

If the *CSV* (or *SRT*) is true, it would seem that we are speaking very loosely indeed when we say, for example, that Barney intends to bathe the baby; for on either view, Barney intends at least this much, that he perform the action of bathing the baby by way of carrying out a certain intention. This is problematic. Agents capable of intentional action are beings with cognitive and representational capacities and limitations. They can intend only what their cognitive and representational capacities permit them to intend. And it is doubtful that very young children, dogs, and many other beings capable of intentional action—and, hence, of having intentions[10]—have the cognitive capacity to intend that an intention of theirs be executed. When Barney's eight-month-old daughter intentionally crawls toward him upon seeing him enter the room, does she intend to crawl toward him by way of carrying out her pertinent intention? Or does she intend simply to crawl toward him or to get to him or something of the sort?

Harman anticipates this objection in a note, remarking that "it is not clear what the test is for saying that [a] child has a concept of intention" (1976, p. 441). Be this as it may, it *is* clear that some sentient beings do have a concept of intention and that others do not. Eight-month-old children seem clearly to fall into the latter group. Now, very young children can have desires and beliefs without possessing concepts of desire and belief.[11] This is true in the case of intentions as well—*unless* intentions are self-referring. On the SRT, as propounded by Harman and Searle, *S* intends to *A* only if *S* intends that his *intention* have a certain result. This requires of all intenders not only that they have a concept of intention but that they have a conceptual grip, as well, on causation and on an intention's resulting in what is intended. The requirement is psychologically unrealistic. Some beings whose behavior is such that we confidently attribute intentions to them are very probably incapable of intending if the SRT is true.[12]

In an effort to meet this objection, one might appeal to a functionalist criterion of content identity. It might be urged that the causal connection between intentions and intentional actions can only—or best—be accounted for on the hypothesis that intentions are self-referring. Consequently, it might be claimed, we can infer that the effective intentions of very young children are self-referring; and since their having self-referring intentions requires that they have a concept of intention, very young children are possessed of a concept of intention. Their having this concept is a matter of their harboring mental states filling a certain functional role.

The success of this reply depends partly, of course, on the merits of the hypothesis that intentions are self-referential. We have seen that the portion of the case for the SRT thus far examined is seriously flawed. The other major arguments for the thesis are refuted in the remainder of this chapter. Whether the suggested criterion of content is adequate is an issue that need not be addressed here.

Now, one can attempt to construct a version of the SRT that does not entail that all intenders have a concept of intention.[13] *S* may believe *of* the aardvark in front of him that it is an animal and yet not believe *that* the aardvark in front of him is an animal, if *S* has no concept of aardvark. Similarly, it might be suggested, an agent can intend (*de re*) *of* his intention to *A* that it result (in a certain way) in his *A*-ing and yet not intend (*de dicto*) *that* his intention to *A* result in his *A*-ing, if he has no concept of intention. On what I shall call the *modest* SRT, all intenders-to-*A* have at least a *de re* intention of the sort just described. And they all intend *that* something (something that others properly term an *intention*) result in their *A*-ing, though they might not identify or represent the pertinent "something" as an intention. (It should be noted that if, as is commonly held, *de re* attitudes are caused in part by what they are attitudes *about*, the modest SRT has the unacceptable result that intentions are partial causes of themselves.)

Does Barney's daughter intend of her intention to get to him that it result in her getting to him? I am confident that she has some mental representation of Barney and of a suitable way of getting to him. And I believe that these representational items figure in an explanation of the bit of intentional behavior in question. But if the modest SRT is true, she must also have a representation of the state or event that is her intention (or, alternatively, of one that *encompasses* her intention) and of its resulting in her getting to him. (Of course, she need not represent the intention *as* an intention.)

There is no easy way to decide whether, in the case in question, the

baby's representational condition involves all of the elements just identified. I suspect that it does not. But in any case, we have not as yet
encountered a convincing reason for endorsing the empirical thesis
about intending entailed by the modest SRT, namely, that all intenders-
to-*A* have a mental representation of the state or event that is their
intention (or of one that encompasses their intention) and of its resulting
in their *A*-ing. And if the empirical thesis is not manifestly false, it is at
least sufficiently uncertain that the safest course is to leave the matter
open. In short, the very fact that the SRT, even in its modest form,
commits us to a stand on the matter is a strike against it—provided that
there is a reasonable alternative that does not force us to come down on
one side or the other of the empirical question.

There is a related difficulty for the SRT. Why is it that we describe our
own and others' intentions in the way we do, if all intentions are self-
referential? When I intend, as I would say, to raise my left arm, do I
realize that I am really intending (in part) to raise my left arm by way of
executing this intention and then simply speak elliptically when asked
what I intend? Here, I think, what we ordinarily say carries some
weight. If a theory of the contents of intentions entails that the common
way of describing intentions is importantly incomplete, there had better
be good reasons for adopting the theory.[14] Searle's acceptance of the
SRT rests upon his endorsement of the CSV. But why *should* we suppose
that a specification of the content of an intention is a specification of the
conditions of satisfaction (execution) of the intention? Searle does not
say.

The point (if it is correct) that the conditions of satisfaction of beliefs
and desires are specified by a specification of the content of these attitudes certainly is not enough to show that this is true of intentions as
well. Perhaps, in the case of intention, the conditions of satisfaction are
only partially fixed by the content of the intention. Perhaps finding an
adequate specification of the conditions of satisfaction of an intention
requires that we also look elsewhere.

The discussion of wayward causal chains in section 1 suggests a rough-
and-ready account of intention satisfaction that does not rely on the
SRT. It is this:

> *RR.* (1) *S* satisfies an intention *N* of *S*'s if and only if *S* executes *N;*
> (2) *S* executes an intention *N* of *S*'s if and only if *S* follows the plan
> component of *N;* and (3) *S* follows the plan component of an inten-
> tion *N* of *S*'s if and only if *S* acts in accordance with the plan and, in
> doing so, is guided by the plan.

Whatever imperfections *RR* may have, it captures, among other things, Searle's correct observation that an intention is executed only if it plays "a causal role in action" (1983, p. 86).[15] (Again, the notion of guidance in *RR*3 is a causal notion.) The important point is that *RR* does this without presupposing that "causal self-referentiality" is a universal feature of intentions. Whether an agent's intention to *A* is self-referring or not, he executes that intention only if the intention plays an appropriate role in the etiology of his *A*-ing. Of course, any attempt to specify the appropriate causal role must come to grips with the problem of wayward causal chains.[16] But in section 1 we saw that representative cases of causal deviance can be handled without our having to fall back on the psychologically unrealistic (or at least unsubstantiated) idea that all intentions are self-referring.

It will prove instructive to notice that even setting aside the possibility of intentional actions that are not intended (Bratman 1984, 1987; Harman 1976, 1986a), the conceptual connection between executing one's intention to *A* and *A*-ing intentionally is not as tight as one might naturally think. Searle assumes that a necessary condition of an agent's having carried out or executed his intention to *A* is that he *intentionally A*-ed (1983, pp. 82–83). However, there are cases that seem to me to falsify this assumption.

The following example, which I have presented elsewhere for another purpose, is a case in point:

> Fred is taking a machine-readable multiple choice test. His strategy is to circle on the question sheet the identifying letters next to the answers that he feels certain are correct and then, after all such circling is completed, to fill in the corresponding spaces on his answer sheet. At this point, he will take up the more difficult questions.
>
> An hour has elapsed, and Fred is reading the forty-fifth question. He is confident that the answer is 'bee', which word appears next to the letter '*a*' on his question sheet. However, as a result of an understandable momentary confusion, he circles the letter '*b*'. As luck would have it, '*b*' is the correct answer. Later, when filling in the answer sheet, Fred looks at the circled '*b*' under question 45 and fills in the space under '*b*' on his answer sheet—intending thereby to provide the right answer. (Mele 1987c, p. 56)

Though Fred provides the correct answer to question 45 by filling in the space under 'b' on the answer sheet, we are strongly disinclined to count his providing the correct answer as intentional. It is just too accidental. Nevertheless, on a plausible construal of the intention with which Fred filled in the space under 'b' on the answer sheet, I can think of no compelling reason to deny that he *executed* that intention. Suppose that Fred's intention with respect to the final answering of question 45 is simply this: that he will provide the correct answer by filling in the space under 'b' on the answer sheet (or, so as not to beg any questions against the SRT, some self-referential analogue of this). It seems quite natural to say that Fed did execute or carry out this intention. After all, he did what he intended; in doing so, he followed the plan component of his intention; and there is no deviant connection between his intention and his filling in the space under 'b' or between that action and his providing the correct answer.

Now, one can *reconstruct* the example in such a way that Fred's intention regarding the answering of question 45 is more complex or detailed than the one that I attributed to him, with the result that he does not execute his intention. Suppose, for example, that Fred intends to translate into the correct response on the answer sheet his circling of the letter that *in fact identifies* his favored prose answer to question 45 and to do this by filling in the space under 'b' on the answer sheet. He clearly does not execute this intention. However, there is no need to suppose that the intention just mentioned or any other unexecuted intention is Fred's actual intention at the time at which he provides the correct answer by marking in the space. It is surely *possible* that Fred has only the simple intention (be it self-referential or otherwise) that I attributed to him. Since this *is* possible, I shall suppose that this is precisely Fred's intention.

It should also be observed that the case of Fred is not the sort of example that brings us to "the limits of our ordinary concept of intentional action" (Brand 1984, p. 30) and therefore generates conflicting intuitions. Our intuitions about this case are quite clear. Fred's providing the correct answer is a nonintentional action.

If the preceding remarks about intention execution are correct, *RR* is in need of revision. But the required modification does not commit us to self-referentiality. *RR* may be reformulated neutrally as follows:

RR′. *S* satisfies an intention *N* of *S*'s to *A* if and only if *S* executes *N* and, in so doing, intentionally *A*-s. (Intention execution is here understood as in *RR*2 and *RR*3.)

(Of course, this leaves a very difficult question unanswered: Under what conditions is it true that an *A*-ing is *intentional*?)

I conclude this section with three interrelated observations. First, even if the SRT gives us the right result in familiar cases of waywardness of the sort discussed in section 1, it does not explain why Fred's providing the correct answer to question 45 is not intentional. A self-referring analogue of the simple intention attributed to Fred, expressed in Harman's fashion, is the intention that Fred's very intention with respect to the answering of question 45 will result in his providing the correct answer by leading him ("in a more or less explicitly specified way") to fill in the space under 'b' on the answer sheet. Expressed à la Searle, the analogue is Fred's intention that that very intention cause an "intention in action" that "presents" and causes its own conditions of satisfaction (see 1983, pp. 95, 128, 167). But in either case (assuming that there are "intentions in action," that they function as Searle claims, etc.), things transpire precisely as Fred self-referentially intends. Still, the action at issue is not intentional.

To account for the nonintentionality of Fred's action, we must look beyond the *content* of Fred's intention to the *etiology* of that intention. The nonintentionality of Fred's action derives from the deviant causation of the plan component of the intention with which he acts, or, more specifically, from the deviant etiology of Fred's belief that the circled 'b' identifies the correct answer.[17] But if we must look beyond content in this case, why should we suppose, as the CSV would have us do, that in more familiar cases of causal deviance, the conditions of satisfaction of the pertinent intention *must* be identified by a specification of the content of that intention?

Indeed—and this is my second observation—the case of Fred *falsifies* the CSV if, as Searle assumes, the satisfaction of an intention depends upon the occurrence of an appropriately corresponding *intentional* action (1983, pp. 82–83). For Fred's providing the correct answer fits an adequate specification of the content of his simple intention (whether that intention is self-referring or not); but the action is nonintentional nonetheless. In short, *not* every intention is such that its conditions of satisfaction are specified by a proper expression of the content of that intention if intentions are satisfied only by appropriately corresponding intentional actions. Searle places an unbearably heavy load on the contents of intentions.

Third, though this is really a matter of reformulating the point just made, Searle is committed to holding—falsely—that Fred *intentionally* provides the correct answer. In the case of intention, "the *specification* of the content is already a *specification* of the conditions of satisfaction" (Searle 1983, p. 13). And, for Searle, satisfying an intention to *A* entails *A*-ing intentionally (pp. 82–83). Thus, Fred intentionally answers the question correctly, provided only that the content of his pertinent intention is satisfied. But as we have just seen, that content *is* satisfied—even

on a self-referential interpretation of the kind favored by Searle. So
Searle must hold that Fred intentionally provides the correct answer;
that is, he is committed to a falsehood.

3. An Argument from the Analysis of Action

I turn now to an argument for the SRT advanced by Alan Donagan.
Donagan claims that in the case of a chosen action,

> *DC.* No proposition that falls short of implicitly describing the event to be
> brought about as an action will do as the content of your choice; for, given
> the variety of ways in which one event can cause another, it will always be
> possible that the event described may be caused by your choice but in such
> a way as not to be an action. (1987, p. 88)

Donagan's working hypothesis is that "actions are events explained by
their doers' choices" (p. 87). If this hypothesis is correct, he contends,
then "in choosing *that a raising of your right arm by you occur* you would
be choosing *that a going up of your right arm occur that will be explained
by your choice*" (p. 88, Donagan's italics). The argument for the consequent of this conditional claim apparently runs as follows:

> 1. In the case of any action performed by choice, the content of the
> choice at least *implicitly* describes "the event to be brought about as an
> action" for the reason given in *DC.*
> 2. But "actions are events explained by their doers' choices."
> ∴ 3. In the case of any action performed by choice, the content of the
> choice at least *implicitly* describes "the event to be brought about" as
> something that will be explained by the agent's choice.

If claim 3 is true, effective choices of actions are at least implicitly self-
referential.

On the face of it, the argument commits a simple fallacy. From the
facts that *S* has a propositional attitude concerning an *X* (or describing
something as an *X*) and that *X*-s are properly analyzed as *Y*, it does not
follow that the content of *S*'s attitude describes the *X* as *Y*. A four-year-
old, Anna, expresses a desire to get a better look at the Sea World
whale: "Let's get a better look at the whale!" she says. But although a
defining feature of whales is that they are mammals, the content of
Anna's desire does not describe the whale as a mammal. She has no idea
that whales are mammals.

Perhaps it will be replied that Donagan requires only that the content of a choice *implicitly* describe in a certain way the event to be brought about. But what is the force of 'implicitly' here? If it is a sufficient condition of a propositional attitude's implicitly describing an X as Y that the attitude concern the X and that Xs be properly analyzed as Y, then claims 1 and 2 do imply claim 3. But claim 3, on this reading, is not enough for Donagan. He wants choices to do important causal work partly in virtue of their self-referential content. Although an agent need not have the concept of choice (1987, p. 158)—in which case the contents of his choices will not explicitly represent choices as *choices*—the content of an effective choice must, for Donagan, in some way express an idea that the agent has about the state whose content it is. If the content of an effective choice were not to do this, the choice would not be "explanatorily"—or "causally"—self-referential (see, e.g., pp. 88, 116): It would be at most *analytically* self-referential, in the sense that a proper analysis of action—what is chosen—makes essential reference to choice as a causal requirement. On the fallacy-avoiding reading of claim 3 under consideration, claim 3 does not yield the needed result. Just consider a four-year-old child's belief that her father knows that grass is green. If knowledge is properly analyzed as justified, true belief that satisfies some complicated condition C, then, on the fallacy-avoiding reading of 'implicitly', the content of the child's belief implicitly describes her father's knowledge as justified, true belief satisfying C. But since the child herself is in no way in possession of a portion of this descriptive content, that portion of the "content" is causally irrelevant to the child's mental and physical life.

Donagan's mistake here resembles Searle's in embracing the CSV. If, as Donagan holds, actions are properly analyzed as events causally explained by choices, then a choice to perform an action will be executed (or "satisfied") only if that choice causally explains an action. Grant this consequent. Then *if* the conditions of satisfaction of any effective choice must be expressed or specified in the content of that choice, effective choices will be self-referring. What Donagan needs is a successful argument that the conditions of satisfaction must be, or are, so specified. And that is something that he, like Searle, lacks.

4. More Unsuccessful Arguments for the Self-Referentiality Thesis

In the present section I refute three additional arguments for the SRT. The first two are advanced by Gilbert Harman (1976). Though Harman and Searle arrive at very similar accounts of the contents of intentions, they do so in quite different ways. Searle's approach is to assume that a proper specification of the content of an intention is a specification of its "conditions of satisfaction" and to ask what constitutes the satisfaction of an intention. Harman's route is more direct.

An Argument from the Instrumentality of Intentions

One of Harman's arguments is as follows (I have numbered the sentences to facilitate discussion):

> <1> One cannot intend to do A without intending to intend to do A. So, <2> the intention to do A contains the intention of intending to do A. <3> Intentions are therefore self-referential. (1976, pp. 440–41)

Harman elaborates 3 into two propositions:

> <4> The intention to do A is in part the intention that one have that very intention. <5> The intention to do A is the intention that, because of that very intention, it is guaranteed that one will do A. (1976, p. 441; cf. 1986a, pp. 85–86)

There are several problems with the argument. I start with 1. If 1 is to entail 2, 1 must assert

> *1'*. One cannot intend to do A without *simultaneously* intending to intend to do A.

(Even then, the entailment does not go through, as I shall explain shortly.) However, the basis given for 1 is

> <6> Forming an intention is something one does as a means of doing something else. So, <7> forming an intention is itself something one does intentionally. (Harman 1976, p. 440)

And 6 and 7 entail at most that one cannot intend to do A without *having* intended to form the intention to do A; that is, 6 and 7 do not establish the required simultaneity.

The following case illustrates the point. Suppose that Rockford intentionally forms an intention to A as a means of bringing it about that he

A-s. Suppose further that his intentional formation of the intention to A is a causal product of his intending to form that intention. Then, at some time t_1 Rockford has an intention to form an intention to A. And at some later time t_2 he acquires, as a result of the former intention, an intention to A; that is to say, he has at two different times two different intentions—and so far, we have been given no reason to think that either is self-referring. The most that follows from 1, if it is entailed by 6 and 7, is that an agent's intending to do A is *causally dependent* upon his having intended to form that intention. The claim about containment in 2 is not warranted by 6 and 7—nor is it warranted by 1, on the *causal* interpretation of 1 that fits 6 and 7.

Suppose that we give 1 the stronger reading 1'. Does 1' entail that "the intention to do A contains the intention of intending to do A"? No. It does not follow from 1' that the second-order intention is a *part* of the intention to do A. We may wish to say that if 1' is true, then, whenever an agent intends to do an A, he has some "larger" intention that is constituted by his intention to do an A and his "intention of intending to do A." But we need a distinct argument to show that this larger intention is properly described as "the intention to do an A."

Another problem concerns 6. We do often speak of our intentions as things that we form. And the expression 'S formed an intention to A' certainly suggests that S's intention to A is a product of some *act* of his. However, if 'formed' is understood literally in this context, the claim that all intentions are formed by the intender is far from obviously correct. When I hear a knock at my office door and say, "Come in," with the intention of inviting the person in, there is no need to suppose that I performed some act of intention formation. Some intentions, like some beliefs and some desires, seem to be quite passively acquired (see ch. 8.3). Furthermore, if *all* intentions are formed, this applies to higher-order intentions (e.g., the intention to form the intention to A); and Harman is faced with an infinite regress of intention formation.

This last issue is worth pursuing briefly. Harman attempts to handle the problem of infinite regress by incorporating the intention to form the intention to do A into the latter intention (1976, pp. 440–41; cf. p. 444 and Harman 1986b, p. 372). However, this strategy is not adequate to the task. Let us grant, for the purposes of making the present point only, that any intention to do A is composed in part of the intention to form the intention to A. Perhaps the story goes as follows: (a) S intends to form the intention to A; (b) this second-order intention generates something such that this product along with the second-order intention together constitute the intention to do A. Now, if all intentions are formed, the second-order intention is formed. And if, as Harman apparently holds, any instance of intention formation is itself intended, then the agent has a third-order intention to form the second-order intention. This third-order intention is itself intentionally formed, and so on ad infinitum.[18] The second-order intention's being part of some larger intention cuts no ice.

Claim 6 is also problematic on other grounds. There is a difference between doing something, *X,* which is a "means of doing something else" and doing *X as* a means of doing something else. Suppose that Barney's going bowling tonight would upset Betty. Then his going bowling is a means of upsetting Betty. But even if Barney knows this, he may go bowling tonight without doing this *as a means* of upsetting Betty. Barney goes bowling as a means of upsetting Betty only if he goes bowling, at least in part, *in order to* upset Betty—only if one of the reasons for which he goes bowling is that his doing so will (or might) upset Betty.

The same point applies to the formation of intentions. Wilma judges that it would be best to diet, but she fears that she will not diet unless she takes some special steps to commit herself to doing so. One such measure that occurs to her is purchasing an expensive, undersized dress, so that she will have additional incentive to lose weight. She may also think that her forming an intention to diet would be a means of getting herself to diet. If (in part) for this reason she does form an intention to diet, she forms this intention as a means of getting herself to diet. But this is a special case. Typically (or so it seems to me) one's reason for forming a particular intention is not that one's forming that intention will, or might, bring it about that one acts in certain ways.

A brief look at an instance of desire formation will prove useful in this connection. Imagine that while looking over a dessert menu you notice a very attractive picture of a hot fudge sundae and, as a partial consequence, form a desire to order one when your waiter returns. Your forming (or acquiring) this desire certainly increases the probability that you will order a hot fudge sundae. But unless you are a special case, you do not form this desire for that reason, that is, in order to increase the probability that you will order a sundae. If asked, you could produce reasons for your desiring to order a hot fudge sundae—for example, that you would like very much to eat one. But (again, unless you are a special case) you will not cite as a reason the fact that your desiring to order a hot fudge sundae is a means of your bringing it about that you do order one or increases the probability that you will order one.

This is true of many intentions as well. Suppose, for example, that in the preceding case you do not merely *desire* to order a hot fudge sundae but in fact *decide* (and, hence, intend) to order one. Presumably, your decision rests on desires and beliefs of yours (the constituents of reasons, on a plausible, Davidsonian account). But it is doubtful that you would view yourself as having decided to order a hot fudge sundae as a means of bringing it about that you do order one. Rather, you decide to order one because you very much like hot fudge sundaes and realize that the most appropriate way to bring it about that you are served one is to order one (or something of the sort).

The Explanatory Coherence Argument

I turn now to the second argument to be examined in this section. Consider the following case. Ward has just broken the tip of the mechanical pencil with which he was writing. He wants to continue to write with that pencil, so he twists the shaft appropriately, thereby producing a new tip. Here, we say quite naturally that Ward intends to produce a new tip by twisting the shaft (appropriately). If, as Harman maintains, intentions incorporate plans, what is Ward's plan? My suggestion is that it is to twist the shaft of the pencil appropriately in order to produce a new tip (of a suitable size). For Harman, however, a proper description of Ward's plan must make essential reference to Ward's intention. Ward's plan is that his intention to A will lead in some specified way to his A-ing.

Setting aside the question what Ward's A-ing *is* on Harman's account, why should we think that this is Ward's plan? Harman's answer is as follows:

(8) Unless Ward "has some idea about how [his] intention will lead to [his] doing A," his "conception of the immediate future will lack explanatory coherence." (1976, p. 443)

("Other things being equal, a given conception of the future . . . is more coherent than another to the extent that the first leaves less unexplained than the second" [p. 435]; and Ward's conception of the future explains more than it would otherwise do if it includes some correct idea about how his intention will result in his A-ing.)

(9) To have an idea of this sort is to have a plan about how one's intention will lead to one's action. (pp. 443–44)

(10) Such a plan is an expression of what one intends. (p. 444)

∴ (11) What Ward intends is that his intention to A will lead in a certain way to his A-ing. (p. 444)

This is an instance of what I shall call the *explanatory coherence argument*.

Again, there is a problem. If Ward does not have a plan about how his intention to A will lead to his A-ing, then his conception of that portion of his future that revolves around his A-ing is less rich, as far as explanation is concerned, than it would otherwise be. But nothing follows from this about what Ward's actual plan is. Moreover, even if it does occur to Ward that his intention will figure, in a manner M, in the etiology of his A-ing, his plan for A-ing need not be a plan about the functioning of his intention. It may simply be a plan that specifies his goal (having a new tip on his pencil) and a particular route that to this goal (appropriately twisting the shaft). If we were required to suppose that Ward formed the intention to A as a means of bringing it about that he A-s, we might be committed to giving a place to Ward's intention in his plan for A-ing. But as we saw earlier, Harman does not establish this requirement. The claim that one's intention must be an element in one's envisaged *means* to one's end (see Harman 1986a, p. 86) is unsubstantiated.[19]

An Argument from Justified Intentions

Just as we may be justified or unjustified in believing that p, we may be justified or unjustified in intending to A (Harman 1986a, p. 83).[20] Now, concerning what Harman has termed "positive intentions,"[21] it might be claimed that an agent is justified in intending to A only if he is justified in believing that his intention to A will (or might) lead to his A-ing. In the absence of such a belief, it might be urged, there is nothing to recommend the intention to the agent, in which case the intention is unjustified.

Even if these claims are granted, a critic of the SRT may resist the further contention that all intentions are self-referring. One might observe that what is true of justified intentions might not be true of others. And one might note that even if everyone who intends to A believes that his so intending will (or might) lead to his A-ing, a distinct argument is needed to show that the belief is a component of the intention or that the content of the *intention* (and not just that of the belief) refers to the intention whose content it is. However, the initial premise itself should be assessed.

Under what conditions is an intention to *A* justified? Here it will be useful to ask a parallel question about instrumental wants or desires. Paul wants to travel to Alaska; and he wants to do so because he wants to study Eskimo culture and believes that he may best do this in Alaska. If Paul's desire to travel to Alaska is justified, must what justifies it include a belief that the desire will (or might) lead to his going to Alaska? Not at all. To simplify matters, suppose that Paul's desire to study Eskimos and his belief that he can do so best in Alaska are both justifed. Then, I submit, it is sufficient for the justification of Paul's desire to travel to Alaska that the desire be properly based on his justi-fied desire to study Eskimo culture and his justified belief that he can best do that in Alaska. Further, I see no reason to suppose that the traveling desire's being properly based upon the others depends upon Paul's believing that that desire will (or might) lead to his going to Alaska. In the absence of any thoughts about what that *desire* will pro-duce (or would produce, if he were to form it), the justified belief/desire pair might issue smoothly in a desire to go to Alaska in such a way as to justify the desire and its acquisition.

The same general point applies to the justification of instrumental intentions as well. To take the same example, if Paul is justified in intending to go to Alaska, this intention will be justified by Paul's justi-fied aims and a justified belief of his to the effect that going to Alaska is a suitable means to his end, provided the intention is properly (e.g., nondeviantly) formed or acquired on the basis of those items. The impor-tant point (echoing one made in reference to the explanatory coherence argument) is that the justification of Paul's intention to travel to Alaska does not rest on a belief about the intention. Paul's pertinent belief is about a connection between his going to Alaska and something else that he wants.

Justified (wholly) *intrinsic* intentions—intentions to *A* in instances in which one's *A*-ing is wanted only for its own sake (see ch. 6)—are no different from justified instrumental intentions in an important respect. What justifies an intrinsic intention to *A* is largely what would justify an intrinsic want to *A*. And what justifies someone in intrinsically wanting to *A* is not typically a belief that one's having that want will (or might) result in one's *A*-ing. The relevant beliefs concern the value of one's *A*-ing. Perhaps intending differs from wanting in that one can intend to *A* only if one does not believe that one (probably) will not *A* (see ch. 8.4) whereas one can want to do things that one believes one will not do. But this difference does not support the view that intrinsic intentions to *A* are accompanied by beliefs that those intentions will (or might) result in one's A-ing, much less the thesis that intrinsic intentions are self-referring.[22]

5. Intentions and Plans

My purpose thus far has been to show that the main arguments for the SRT are unsuccessful and that the thesis is problematic. However, an alternative to the SRT has been emerging. The remainder of this chapter develops it.

There is a close conceptual connection between intentions and plans. Indeed, though it is apparently somewhat idiosyncratic on this matter, *The American Heritage Dictionary* defines 'intention' as "a plan of action." The plan element of an intention, on the view that I shall develop here, need not be complex or detailed. In the limiting case, as I have mentioned, one's action plan is a representation of one's performing a basic action of a certain type. In other cases, one's plan is a representation of one's prospective A-ing and of the route to A-ing that one intends to take. Action plans may be formed in the course of practical reasoning about how to achieve some end that one intends to achieve; but they need not be formed in this way. In general, I no longer have to construct a plan for getting to work or for entering various directories in my computer; for I now have standing plans for these projects.

The American Heritage Dictionary notwithstanding, intentions are not uncontroversially *identified* with plans of action. Intentions, as I have argued, have a conative or motivational dimension. They are psychological items of a sort that can *move* us to act intentionally. However, plans of action, on the construal that I have adopted, are not motivational (see ch. 8.3).

Though intentions have a motivational dimension, I see no need to maintain that that feature must be captured in a proper expression of the *content* of an intention. A proper expression of the content of S's belief that p is true does not make reference to the element of assent or acceptance that his believing that p is true involves. Similarly, a proper expression of the content of S's intention to A might not make reference to the motivational aspect of intending. Assent is carried in the *attitude* of believing, not in the content of particular (first-order) beliefs. Similarly, motivation may be carried in the attitude of intending, rather than in the content of particular intentions.

According to the view to be developed here, the content of an agent's intention to A is *simply* the plan component of his intention to A; what distinguishes intentions from plans is a function of the *attitude* of intending. On this view, the content of an agent's intention to *A* is his representation of his prospective *A*-ing and of the route, if any, that he intends to take. For lack of a better name, I shall call this view the *modest plan view* (MPV).

6. Accommodating Data

What data are to be accommodated by an account of the contents of intentions? Section 1 addresses one important datum: there is a difference between intentional and unintentional actions. We do not want an account of the contents of intentions that will prevent us from making this distinction, even in tricky cases involving wayward causal chains. If an account of the contents of intentions actually helps to resolve the problem of causal deviance, that would surely be a welcome result; but we should not require of a theory of the content of intentions that it single-handedly resolve the problem. In any case, as is clear from section 1, the MPV does not prevent us from distinguishing the unintentional actions described by Harman from hypothetical intentional counterparts. And Harman presents us with representative instances of both of the species of causal deviance that have attracted significant attention in the literature on intentional action.[23]

A related datum is that intentions have, in Searle's terminology, "conditions of satisfaction." We want an account of the contents of intentions that is compatible with intentions' being "satisfiable." We need not suppose that the conditions of satisfaction of each intention are built into the content of the intention. Indeed, section 2 demonstrates that the content of Fred's intention to provide the correct answer to question 45 does not capture that intention's conditions of satisfaction. And the MPV does not militate against intentions' being satisfiable. If the MPV is true, it simply is not the case that intention satisfaction consists wholly in *content* satisfaction. There is also a distinct causal requirement. An intention is "satisfied" only if behavior in which it issues is guided by the intention-embedded plan—only if the intention's resulting in that behavior depends appropriately on its content.

Other pertinent data are provided by our evidence about the cognitive/representational capacity of beings who have intentions. I argued in section 2 that the SRT conflicts with some of these data and that even the "modest" SRT commits us to a stand where the safer course is to remain agnostic. The requirement that all intentions be self-referential is psycho-

logically unrealistic or at least, in the case of the modest SRT, unsubstantiated (even setting aside, in the latter case, the apparent commitment to
self-causation).

The MPV does not make this requirement. One of its virtues is that it
does not require of intenders more than we can reasonably expect of
them and that it does not commit us to a position on an empirical issue
that is better left open. On the positive side, we have good reason to
believe that agents of intentional actions follow—and hence *have*—
plans of action. The plausibility of treating such plans (or portions of
them) as aspects of intentions derives at least partly from the conceptual
connection between intentions and plans.

In developing the view that the content of an agent's intention to A is
precisely the plan component of his intention to A, I shall leave open a
number of questions about plans. I have suggested that the plan component of an agent's intention to A is his representation of his prospective
A-ing and of the route, if any, that he intends to take; but I have not
endorsed a position on what form this representation takes. I do not say,
for example, whether intended routes are represented (by human beings) wholly in declarative sentences, whether they are represented in a
natural language or a language of thought, or whether the representation is exclusively propositional. Nor do I take a position on the extent to
which the plan component of an intention is conscious or accessible to
consciousness. These issues are intentionally left open.

7. Content's Basic Role

The most fundamental role of the representational content of an intention (i.e., of the plan component of an intention) is to *guide* behavior.
Sometimes the guidance required is relatively slight: for example, when
what the agent intends is, for him, a basic action—roughly, something
that he can do without first having to perform some distinct action.[24] In
such cases, the basis for guidance in the content of an intention might lie
simply in the intention's identifying the agent's target, as it were, perhaps his snapping his fingers or winking. In other cases, much more is
required by way of guidance.

Even when what is intended is routine and very simple behavior for
the agent—say, buttoning his shirt—presumably a great deal is going on
representationally. The activation of (representational) motor schemata,
for example, may help to explain the occurrence of particular finger
motions involved in the buttoning.[25] And the monitoring of feedback

contributes to the development of the agent's intentional behavior. Do "low-level" representations of minute "to-be-performed" finger motions and the like (Gallistel 1980, p. 368) enter into the content of the agent's intention to button his shirt? And is the monitoring of feedback a function of intention?

Here, it is useful to have at least a rough idea how representations of the sort at issue might be realized. Physiological psychologist C. R. Gallistel offers an illuminating speculative account of the neural embodiment or realization of a motor schema that might be involved in a certain target tracking task (1980, pp. 367–73). The account conveys a firmer sense of the location of motor schemata in the etiology of intentional action than do various functional definitions.

The task in question is "to keep the tip of a . . . pointer on top of a sinusoidally undulating target, while the experimenter varies the frequency of the undulation." "At higher frequencies of undulation," Gallistel writes, subjects "generated their own sinusoidal movements and adjusted the parameters of their movements so as to match the trajectory of the pointer to the trajectory of the target" (1980, pp. 367–68). Gallistel speculates that the schema involved is embodied in a "neural oscillator . . . whose phase, period and amplitude have been adjusted to correspond with the target's." The subjects "represent the trajectory of the target by means of" such an oscillator; and the "neural embodiment" of the stored representation "records the strengths of six signals," including "the strength of the signal required to make the period of the internal oscillator match the period of external oscillation." Further, it is supposed, "an appropriately adjusted oscillator is not only the last stage of the perceptual process . . ., but also the first stage of the motor process" (p. 369). Thus, "the process of perceiving a sinusoidal movement culminates in the creation of precisely those neural signals that are needed to direct a corresponding voluntary movement." An agent who intends to do his best to comply with the experimenter's request may succeed in keeping the pointer on the target in virtue of guidance provided by a motor schema of the sort just characterized.

Some psychologists, it should be noted, take the representational content of motor schemata to run even deeper. For example, Donald MacKay, citing Klapp and colleagues (1979) and Lashley (1951) for support, argues that motor schemata involved in handwriting have "lower-level components" that represent "the neuromuscular activity required to achieve" the movement represented by their "higher-level components" (1981, p. 630). Gallistel denies this (1980, pp. 370–71).

Needless to say, I shall not take a stand on the disagreement between

Gallistel and MacKay. The point of the preceding two paragraphs is simply to convey a sense of just how deep motor schemata might run. Now, I argued in chapter 10 that not all items that figure motivationally in the initiation and sustaining of an intentional action need be built into the initiating and sustaining intention. A proximal intention to A may depend in part for its efficacy upon the presence of motivation to A that is not itself incorporated into the intention. This observation yields a moral that is directly relevant to the questions at hand. When, proximally intending to A, an agent A-s intentionally, not everything that enters into the proximal cause of his A-ing—or even into a wholly psychological or mentalistic characterization of that cause—need enter as well into his intention to A.

Thus, even though monitoring and motor schemata (or some functional, representational equivalent of the latter) may play proximal causal roles in the guidance of an intentional action, the fact that such roles are played in the case of a particular intentional action does not itself license the inference that the roles are filled by an *intention*. Consider behavior of a kind that has become routine for an agent—again, for example, buttoning his shirt. And consider the proximal intention of a particular experienced shirt buttoner to button the shirt that he has just put on. On the MPV, the content of that intention is a plan for buttoning his shirt. In normal cases, that plan is, by default, the agent's normal plan for that activity. Perhaps this agent normally starts with the top button and moves downward, buttoning each successive button in turn; and his so doing in a particular normal case will be explained in part by his intention's incorporating his normal plan. But in the process of buttoning, a host of muscle movements are made, movements whose occurrence may be partially accounted for by low-level representations of, for example, various trajectories of "to-be-performed" movements of the agent's thumb and forefinger; and the agent's progress is monitored. Are these representations part of the plan incorporated in the agent's proximal intention to button his shirt? If his buttoning his shirt is guided in part by low-level representations of the sort identified, does his intention incorporate these representations? And is it part of the function of his intention to monitor his progress?

Let us take monitoring first. I am inclined not to move any further than necessary from commonsense conceptions of intention. And intentions, standardly conceived, do not monitor behavior. That role is reserved for something else—something perceptual or quasi-perceptual. Fortunately, no move at all is required. The account of intention taking shape in the second half of this book in no way precludes the functions of intention from depending upon intention-external representational (or motivational) states. Intentions may depend for their efficacy upon a host of conditions that do not themselves enter into intentions. Agents may modify their intentions in light of feedback received by perceptual and quasi-perceptual monitors. And adjustments in intentions may be relatively automatic results of receipt of feedback in certain cases. But none of this implies that intentions themselves serve as monitors.

Low-level representations figuring in the production of minute muscle movements that occur in the course of an agent's buttoning his shirt also seem not to be countenanced by standard conceptions of intention as parts of the representational content of a normal agent's intention to button his shirt—probably because of the apparent inaccessibility of these representations to consciousness. However, there is an important difference between the question whether intention is properly regarded as incorporating such representations and the question whether intention functions as a monitor. An affirmative answer to the latter question gives intention a *kind* of function not countenanced by commonsense conceptions of the state. But on standard conceptions, intentions do initiate and guide behavior in a way that depends on their representational content. The question here is one of *degree*. How deep does the representational content of intention run? This is a partly empirical and partly conceptual question that has, I think, no clear answer. The content of an intention is its plan component; but just how far that plan extends—whether it extends, for example, to motor schemata or functional representational equivalents—is an issue that I shall leave open. Perhaps the effective functioning of intention in the etiology of intentional action depends upon intention-extrinsic representational monitoring *and* guidance events.[26]

8. Intention and Belief Again

I argued earlier that "normal" intentions are such that S intends to A only if S does not believe (at the pertinent time) that he (probably) will not A (see ch. 8.4). Obviously, it does not follow from the truth of this thesis that the representational content of an intention includes the content of a belief; for the thesis does not attribute a belief to intenders. Rather, it asserts that intenders *lack* beliefs of a certain kind.

Even when someone who intends to A does believe that he (probably) will A, the content of that belief is no part of his intention on the MPV. Perhaps it is true in some cases of this sort that the agent would not

intend to A if he did not believe that he (probably) would A. It may be
that in the closest possible worlds in which he lacks this belief, he believes that he (probably) will not A. But it does not follow from this that
his belief is a *part* of his intention or that the content of the belief enters
into the content of his intention. Not everything that is required for a
person's possessing an X is part of the X that he possesses.

This concludes my account of the constitution and functional roles of
intention. Next on the agenda is the acquisition of intentions. How do
our intentions come to be present in us?

Notes

1. Harman adds:

More specifically, a positive intention to do A is also the intention that,
because of that very intention, one will do A. A conditional intention to do
A, if C, is also the intention that, if C, one will, because of that very
intention, do A. And a negative intention to do A is also the intention that
that very intention to do A will ensure that one will not decide to do
something other than A. (1976, p. 441; cf. 1986a, pp. 80–81)

2. "Intentions in action" are self-referential as well for Searle (1983, p. 94).
3. See also Ginet 1990, pp. 35–36; Velleman 1989, pp. 96–98.
4. See, e.g., Chisholm 1964; cf. Frankfurt 1978, p. 157, on causal analyses of
action. Notice that a bit of behavior may fail to be an intentional action for either
of two general reasons. It may not be an action at all; or though an action, it may
not be intentional. Causal accounts of what it is for an action to be intentional
(unlike causal accounts of what it is for an event to be an action) cannot be
falsified by waywardly caused nonactions. However, philosophers have not always been careful to distinguish actions from nonactions in this connection.
Thalberg (1984) rightly emphasizes this point.
5. A third type of case—first noticed, I believe, by me (Mele 1987c)—is
discussed in section 2.
6. For essentially this distinction and for the analogy with rules, see Brand
1984, pp. 240–41. Plan following plays a central role in Brand's formal folk-
psychological analysis of intentional action (pp. 28–29). The analysis is designed
to handle cases of wayward causal chains such as those presented by Harman.
I should mention that when Brand ascribes self-referentiality to intentions
(1984, pp. 90–100), he is claiming that a proper expression of the content of an
intention makes essential reference to the *agent* whose intention it is. This sort of
self-referentiality obviously is quite different from the kind with which I am
concerned in this chapter.
7. Brand 1984, p. 20. See also Thalberg 1984, pp. 257–59. For Brand, this

proximate causation is a necessary condition of an agent's acting at all (p. 20). He would deny, for example, that Betty contracted her finger, that is, that she performed that action. Thalberg, too, is inclined to deny that there is an action of finger contracting or trigger pulling in cases of this sort (p. 252). Others (e.g., Wilson 1989, ch. 3) embrace a much more inclusive conception of action according to which even uncontrollable bodily motions occurring during an epileptic seizure count as actions. On Wilson's conception of action, see ch. 13.1.

8. Cf. Brand's contention that "the action of Richard's clapping his hands begins in the brain" (1984, p. 20). Incidentally, a proximal intention to *A* may proximately cause an overt *A*-ing without triggering actional mechanisms. If, while tugging at a weight, I consider giving up my attempt to move it but form the intention to continue trying, my forming that intention might cause my continuing to tug and its so doing may consist partly in its causing the operative mechanisms to remain operative.

9. Does this indicate that Wilma's intention was in part an intention to produce cutting motions of the saw by way of executing that very intention? See sec. 3.

10. I am not assuming here that all intentional actions are intended actions. My assumption is weaker: every case of intentional action involves the agent's having some pertinent intention or other (see chs. 8.2 and 10.3). Thus, I again leave it open whether, as Harman (1976, 1986a) has claimed, certain unintended but foreseen behavioral results of intended actions may themselves be intentional. (On the intentional actions of animals, see Searle 1983, p. 101.)

11. For an opposing view about belief, see Davidson 1982a. Jeffrey 1985 is an instructive rebuttal.

12. Some recent psychological work advances the thesis that "infants . . . impute mental states to themselves and to others" (Bretherton, McNew, and Beeghly-Smith 1981, p. 346). Of course, whether *intention* is among the states imputed depends upon what intention is. Given the nature of the contents of intentions on the SRT, it is less likely that very young children impute intentions to themselves and others if the SRT is true than it is if intentions have the simpler representational structure that I claim for them later in this chapter.

The contention about infants in Bretherton, NcNew, and Beeghly-Smith 1981 is, of course, controversial. Wellman concludes from a survey of psychological studies that "the earliest awareness of the difference and independence of the internal and external worlds is acquired by about 2½ years of age" (1985, p. 176). On the assumption (endorsed by Wellman p. 172) that some grasp of this difference is presupposed by the ascription of mental states to oneself and others, Wellman's conclusion implies that Bretherton, McNew, and Beeghly-Smith are mistaken.

13. Donagan embraces such a version (1987, p. 158).

14. Someone might claim, of course, that ordinary descriptions of our intentions implicitly treat intentions as self-referring. Consider the utterance 'It is snowing'. Utterances of this sort typically refer to particular places even though

they do not explicitly mention them. It might be claimed that garden-variety descriptions of intentions function analogously in the relevant respect, as Gilbert Harman pointed out to me.

15. A challenge to the causal thesis is rebutted in chapter 13.

16. For Searle's investigation of causal deviance, see Searle 1983, pp. 107–11, 135–40.

17. It is worth noting that the problem posed by the case of Fred is not one of consequential or antecedential waywardness. There is nothing deviant about the connection between Fred's intentionally filling in the space under 'b' on the answer sheet and his providing the correct answer. This is a straightforward instance of noncausal level generation (see Goldman 1970, pp. 20–44). Nor is there anything wayward about the causal connection between Fred's intention to provide the correct answer by filling in the space under 'b' on the answer sheet and his providing the correct answer by filling in the space. This portion of the etiology of Fred's behavior proceeds quite normally.

Nevertheless, the example of Fred does involve a wayward causal chain. Things go awry prior to his forming (or acquiring) the proximal intention to provide the correct answer by filling in the space under 'b' on the answer sheet. The basic deviance is in the etiology of Fred's circling the letter 'b' on the *question* sheet. This is an instance of what I have dubbed *tertiary* waywardness (Mele 1987c). Tertiary waywardness has attracted little attention; but see Adams 1989 and Adams and Mele 1989. (Moya [1990, pp. 126–27] misrepresents tertiary waywardness.)

18. Harman claims not only that "forming an intention is itself something one does intentionally" but also that "when one forms the intention to do *A,* one intends to intend to do *A"* (1976, p. 440). Provided that '*A*' stands not only for actions essentially involving peripheral bodily movement but also for such mental actions as forming intentions, the latter claim implies that when one forms a second-order intention one intends to do that.

19. See also Harman 1986b, where the assertion that effective *willing* is self-referential rests upon the undefended contention that to will to bring about *A* is "to will that one should will in such a way that one brings about *A"* (p. 373). A version of the explanatory coherence argument appears again in Harman 1986a. Like the version just examined, it centrally involves the contention that one who harbors a positive intention "thinks of the connection between one's intention and some further result as a necessary part of one's means of accomplishing that result" (p. 86). But, again, the need to suppose that one's *intention* enters into the envisaged means to one's end is not established.

20. I am grateful to Harman for correspondence that generated this subsection.

21. See n. 1

22. Perhaps it will be suggested that at least normally, agents *tacitly* believe of their intentions to *A* that they will (or might) result in their *A*-ing—in the sense that if the question were explicitly to arise, they would have explicit occurrent beliefs to this effect. Again, however, an argument would be needed to show

that the tacit beliefs are components of intentions or that it is not merely the contents of these beliefs but the contents of intentions that refer to intentions.

23. On various kinds of causal deviance, see sec. 1 and n. 17; also see Mele 1987c.

24. On basic action, see Goldman 1970, pp. 63–72.

25. For an instructive discussion of motor schemata, see Brand 1984, ch. 9.

26. Notice that even a relatively modest conception of the constitution of proximal intentions is compatible with the view that intentional actions have intentions as *proximate* causes. If action begins in the brain, the functioning of motor schemata in the production of a bodily motion may be a *constituent* of an action; and the schemata may be proximately activated by the acquisition of an intention.

12

Acquiring Intentions

If intention plays an important role in the production of intentional action, a robust theory of the explanation of intentional action will provide an account of the production of intentions themselves. In sections 1 through 4 I limit my investigation to intentions formed or acquired on the basis of practical evaluative inference and to the role of various kinds of evaluative judgment in the etiology of these intentions. Section 5 addresses varieties of intention acquisition that do not involve such inference.

A common product of practical inference, I shall suppose with many others, is a judgment to the effect that it would be best to do something. When we judge it best to A and things go smoothly, we intend to A. But there are exceptions. In some instances of incontinent or akratic action, what we judge best is *not* what we intend. Akratic breakdown in the transition from judgment to intention is my point of departure for an investigation of the connection between practical evaluative inference and output intentions. Often we may begin to see how something functions by locating sources of malfunction.

1. The Problem and Some Background

Just as, owing to so-called weakness of will, we may act against our best judgments, we may akratically fail to intend in accordance with them.[1] The simplest illustrations are garden variety cases of self-indulgence.[2] Al judges it best to quit smoking on the basis of practical reasoning addressed to the practical question, "What shall I do about my smoking?" Although it is evident to him that there is something to be said for his smoking, namely, that he enjoys it, he judges that his reasons for not smoking are significantly better; and he judges accordingly, without qualification, that it would be best to quit. Still, Al does not intend to quit. Rather, he decides to indulge himself. People are not perfectly rational; and it seems that only someone firmly in the grip of a theory would deny the possibility of such apparently common instances of self-indulgence (Mele 1987a).

My use of the expression 'practical evaluative inference' instead of the more customary 'practical inference' or, alternatively, 'evaluative inference,' has a point. Practical inference, as I shall understand the notion, is, roughly, inference that is both addressed to the question "What shall I do?" (or a question to that effect) and sustained by motivation to settle the practical issue raised by the question. Not all inference about action counts as practical inference in this sense. Wally's reasoning about what it would be best for Wilma to do, for example, is not practical inference in my sense. Nor need Wally's reasoning about what it would be best for *him* to do be practical inference. If Wally reasons about the latter topic purely as an academic exercise, with no inclination to be guided by his reasoning in his subsequent behavior, he is not engaging in practical inference in my sense. Still, I hold, with the support of a lengthy tradition, that at least some (cogent) practical reasoning is evaluative, in the sense that among its premises are the propositional contents of evaluative judgments supporting an evaluative conclusion. For example, one may attempt to decide one's practical question "What shall I do?" *by* determining what it would be *best* to do (see Bratman 1979); and the reasoning involved in this determination will make use of premises provided by evaluative judgments.

My concern in much of this chapter is with what I shall call *unqualified* best judgments. Someone who judges that it is financially (or aesthetically, militarily, etc.) best to A is not, by that judgment alone, rationally committed to A-ing. He may consistently judge, as well, that all things considered, it would be best not to A; and he may rationally act accordingly. An unqualified judgment that it is best to A is a judgment that is detached in a sense from the considerations that support it; it is, we may say, a judgment that it is best *simpliciter* to A. Some such judgments may be prompted by all-things-considered better judgments.[3] Others may issue from qualified best judgments made from a narrower perspective that the agent takes to be evaluatively overriding or from qualified best judgments unopposed by other such judgments. In any case, an unqualified judgment that it would be best to A *rationally commits* the agent to action, in this sense —that as long as he consciously holds the judgment, he cannot rationally take himself to have, from his own point of view, better (or equally good) reason not to A than to A. (As the parenthetical clause indicates, I understand 'best' as 'uniquely best'.) Uncompelled, intentional action that is at odds with such a judgment would be subjectively irrational: it would be irrational from the agent's own point of view, the point of view reflected in the judgment.

If, as I should think, someone can judge that it is best *simpliciter* to *A,* purely as the upshot of an academic exercise and with no attendant inclination to *A,* some judgments that it is best *simpliciter* to *A* might not be genuinely practical judgments. However, any best judgment nonwaywardly produced by *practical inference* is a *practical* judgment—a judgment that is practical not only in its subject matter but also in its disposing one (to some degree) to intend and act accordingly.[4] (I return to this point in section 2.) Since my concern here is with judgments so produced by practical inference, I shall simply restrict the class of best judgments considered to best judgments so produced. In what follows, the reader should understand 'judgment that it is best *simpliciter* to *A*', 'best judgment', and the like, to refer only to nonwayward products of practical inference, unless otherwise indicated.

The occurrence of akratic failures to intend in accordance with an unqualified best judgment shows that unqualified best judgments are not identical with intentions and that their formation is not causally sufficient for the formation or acquisition of corresponding intentions.[5] There is, however, *some* important connection between best judgments and intentions if, as I suggested earlier, our intentions accord with our best judgments when things go smoothly. In addition to any conceptual connection that there may be, one naturally supposes that there is a *causal* connection. If forming best judgments on the basis of practical reasoning were incapable of contributing to the acquisition of a corresponding intention, forming the judgments would be practically useless; and it would be pointless to attempt to answer a practical question by trying to determine what it would be best to do. Supposing that there is a contribution, but only a *noncausal* one, leaves us with a very large mystery. One might ask, in light of the occurrence of akratic failures of the sort mentioned, what must be added to an unqualified best judgment to provide causally sufficient conditions for the acquisition of a corresponding intention. My own track is a bit different.

2. Intentions by Default

The acquisition of an intention to *A,* I suggest, is the *default condition* of the formation of an unqualified judgment that it is best to *A.*[6] The suggestion, roughly, is that normal human agents are so constituted that in the absence of preemption, judging it best *simpliciter* to *A* issues directly in the acquisition of an intention to A. Even though the formation of an unqualified judgment that it is best to A is not itself causally sufficient for the production of an intention to A, forming the judgment does play a central role in the etiology of an intention resulting by default—a role analogous to that played by events triggering default instructions in computing.

This is not to say, of course, that the route between unqualified best judgment and resulting intention is always a default route. There are, as we shall see, other routes. However, postulating a default procedure of the sort at issue helps to explain the normally easy transition from best judgment to intention. Certainly, no conscious intervening step is needed in the easy cases; nor, in these cases, is the exertion of any special effort of self-control on the part of the agent required to bring it about that his judgment issues in a corresponding intention.

Sometimes, of course, we move easily from judging it best to A to *deciding* to A. But because *in* deciding to A one forms an intention to A, deciding to A is not an *intervening step* between the judging and the acquiring of a corresponding intention. A smooth transition from judgment to decision *is* a smooth transition from judgment to intention.

The converse, as I have argued (ch. 8.3), is false. Deciding is one mode of intention acquisition—an active, or intention-*forming,* mode. But intentions are often passively acquired; that is, they are often acquired independently of an *action* (like deciding) of intention formation. When I intentionally unlocked my office door this morning, I intended to unlock it. But since I am in the habit of unlocking my door in the morning and conditions this morning were normal, nothing called for a *decision* to unlock it. The requirements for deciding are stronger than those for intending.[7]

The suggestion that the acquisition (i.e., the formation or the *mere* acquisition) of an intention to A is the default condition of the formation of a judgment that it is best *simpliciter* to A may be given an explicitly dispositional formulation. Normal human agents are disposed to intend in accordance with unqualified best judgments (nonwaywardly produced by practical inference); and the disposition is such that in the absence of preemption, one who forms such a judgment in favor of A-ing straightaway acquires an intention to A. When there is an akratic failure to intend in accordance with such a judgment, something blocks the normally smooth transition from best judgment to intention; something preempts the default value.

A partial account of the blockage may be gleaned from recent work on akrasia. Though the agent judges it best to A, he may be more motivated not to *A,* since best judgments are formed in significant part on the basis of one's *assessment* of one's reasons for action; and these assessments need not be in line with the *motivational force* of the evaluated items. I have argued that one's assessment of reasons often plays a significant part in the etiology of one's *intentions,* as well, and that an agent may consequently intend to *A* while being preponderantly motivated to refrain from *A*-ing.[8] But if assessment of reasons has a stronger grip on best judgments than on intentions, there is room also for akratic failures to *intend* in accordance with our best judgments. And we have every reason to believe that the grip of assessment *is* stronger in the former case. Whereas a rationally formed judgment that it is best to *A* articulates the central evaluative thrust of the collection of one's assessments of reasons, intending to *A* goes further—involving, as it does, the agent's being *settled* (often revocably) upon *A*-ing. Best judgments settle, in the agent's mind, the question what it would be best to do; intentions settle for the agent the question what he *will* do or try to do. Intending involves a conative commitment. And an imperfectly rational conative system, in the presence of strong competing motivation, might not be properly engaged by assessments of reasons and the best judgments that they yield.

None of this, incidentally, should be taken to imply that evaluation cannot influence the motivational strength of pertinent items or, conversely, that the motivational strength of an item cannot affect evaluation. Influence can—and often does—go both ways. The crucial point is that even granting mutual influence, motivation and evaluation are not always in mutual alignment, thus opening the possibility of various kinds of akratic episode.

What accounts for the aforementioned dispositional nature of unqualified best judgments nonwaywardly generated by practical inference? Partly, the nature of practical inference itself. It is inference driven by motivation to settle a practical question. The motivation that drives practical inference is also motivation to intend and act in accordance with the evaluative conclusion. In addition, unqualified best judgments are *strong* evaluative judgments in that they rationally commit the agent to appropriate action in the sense I have explained. Indeed, it seems that it is partially *constitutive* of being a rational agent (or, more precisely, a rational agent who makes unqualified best judgments) that one is disposed to intend and act in accordance with one's unqualified best judgments.[9] An attempt to imagine an agent who is not so disposed—or someone who, as often as not, intends and acts against his best judgments—might end in incoherence. When a person's reported best judgments are only loosely correlated with his intentional actions, our natural inclination is to suppose that his reports are often false. In this way, we may begin to render his behavior as a whole (including verbal behavior) intelligible or interpretable.

Not all opposition to an unqualified best judgment will preempt the default value. Often, in the course of practical inference, we judge it best to forgo the satisfaction of some desires in favor of satisfying others. When this happens, the desire for the lower-ranked object often survives. However, in an efficient system, not every opposing desire will prevent the acquisition of an appropriate intention; *nor* will every such desire prevent the *default procedure* from generating the intention.

There is an important distinction here. In some cases, motivational opposition to one's best judgment prevents the acquisition of the appropriate intention and even figures in the production of an akratic intention. In others, a "continent" intention is formed even though the default route to intention is blocked by the opposition. (We shall see that *something else* can settle the matter by producing the intention.) In a third kind of case, the default process generates its normal result even in the face of opposition.

What we need is a principled way of carving up the territory. Consider continent intentions formed or acquired in the face of opposition to one's best judgment. In *which* such cases are the intentions simply products of the default process? In which must something else step in to produce them? Further, why is it that when the default process is blocked, we sometimes do, and sometimes do not, intend in accordance with our best judgment?

A plausible, if somewhat schematic, answer to the former question is that an intention is produced (in the normal way) by default, as opposed to being produced via a distinct causal route, when and only when (barring causal overdetermination, the assistance of other agents, and science fiction) no intervening exercise of *self-control* is responsible for the production of the intention. If the move from best judgment to intention does not require a special intervening effort on the agent's part, the intention's presence typically may safely be attributed to the operation of the default procedure.

Self-control also figures importantly in a schematic answer to the question about the formation or nonformation of intentions when the default route *is* blocked. Barring the operation of higher-order default processes, overdetermination, and the like, whether an agent intends in accordance with his best judgment in such cases will depend upon his own efforts to control what he intends. In simple cases of self-indulgence, he makes no effort at all to form the appropriate intention. In other cases, he might attempt in any number of ways to get himself to intend the behavior that he judges best. He might try focusing his attention on the desirable results of the course of action judged best or on the unattractive aspects of the opposing alternative. He might generate vivid images of both or utter self-commands. If all else fails, he might seek help from a behavioral therapist. Whether his strategies work will depend upon the details of the case; but strategies such as these certainly *can* have a salutary effect, as empirical research on delay of gratification and behavior control amply indicates.[10]

I close this section with a brief commentary on the ingredients of intentions. To say that the acquisition of an intention to A is the default condition of forming a corresponding unqualified best judgment is not to say that the ingredients of the intention are present in the best judgment itself. Intending to A involves being settled upon A-ing (or, in some cases, being settled upon trying to A); and an agent is not in the latter condition until an appropriate intention is acquired. Though the best judgment recommends this condition, as it were, it does not incorporate it. Acquiring an intention on the basis of a best judgment constitutes genuine progress toward action. The default procedure that I have been discussing should be understood in part as constituting a disposition to become settled upon courses of action judged best immediately upon forming the judgment.

An intention to A also includes a *plan* for A-ing, or so I have argued. An intention-incorporated plan, again, is a representation of one's A-ing and of the intended route to A-ing (when there is one: in some intentions for the nonimmediate future, there is no represented route). While finishing lunch, I judge it best to mow my lawn next. The judgment itself incorporates a representation of my mowing my lawn. But my intention is representationally richer. In normal circumstances, a proximal intention to mow my lawn incorporates my normal lawn-mowing plan, a plan stored in memory. Proximal intentions for familiar actions typically derive their representational content in part from items other than corresponding value judgments. And typically, the content is acquired, at least partly, by default: in the absence of preemption, one's proximal intention to A incorporates one's normal plan for A-ing. In other cases, central elements of an action plan are generated in the course of practical reasoning. However, even then, execution of the plan will typically benefit from stored subroutines for familiar component actions; and an inclusive view of the contents of intentions makes the representational content of pertinent subroutines part of the content of the proximal intention.

3. More Intentions by Default

So far, I have addressed only intentions prompted by unqualified best judgments formed on the basis of practical inference. In the present section, I briefly explore the possibility of intention-producing default processes for other evaluative pronouncements of practical inference.

When, on the basis of practical inference, someone holds a judgment that, *all things considered,* it is best to *A,* must he proceed to form an unqualified judgment that it is best to *A* in order for the process of practical inference to issue nonwaywardly in an intention to *A*? Here a proponent of the default line that I have been sketching has at least two options: (1) there is a default process directly linking all-things-considered best judgments to intentions; (2) claim 1 is false—but there is a default process linking all-things-considered best judgments to unqualified best judgments, which in turn are linked by default to intention.

Felicia, who means to buy a house, is deliberating about which of three houses to buy. She has decided to consider financial data first and then weigh other factors. Felicia judges that it would be financially best to buy house *A.* Moreover, the financial considerations now seem to her so weighty that she does not proceed to weigh other factors. To cut a potentially long story short, Felicia intends to buy house *A,* on the basis of practical inference.

At least three options are open to default fans: (1) there is a default process directly linking qualified best judgments made from the per-spective of a particular category of value (financial, aesthetic, etc.) to corresponding intentions; (2) claim 1 is false—but there is a default process linking such judgments to *un*qualified best judgments, which in turn are linked by default to intention; (3) both of the preceding are false—but there is one default process linking judgments like Felicia's to all-things-considered best judgments, another linking the latter to unqualified best judgments, and yet another linking the unqualified judgments to intentions.

In the absence of a decisive argument, one should keep an open mind about the various options identified. What I want to emphasize is that default procedures linking value judgments to corresponding intentions need not be limited to procedures for unqualified best judgments. It is reasonable to suppose that there are default processes linking (perhaps only indirectly) all-things-considered and other qualified best judgments to corresponding intentions.

4. The Rationality of Intentions by Default

I have already commented briefly on the rationality of intentions issuing by default from unqualified best judgments. More remains to be said, especially by way of countering skepticism about the benefits for agents of acquiring intentions by default. If a default procedure of the sort that I have been discussing is counterproductive in a way that would render human behavior less rational than we have reason to believe it to be, we would have grounds for denying that the procedure is realized in us.

Someone who judges that it is best *simpliciter* to *A* cannot consistently judge that it is better (or probably better) *simpliciter* to do something else. Still, it seems, one may consistently hold the former judgment *and* the judgment that it *might* be better *simpliciter* to do something else. What should a person who holds these last two judgments intend? This depends upon a number of factors, including the strength of his conviction in his judgments, the kind of 'might' at issue (Is it mere logical possibility that he has in mind or something with more bite?), and what is at stake. Under certain conditions, further consideration might be called for before a rational intention to *A* can be formed. An ideally rational default procedure will not generate an intention to *A* in such cases prior to such consideration: the default value will be preempted.

Now, one might urge that a judgment that it is best *simpliciter* to *A* must in some way incorporate, or be partially based on, a judgment that it is better *simpliciter* to *A* than to consider the matter further, on the grounds that further consideration is an *alternative* to *A*-ing. But with the exception of cases in which the opportunity to *A* will soon be lost, further consideration does not preclude *A*-ing—one can *A* *after* further consideration. Notice also that if we always had to consider whether we should do something *other than* engage in further consideration, we would get very little done. Here, too, it would be nice to have a default procedure (see Bach 1984, pp. 46–48).

If someone judges that it is best *simpliciter* to *A,* would it be rational of him to intend at the time to *A* at once? The question is too vague to be answered directly. Practical evaluative judgments include, at least implicitly, temporal indices. The indices may be very inclusive, as in 'It would be best to *A* before the end of the next decade', or quite exclusive. Corresponding rationally generated intentions must have the same temporal indices as the judgments that produce them. Though Hector is justifiably convinced that it would be best *simpliciter* to *A* within the next six months, it might not be rational of him to intend (now) to *A* now. Perhaps he knows that his *A*-ing now would interfere with other things that he rationally wants to do now and believes that his *A*-ing later would not interfere with future plans. Perhaps Hector should intend now to *A* within the next six months; but given the details of the case, he should not intend (now) to *A* now.

If Hector thinks it best not to *A* now, what is the point of forming the intention now to *A* within the next six months? Would it not be rational simply to hold on to the best judgment and to form at some later time the intention to *A*, when the time for *A*-ing is ripe? If it would, a default process that generated the intention now to *A* later might be doing more than it should. Here there is an easy answer. Intentions for the nonimmediate future promote planning and the coordination of projects and activities.[11] (To do this, they need not be *unrevisable*, of course.) If we crossed all our bridges when we came to them, we might end up wandering aimlessly. There is no good reason to think that a default procedure linking unqualified judgments about temporally distant action to corresponding intentions would be counterproductive.

5. Other Varieties of Intention Acquisition

I turn now to the etiology of intentions not acquired by way of practical evaluative inference. Any such intentions will be acquired either via practical *nonevaluative* inference or independently of practical inference of any sort.

Robert Audi advances the following as "the simplest basic schema for practical reasoning":

M_1. Major premise: I want *X*.

M_2. Minor premise: My *A*-ing would contribute to bringing about *X*.

C. Conclusion: I should *A*. (1982a, p. 31; cf. 1989, p. 99)

The schema obviously is not deductively valid. But there may be some rule of practical inference that licenses the inference to 'I should *A*' in certain cases in which an agent assents to instances of M_1 and M_2. To be sure, the rule cannot be as simple as 'Whenever you want X and believe that your A-ing would contribute to your bringing about X, conclude that you should A'. This would recommend our concluding that we should A even when our performing a competing action B would, by our own lights, secure a much greater end. But might there be a *default* rule or instruction linking acceptance of instances of M_1 and M_2 to acceptance of instances of C? Perhaps when one wants X, believes that one's A-ing is a means to X, lacks competing wants, and harbors no reservations about A-ing, drawing the conclusion that one should A is in order.

There is, however, a serious pragmatic problem with any such default rule. What practical work is the judgment 'I should A' supposed to do in cases of the sort at issue? Given the background conditions and acceptance of the premises, a more productive default result would be an intention to A. Alternatively, the immediate result might be a *want* to A that is linked by default to a corresponding intention. When there is an evaluative "major" premise, there is an important practical function for acceptance of an evaluative conclusion—accepting the conclusion may serve as a proper link between accepting the premises and acquiring a suitable intention. But in the absence of an evaluative premise, insistence on an evaluative conclusion for practical inference should strike one as forced.

John has an unopposed desire to drink a beer. When he opens the refrigerator, he notices several cans, all brand X. He reaches for one of the beers, intending to drink it. Here we have what might be regarded as a very modest process of practical inference, one that starts with an unopposed desire to drink a beer and involves some representation of the thing that John picks up as a beer. One might hold that the process involves a modest evaluative judgment about the beer that John picked up, something to the effect that it is an acceptable beer: if the can were open or covered with drippings from a higher shelf, John might have selected another. Alternatively, it might be enough that John *not* deem the beer *unacceptable*. In either case, the most likely upshot of the inference is not an evaluative judgment, but a desire or intention to take a particular can of beer from the fridge.

Some readers might be disinclined to count John's psychological process as practical *inference*, on the grounds that there need be no *conscious* inference in John's move from desire and representation to a further desire or an intention (see Audi 1982a, pp. 34–35; Audi 1989, pp. 108–12). Others will have no such reservations (see Goldman 1970, ch. 4.3). For present purposes, there is no need to adjudicate the issue; for in either case I have identified a process of intention acquisition not involving practical *evaluative* inference. Suppose that there is practical inference here and that John's "second" premise is the content of an evaluative judgment to the effect that a particular beer is acceptable. Even then, this is not an instance of evaluative inference (as I have characterized such inference); for although there is a conclusion, there is no *evaluative* conclusion.

John's case may or may not be an instance of intention acquisition in the absence of practical inference, depending upon how strictly practical inference is to be construed. Are there any *clear* cases of the sort at issue? Even sudden or impulsive intentional actions may issue from practical inference in an inclusive (Goldmanian) sense. The driver who, upon noticing a dog running into the path of his car, acquires an intention to hit the brakes, presumably wants to avoid the animal and represents his hitting the brakes as a means. This is a proper basis for practical inference, liberally construed. But consider certain instances of what I have termed *wholly intrinsic* intentions (ch. 11.4). In chapter 6.2 I sketched an example in which a man, Chris, who is in the habit of whistling while he works alone in his tool shed, finds himself whistling (in his shed) a Vivaldi tune and continues to do so as a wholly intrinsically motivated action. Supposing that Chris intends his whistling, what accounts for his having the intention?

There is a familiar distinction between *occurrent* and *latent* beliefs and desires.[12] For example, many cigarette smokers are strongly disposed to have an urge or desire to smoke when they see someone else smoking. This *disposition* is a latent desire. The activation of the disposition yields an occurrent desire to smoke—a desire to smoke that plays a role in the agent's psychological economy at a particular time. Similarly, the reader's belief, just prior to reading this sentence, that Dallas is in Texas was a latent belief, a belief that was rendered occurrent by reading it. Plainly, the beliefs and desires involved in practical inference must be *occurrent* psychological items. For example, the conjunction of Chris's latent desire to whistle while working alone in his shed and his awareness of his activity and surroundings is not itself a proper basis for practical inference. Now, one might suppose that owing to his latent desire and the awareness just mentioned, Chris acquires an occurrent desire to whistle. This itself is not an instance of practical inference: it is merely the activation of a latent desire. But imagine that the occurrent want leads by default to a corresponding intention (where the pertinent default instruction is a very simple one, perhaps 'If you want to A and have no competing wants, then intend to A'). Is *that* a practical inference? I do not see why it should be so counted.

My concern here, in any case, is with explanation, not classification. How are intentions acquired? In sections 1–4 I attempted to shed light on the causal connection between evaluative upshots of practical evaluative reasoning and corresponding intentions. Even the presence of all-things-considered and unqualified judgments that it is best to A is not sufficient for the production of a corresponding intention, as familiar instances of akrasia show. In other cases a default procedure can do the required causal work. In yet others, the agent is left to his own intentional devices. He must successfully exercise self-control. Precisely why our intentions sometimes fail to accord with our best judgments, and how exercises of self-control can produce, or fail to produce, continent intentions, are, to be sure, intriguing questions. But I have answered exactly parallel questions about incontinent and continent *actions* at length elsewhere (Mele 1987a, chs. 1–7). With a view to focusing attention on intentions by default, I have elected not to present cognate answers here.

The present section took up instances of intention acquisition not involving practical evaluative inference. Here again, as we have seen, the default hypothesis is an attractive one. Indeed, we should be surprised if a default route were not a *normal* route in such cases.

Notes

1. On akratic failures to intend, see Audi 1979, p. 191; Davidson 1980, ch. 2; Davidson 1985a, pp. 205–6; and Rorty 1980.

2. On self-indulgence, see Mele 1987a, pp. 28–29.

3. On this and the point in the preceding sentence, see Davidson 1980, ch. 2.

4. The qualification 'nonwaywardly' is motivated in part by the possibility of cases in which what *starts* as a process of practical evaluative inference degenerates into nonpractical (or theoretical) evaluative inference. In such cases, the process of inference may issue in a best judgment wholly devoid of motivational force. Such a judgment is not a practical one.

5. Donald Davidson (1980, ch. 5) has claimed that a certain kind of evaluative judgment *is* an intention. Fortunately, there is no need to rehearse familiar objections; for Davidson has since made it clear that he was using 'judgment' in an unconventional sense. For some telling objections to Davidson's claim (straightforwardly interpreted), see Bratman 1985; Mele 1983; Mele 1987a, ch.

2.1; and Pears 1984, ch. 9. For clarification of Davidson's intended meaning, see Davidson 1985a, esp. pp. 211 and 220.

6. For a stimulating discussion of psychological default procedures, see Bach 1984.

7. Kent Bach claims that intentions, unlike decisions, cannot be conclusions of practical inference, on the grounds that "conclusions must be events, since they are outputs of real-time cognitive processes" (1984, p. 39). Without taking a stand on whether something other than an evaluative judgment can properly be counted as a conclusion, strictly speaking, of practical evaluative inference, I shall observe that *acquiring* an intention is an event.

8. See ch. 9; Mele 1987a, chs. 3 and 7; and Mele 1984.

9. This is a familiar Davidsonian theme. See, e.g., Davidson 1985b.

10. For a discussion of the practical potential of strategies such as these in effective self-control and of pertinent empirical literature on the topic, see Mele 1987a, pp. 23–24 and chs. 4–6. Ultimately, of course, exercises of self-control are aimed at influencing *action;* but controlling what one intends is a means to this end.

One will naturally wonder what can prevent someone who can intend to exercise self-control for the purpose of bringing it about that he intends and acts in accordance with his best judgment from simply and directly intending to do the action judged best. For an implicit answer, see Mele 1987a, ch. 5. Sometimes intentions to exercise self-control are easier to come by than the intentions that they are aimed at producing.

11. This is a major theme in Bratman 1987.

12. See, e.g., ch. 3.1; Alston 1967; Goldman 1970, ch. 4. The terminology varies.

13

Conclusion: An Unsuccessful Brief
Against "Causalism"

I have been guided in much of this book by the popular idea that our intentional attitudes play significant causal roles in the production of our intentional behavior. What I regarded as the most threatening challenge to that idea was addressed in chapter 2. That challenge grew out of recent literature in the philosophy of mind on the causal relevance of intentional attitudes generally. However, within the philosophy of action itself, there has been resistance to the thesis at issue. The "logical connection argument" (see ch. 2.1) was, for a time, deemed an insurmountable obstacle to a traditional, intentionalistic, causal approach to action-explanation. Related charges of explanatory vacuity were made (see ch. 4). And some claimed that instances of causal deviance (see ch. 11) showed that no causal characterization of action or intentional action could possibly succeed.

In the present chapter, I reopen some of the old disputes—but only indirectly, via an examination of a recent attack by George Wilson (1989) on the causal approach (what he terms "causalism") and of an alternative position advanced in different forms by Wilson (1989) and Ginet (1990). I read Wilson's and Ginet's books after the preceding chapters were substantially complete. Each of Wilson's major objections, it seemed to me, had a chance for success only against a "causalism" considerably cruder than the one advanced here. And I saw little to recommend the alternative position. One way to emphasize in a concluding chapter some of the merits of my view while also addressing worries about "causalism" not explicitly taken up earlier in the book, I thought, would be to pit my view against Wilson's objections and against his and Ginet's alternatives.

1. Wilson's Attack and Alternative

Wilson advances a teleological alternative to "causalism." He argues that his teleological view *is* an alternative and then attempts to motivate acceptance of it as a *better* alternative by undermining causalism. Wilson's attack against causalism consists primarily of a collection of arguments from causal deviance and an extension of an argument of Michael Bratman's against the "simple view" of the connection between intention and intentional action (see ch. 8).[1]

Arguments from Deviance

Wilson's arguments from causal deviance feature the standard fare—what Brand terms "antecedential" and "consequential" waywardness (see ch. 11.1). Three-fourths of the way through his chapter 9, devoted to advancing these arguments—and after eight alleged counterexamples featuring deviance—Wilson comes close to observing that a proponent of a causal account of intentional action might try to circumvent cases of antecedential deviance by requiring (roughly and partially) that intentional actions be *proximately* caused by intentions. (This, recall from chapter 11.1, was a suggestion developed in Brand 1984.)[2] As Wilson puts it, "Some but not all of the various counterexamples suggest that the agent's intention must not cause the action *by* first causing some state of nervous or affective agitation that, in turn, is an important causal factor of the action" (1989, p. 252).

Wilson contends that the suggestion is too strong, and he defends that claim by observing that sometimes "intentions cause states of nervous agitation that positively *enable* the agent to perform the type of action intended" (1989, p. 252). He offers the example of a weight lifter whose "intention to lift the weight then caused a rush of nervous excitement that was, in fact, necessary for him to budge the great weight even slightly from off the floor."

This point and example leave the requirement of proximate initiation untouched. What is required is not that intention-inspired nervousness, agitation, and the like, play no role in the etiology of intentional action, but rather that they not fill a causal gap between intention and action, in which case the intention would figure only *mediately* in the production of the corresponding action (see ch. 11.1). In Wilson's example, there is no causal gap between the intention and the beginning of the lifting that is filled by nervousness. Rather, the intention proximately initiates the lifting (which action, on the view suggested in chapter 11.1, begins prior to the weight's rising from the floor) while also producing nervousness that is required for the agent's even budging the weight.

Proximal intentions, it should be recalled, typically are not momentary states. Presumably, the intention to lift the weight, in the case at hand, is at work as long as the lifting continues. Even if, for some reason, nervousness were required for the occurrence of the agent's muscular movements themselves, a nervousness-producing intention to lift the weight that results in an intentional lift would, in conjunction with the nervousness that it causes, figure in the proximal initiation of those movements.[3] If, alternatively, the causal role of an intention to lift the weight were exhausted by the intention's issuing in nervousness and the nervousness were somehow to result in the upward movement of limbs and weight independently of any pertinent intention present at the time, the "weight lifting" would not be intentional. We would have then a case that aside from its failure to proffer an intuitively appealing mechanistic explanation of the focal occurrence, is on all fours with familiar instances in the literature of nonintentional occurrences caused by intention-inspired nervousness—for example, a case in which an agent's intention to drop some poison into his colleague's cup of tea so agitates him that his hand shakes uncontrollably, with the result that the poison falls from his trembling fingers into the tea (see ch. 11.1). The resources presented in chapter 11 are ample for handling each of the cases of deviance advanced in Wilson's chapter.[4] (See also ch. 10.3–4 on the causal sustaining role of proximal intentions.)

Extension of Bratman's Attack on the "Simple View"

The "simple view" (criticized in chapter 8) maintains that for any S and any A, if S intentionally A-ed, S intended to A. Michael Bratman (1984; 1987, ch. 8) has advanced a much-discussed objection to the view, featuring an example involving a pair of video games. I shall not rehearse the example here. Suffice it to say that if the counterexample offered is successful, the simple view is false.

As I observed in chapter 8, one may give up the simple view while holding on to the idea that an agent intentionally A-s only if a pertinent intention plays an appropriate etiological role vis-à-vis the A-ing. In some cases, I claimed, that intention is an intention to *try* to A.

Wilson contends that this idea "cannot possibly go very far." The problem, he thinks, is that to try to *A* is (roughly and for the pertinent range of cases) to perform an action that is intended to *A*. Therefore, the object of an intention to try to *A* invokes, at one remove, the **very** concept of an 'intention in action' that the causalist is attempting to explicate. The would-be reduction seems, in this maneuver, to have gone circular. If we do not understand what is said to be intended when a person is said to intend to try without already having the concept of 'intention in action,' then intentions to try are unsuitable elements in the reductive project of causalism. The obvious and most natural modification of the Simple View seems unavailable to the causalist, and it is hard to see what natural alternative remains. (1989, p. 270)[5]

Wilson's objection rests on (among other things) his assumption that "causalists" want to explicate his notion of an "intention in action." Do they? Before we can be sure, we must consider what Wilson takes an intention in action to be.[6]

In introducing the notion, Wilson writes:

Suppose that a person performs a certain definite movement of her hand, and, *in* performing that movement, she intended to flip the switch. It follows from an assertion that describes this fact that she intended *concerning that very movement* that it flip the switch. And if *in* flipping the switch, she intended to turn on the light, then it follows that she performed *some* act of flipping the switch, and that she intended *concerning that act* that it (by flipping the switch) was to make the light turn on. In other words, . . . ascriptions of intentions in action are statements that are *de re* with respect to an action-token of the action-type the agent has been said, in that very ascription, to have performed. (1989, p. 120)

The vocabulary here certainly has an odd ring. There is no standard sense of 'perform' in which people perform movements of their hands.[7] (Of course, people do move their hands, and they perform actions of moving their hands.) Further, the intelligibility of the supposition that a person intends, concerning a movement of hers, that *it* flip a switch depends on the intelligibility of the idea that movements (sometimes) flip switches. And that looks for all the world like a category mistake. *Agents* flip switches by moving their bodies in various ways. To treat movements or "acts" as items that flip switches is to treat them as agents.

More important, I do not see why the second sentence in the passage just quoted should be accepted. We might say that in performing a certain hand movement, Wilma intended to flip the switch and mean only that she moved her hand as she did then because she intended at the time to flip the switch then. We need not at all be claiming that

Wilma intended of that movement that it flip the switch or that Wilma intended anything of that movement.

This is not to say that there are no *de re* intentions. Indeed, I was willing to countenance *de re* intentions of another sort in chapter 11.2. And it might happen that people sometimes intend of certain bodily motions of theirs that those motions have certain effects. For example, Sam might intend of the present motion of his arm that it cause Tina to look his way.

Where does this get us? Consider a claim just quoted, which is central to Wilson's attack on the successor to the simple view at issue: "To try to *A* is (roughly and for the pertinent range of cases) to perform an action that is intended to *A*" (1989, p. 270). I argued in chapter 8 that one can intend to try to *A* without intending to *A,* and I see no reason to think that intentions *of* movements that they have certain effects (or intentions of *actions* that they *A*—if the notion is intelligible) must be treated differently. Sally, because she thinks that her chances of attracting Tom's attention are remote, might intend to *try* to attract his attention by raising her arm without intending to attract his attention by so doing and without intending *of* her movements that they attract Tom's attention. What, then, *does* she intend of those movements? My preferred answer is *nothing.* But if she does intend something of those movements, it might be that they constitute an indication of her presence that has some chance of attracting Tom's attention.[8]

It is worth recalling Belton's case in chapter 3.3. Belton wants to try to solve a certain chess problem because he is convinced that the very trying will win him fifty dollars. Still, Belton is indifferent to his actually *solving* the problem; and he thinks it very unlikely that he will solve it. In light of the discussion of *intending* to try in chapter 8, it is a small step to the supposition that Belton intends to try to solve the problem while having no intention to solve it. Now, Belton's trying encompasses the performance of mental acts. But he does not intend of those acts that they solve the puzzle. If he intends anything of them, it is that they convince Brett (whom he believes to be psychic or omniscient) that he (Belton) is trying to solve the problem, or that they win him the fifty dollars, or something of the sort.

The remainder of Wilson's attempted extension of Bratman's argument is quite revealing. "The fundamental difficulty" for the "causalists," he maintains, "is that an intention for the future is always an intention to perform an *intentional* act of some kind" (1989, p. 270, my italics).[9] (He treats proximal, or " 'present-directed' intentions, as the causalist conceives of them, [as] intentions of the same form except that they have been 'updated' to the time of acting" [p. 271].) To illustrate his point, Wilson adduces several cases, the most detailed of which is addressed shortly. The intended upshot of his discussion is that "every 'nonderivative' ascription of intention for the future (and of present-directed intention, as the causalist conceives it) involves in the propositional specification of its object, an instance of the concept of 'intention in action' [in which case] it appears to be an absolutely ground-level mistake to think that any kind of noncircular reduction of intention in action in terms of other related intentions is possible" (pp. 274–75).

Wilson examines in this connection the example of a man, Scott, who intends to signal an accomplice in church tomorrow by "wiggling his forefinger" (1989, p. 271). He correctly observes that if, at the appointed time, "a weird muscle contraction . . . causes an involuntary wiggling of the finger," Scott has not executed his intention. The wayward wiggling was not, he says,

> the realization or fulfillment of the intention Scott had formed. The reason that this is so is that we need to capture the idea that
> Scott intends to wiggle his finger intentionally during the service

or that

> Scott intends to perform an intentional act of wiggling his finger during the service. (p. 272)

Wilson's mistake here should be familiar from my discussion in chapter 11.2–3 of Searle's and Donagan's view of the contents of intentions. Searle maintains, as I observed, that a proper expression of the content of an intention to *A* specifies the conditions under which it is true that the intention is executed—or (what comes to the same thing for him) the conditions under which it is true that in executing the intention, the agent *intentionally A*-s. But, as I argued, Searle's view on this point is *false*. He places an unbearably heavy load on the contents of intentions. And *only if* a view like Searle's were true would Wilson's argument go through. If the conditions under which it is true that an intention is executed need not be specified in a proper expression of the content of the intention, then we need not, in order to distinguish Scott's unintentional finger wiggling from a counterpart intentional one, suppose that "Scott intends to wiggle his finger intentionally during the service." Scott's finger wiggling—if, indeed, what happens merits that description—may be unintentional simply because his intention to wiggle his finger did not play a suitable causal role. (For further details, see ch. 11.)

Wilson's Alternative

In fairness to Wilson, his preferred alternative to "causalism" should be addressed. In chapter 1.3, I sketched a challenge posed by Donald Davidson for critics of the causal approach to action-explanation at issue here. In a nutshell, it is this: "If you think that when we act intentionally we act for reasons, provide an account of the reasons *for which* we act that does not treat (our having) those reasons as figuring in the etiology of the relevant behavior."

Wilson admirably takes up the challenge. I quote a late statement of his teleological view as illustrated in a discussion of a man who climbs a ladder to fetch his hat:

> The teleological alternative informs us that the man's desire to retrieve his hat is relevant to explaining why he went up the ladder in virtue of the fact that *this* was a desire he went up the ladder in order to satisfy. He went up the ladder for the *conscious* purpose of satisfying his desire to retrieve his hat. But then, this is just the fact that his movements up the ladder were *intended* to promote the satisfaction of this desire. It is these teleological truths about the man that support the claims that
> He went up the ladder because he wanted to retrieve his hat
>
> and
>
> He went up the ladder because he (thereby) intended to satisfy his desire to get his hat. (1989, pp. 287–88)

As Wilson notes, "causalists" who accept "teleological descriptions" of the sort present in this passage take them to be descriptions of causally relevant items (pp. 215–16). For example, that the man went up the ladder *in order to* satisfy his desire to get his hat is understood as a matter of that desire-state's playing a suitable role in the etiology of his climbing the ladder.[10] If Wilson had succeeded in undermining "causalism," this response would be inappropriate. But even though his critical arguments fail for reasons that I have sketched, more can be said.

Suppose that the man left not only his hat on the roof but also a cumbersome tool kit and a basket of bricks. Suppose, further, that he wants to fetch each, that he knows that he cannot get them all at once, and that as he starts up the ladder he is undecided about which item(s) to retrieve this time. Imagine that at some point on his way up the ladder, the man forms or acquires an intention to get a particular item *x* on the current trip, and that he moves the rest of the way up with that intention.

Let us ask now in virtue of what it is true that "he went up the ladder [the rest of the way] because he (thereby) intended to satisfy his desire to get [*x*]"? Wilson's answer in the passage at issue is that "his movements [the rest of the way] up the ladder were *intended* to promote satisfaction of this desire." But suppose now that although his movements up the ladder were indeed intended to promote this, his so intending played no causal role in the production of those movements. Suppose that once he decided to get *x,* his body moved as it did only because random *Q* signals from Mars just then started providing exactly the right input to his muscles and that even so, it seemed to the agent that he was in fact moving himself up the ladder in just the way that he had been doing. (The *Q* signals struck the man just as bizarre *Z* rays from Venus had prevented events in the man's brain from causing muscle contractions and the like.) In that event, I submit, he did not *climb* the rest of the way up the ladder—much less do so intentionally. Although his body continued to move up the ladder as it had been and although he *intended of his movements* that they "promote satisfaction of [his] desire," he was no longer the agent of the movements. Here, I think, intuitions are clear.

More important for present purposes, even though there is a reading of 'The man went up the ladder' on which the sentence is true, it is *false* that "he went [the rest of the way] up the ladder because he wanted to retrieve [*x*]" and false as well that "he went [the rest of the way] up the ladder because he (thereby) intended to satisfy his desire to get [*x*]." Rather, he went the rest of the way up the ladder because the *Q* signals provided such and such input to his muscles.

This is, to be sure, a highly contrived case. But it lays bare a point that might otherwise be hidden from view. Our bodily motions might coincide with our desires or intentions and even result in our getting what we want or what we intended to get (or what we intended our motions to promote), without those motions being *explained* by the desires or intentions. (For a closely related observation about plans, see chs. 8.2 and 11.1.) The challenge for Wilson is to get want-to-behavior and intention-to-behavior explanation into the picture while not relying on want-to-behavior and intention-to-behavior *causation.* The case at hand shows that in the passage in question Wilson fails to do this.

One might suggest that the case fails on the grounds that since the man was not the *agent* of the movements or motions in question, the movements were not "the *man's* movements" and hence were not movements of the sort with which Wilson is concerned in the quoted passage. Two observations are in order. First, if the correct diagnosis of the man's not being the agent of the movements is that a pertinent desire or intention of his did not play an appropriate causal role in the production of those movements, then "causalism" is vindicated. Second, the reply at issue is not open to Wilson. Just as his broad conception of action commits him to holding that Scott "helplessly *performed*" the "wiggling of the finger" that was caused by "a weird muscle contraction" that "seized" him (1989, p. 271; my italics), it commits him as well to holding that the "movements" on the ladder were performed by our man. Noteworthy in this connection is Wilson's claim that "a man performs a convulsive and spasmodic movement when he clutches and cannot loose a live electric wire, and someone undergoing an epileptic seizure may perform a series of wild and wholly uncontrollable movements" (p. 49). Wilson regards the broadness of his conceptions of performing and acting as a virtue, and the broad conceptions figure significantly in his attack on causalism (as in Scott's case and various examples of causal deviance).[11]

A possible reply that *is* open to Wilson merits brief mention. Wilson claims that the points about desire and conscious purpose in the first two sentences of the quoted passage under consideration constitute (*F*) "the fact that [the man's] movements up the ladder were *intended* to promote satisfaction of [the relevant] desire" and that *F* supports the two 'because'-claims in the passage. The case at hand shows that *F* (given Wilson's construal of a person's movements) may be true even while the 'because'-claims are false. But Wilson might just scrap *F* and contend that the points about desire and conscious purpose "support" the 'because'-claims (or at least the first 'because'-claim) directly.

Once *F* is abandoned, it will be appropriate to ask for another account of the truth conditions of '*S X*-ed *in order to* satisfy desire *D*' and '*S X*-ed *for* the conscious purpose of satisfying *D*'. Since Wilson's attack against a "causalist" approach to an account of the truth conditions is unsuccessful, the burden is on him to show why the account that he might advance is preferable to a causalist one.

2. Ginet's Alternative

Carl Ginet offers a response to a burden of the kind just placed upon Wilson (1990, ch. 6). Consider a "reasons explanation" of the form " '*S V*-ed in order (thereby) to *U*' " (p. 137). "The only thing *required* for the truth of a reasons explanation of this sort," Ginet writes, "besides the occurrence of the explained action, is that the action have been *accompanied* by an intention with the right sort of content" (p. 138). In particular, it is not required, on his view, that the intention figure in the causation of *V* or any part of *V*. "Given that *S* did *V*," Ginet contends, it is sufficient "for the truth of '*S V*-ed in order to *U*' " that "concurrently with her action of *V*-ing, *S* intended by *that* action to *U* (*S* intended *of* that action that by it she would *U*)." He adds, "If from its inception *S* intended of her action of opening the window that by performing it she would let in fresh air (from its inception she had the intention that she could express with the sentence 'I am undertaking this opening of the window in order to let in fresh air'), then ipso facto it was her purpose in that action to let in fresh air; she did it in order to let in fresh air" (p. 138).

Since Ginet does not share Wilson's broad conception of action, his thesis might not be subject to a counterexample of the sort developed in the preceding section. For Ginet, if, in the absence of any pertinent *volition* of *S*'s, mysterious rays from Alpha Centauri were to cause *S*'s body to move in such a way as to bring it about that a window opens, the agent would not have performed the actions of opening the window and letting in fresh air.

Is the condition that Ginet offers sufficient, as he claims, for the truth of '*S V*-ed in order to *U*'? Attention to desire will prove illuminating. Suppose that "concurrently with her action of" opening the window, *S desired* "by that action" to let in fresh air. Would it follow that *S* opened the window *in order to* let in fresh air? No. Suppose that *S* had at the time not only a desire to let in fresh air but also a desire not to let in fresh air and to let in stale air. People in the room are smoking cigars, and she acquires, as a partial consequence, competing desires. She desires to let in fresh air to make the atmosphere in the room more bearable for her, and she desires to let in only stale air so that the smokers might see just how unpleasant polluted air can be. She is, moreover, uncertain whether the air outside is stale or fresh, but thinks that it is more likely to be stale. Suppose that at the time of action, she wants more of her opening the window that it let in stale air than that it let in fresh air. In that event, we would be disinclined to maintain that she opened the window *in order to* let in fresh air, even though she had at the time a *de re* desire of her opening the window that it let in fresh air. Other things being equal, if it is true at all that she opened the window in order to _____, 'let in stale air' is a better candidate for filling in the blank than 'let in fresh air'.

Is there something special about *de re* intentions in virtue of which they turn Ginet's trick even though *de re* desires, as a class, do not?

Ginet writes: "The content of the intention is . . . the proposition 'By this V-ing (of which I am now aware) I shall U'. It is owing to this direct reference that the intention is about, and thus explanatory of, *that particular* action" (1990, p. 139). Of course, if intentions can have such propositional content, so can desires. But in the case just sketched, a desire having the "direct reference" that Ginet identifies is *not* "explanatory of" the action. So direct reference is not sufficient, and there must be something special about intending.

Before asking what that special feature is, it is worth noting that the proposition identified by Ginet as "the content" of the intention can be the content of a predictive belief. (Indeed, since 'shall' in the first person standardly expresses simple futurity, the proposition identified is *best* suited to a predictive belief.) But, of course, someone who V-s can believe that by (that) V-ing he will U and yet not V in order to U. (Just now, when typing the word 'But', I believed that by so doing I would cause the word to appear on my computer monitor; but I did not type the word 'But' in order to cause it to appear on my monitor. It is the record on my hard disk that concerns me.) So, again, there must be something special about intending, in virtue of which the mere possession of a *de re* intention about an action explains that action. What is it?

Ginet tells us that an intention of the sort in question, being an intention about a particular action, "could not begin before the particular action does" (1990, p. 139). However, he says, the action need not be complete before one can have an intention about it: "It is enough if the particular [action] has begun to exist."[12] So imagine that for some reason or other, S gets up to open the window and then, while in the process of opening it, acquires an intention N, of her opening the window, that by so doing she let in fresh air. Would she have opened the window— performed that action—even if she had not acquired N? Perhaps. Maybe she set out to open the window in the first place to get a better view of the street, and perhaps she would have opened it (simply for that purpose), if she had not acquired N or any other intention concerning her letting fresh air into the room. Even then (i.e., even if the counterfactual is true) N might properly figure in an explanation of S's opening the window. For one thing, the completion of that action might be causally overdetermined by N and S's intention to get a better view. N would not causally explain the entire action (from the beginning on), since N was not present until the action was already in progress. But it might nevertheless enter into a causal explanation of the action's being completed.

In the preceding section we saw how a *de re* intention might just be along for the ride, as it were, and not explain the movements about which it is an intention. Does Ginet circumvent a related nonexplanatory rider problem? Just to pump intuitions, let us consider a case that would be question begging if it were not employed simply for that purpose. Imagine that God, who is omniscient and never lies, tells us that S had the following two *de re* intentions while opening the window and that both were present at the time of the completion of that action: S had the intention $N,$ of her opening the window, "that by it she would" let in some fresh air; and she had the intention $O,$ of her opening the window, that by it she would gain a better view. Suppose that God tells us, as well, that one and only one of these intentions explains S's opening the window while refusing to say which one. And suppose that we believe what God says.

Under what conditions would it be true that S's opening the window was explained by N—or, alternatively, by $O?$ A natural answer is that the intention that explains S's opening the window is the one that figures suitably in the etiology of that action or of S's completing the action. Thus, if O helps to produce bodily movements involved in her opening the window but N plays no causal role at all in the production of any part of the action, we would say (given that we believe God) that O is the explanatory intention and that N is just along for the ride.

Let us now delete God from the story and suppose that a mad scientist, without altering the neural realization of N itself, renders that realization incapable of having any effect on S's bodily movements (and any effect on what else S intends) while allowing the neural realization of O to figure normally in the production of movements involved in S's opening the window. Here, it seems clear, O helps to explain S's opening the window, and N does not. Indeed, N seems entirely irrelevant to the performance of that action. And if that is right, Ginet is wrong; for on his view, the *mere presence* in the agent of an intention about her V-ing (where V-ing is an action) is sufficient for that intention's being explanatory of her action.

Can Ginet plausibly retreat to the following position: if (1) "concurrently with her action of V-ing, S intended by *that* action to U" and (2) S had at the time no other intention or desire that helped to explain, either in whole or in part, her V-ing, then (3) the intention just mentioned is explanatory of her V-ing even if it is, at the time, incapable of playing a causal role in the production of (any part of) that action? This conditional assertion will seem to some to be a nonstarter. Even if a V-ing is an *unintentional* action, readers may claim, some associated intentional action will have been caused in part by a desire or intention, and the desire or intention will help to explain V's occurrence. For example, if, when opening a window, I unknowingly let in a fly, one might claim that, say, an intention to open the window, partly in virtue of its figuring suitably in a causal explanation of my opening the window, also figures in a causal explanation of my unintentional action of letting in the fly.

Ginet will have none of this, however. He argues that agents sometimes act in the absence of any relevant desire or intention whatever. Some volitions, he claims, are cases in point, as are some associated "exertions" of the body. For example, he contends that "a voluntary exertion could occur [owing to an associated volition] quite spontaneously, without being preceded or accompanied by any distinct state of desiring or intending even to try . . . to exert, and it would still be an action, a purely spontaneous one" (1990, p. 9). In the case of a *voluntary* exertion of the body, Ginet says, "clearly, a causal connection between the willing and the body's exertion is required" (p. 39). But the volition itself, for Ginet, need not be caused (even in part) by, or concurrent with, any desire or intention.

So let us suppose that in S, standing within arm's reach of a window, a steady stream of volitions spontaneously springs up (volitions being momentary actions [Ginet 1990, pp. 32–33]), as a result of which S's body moves in such a way as to come into contact with the window and smoothly open it in a conventional way. And let us suppose as well that all this happens in the absence of any relevant intention or desire. Since the volitions produce the bodily movements that in turn cause the window to open, we have the makings of a causal explanation of all but the volitional element in S's opening the window. (The first and spontaneous volition in the stream is the "initial part or stage" of the voluntary exertion and the action [p. 30].) And the volitional element, on Ginet's view, needs no explanation at all.

Suppose now that we augment the case by supposing that S intends of her opening the window "that by it she" will let in some fresh air but that her intention N is incapable of playing a causal role in producing the bodily movements or members of the volitional stream. I do not see how N can have any more explanatory significance in the present case than it did in the godless two-intention case, that is, none at all. One might be tempted to think that the intention is explanatory of the action on the grounds that in the absence of *any* relevant intention or desire, S's opening the window—that action—would be incomprehensible. But if Ginet is right, such an action requires no intention or desire at all for its occurrence: a spontaneous stream of volitions can do the work. Moreover, for readers who think it absolutely bizarre that in the absence of any relevant intention or desire, a steady stream of volitions of a kind suitable for window-opening bodily movements would occur in an agent and who therefore want to bring some intention or desire into the explanatory picture, the best candidate, for reasons identified earlier, would be an intention that is *causally explanatory* of the supposed occurrence of the causally effective volitions.[13]

My aim in part I of this book was twofold: to show that a traditional, causal, intentionalistic approach to the explanation of intentional action is alive and well (ch. 2) and to refine a standard belief/desire model of action-explanation while leaving intention standing largely in the wings. The function of part II (with the exception of the present chapter) was to correct a major deficiency in belief/desire models. To that end, intention was thrust to center stage. As has become increasingly clearer to students of action since the mid-1970s—philosophers and psychologists alike—intentionalistic accounts of intentional behavior that ignore intention are radically incomplete. In any case, if intention plays the functional roles identified for it in part II and if, as I have argued, intention is irreducible to belief/desire complexes, relatively pure belief/desire models of action-explanation must be discarded. That negative point has been overshadowed, I hope, by the positive strides taken here toward a more promising model.

I have not pretended to offer a complete account of the psychological springs of action. Rather, I concentrated only on a certain central range of items relevant to causal, intentionalistic explanation of intentional behavior: motivation (or wanting, in a broad sense), belief, reasons or reason-states, practical reasoning, and intention. Moreover, some members of the range were accorded considerably more attention than others. Perhaps there are grounds for hope, however, that my efforts in assembling important segments of the puzzle will make it easier to see how other pieces fit.

Notes

1. The material just mentioned appears in the last three chapters of Wilson 1989. It is preceded by seven chapters addressing the logical form of action sentences, the concept of intention, teleology, and reasons for action.

2. Brand's work is not mentioned in Wilson's book.

3. Here I am simply setting aside cases in which a nervousness-producing intention to lift the weight issues in a distinct intention to lift the weight that has a more direct causal role in the lifting. Such cases pose no special problems.

4. See also Bishop 1989, chs. 4 and 5, for a discussion and account of the causal connection between "basic" intentions and "basic" intentional actions. Bishop's account (p. 172), if successful, enables us to distinguish basic intentional actions from nonintentional counterparts occurring in instances of antecedential waywardness.

5. Here and elsewhere in the chapter, I have substituted my preferred variables for Wilson's.

6. Wilson (1989, p. 242, n. 8) observes that his notion is not Searle's. On Searle's (1983) conception of an intention in action, see ch. 10.3.

7. Wilson (1989) develops his own sense of 'perform' in ch. 3.

8. I have been employing, and will continue to employ, Wilson's terminology. Readers should bear in mind, however, that such expressions as 'She intends of that movement that it attract Tom's attention' and 'That movement was intended to light the match' are ambiguous in a way accounted for by the fact that the verb 'move' has both a transitive and an intransitive use. A bodily movement may be a mere bodily motion (e.g., the motions of a sleeping man's chest) or, alternatively, an instance of an agent's moving his body. See Hornsby 1980, ch. 1, for a discussion of the difference.

9. Cf. Ginet's claim that, "if I intend to do a certain thing, I intend to do it intentionally: I intend that I do it and that my doing it be a carrying out of that very intention" (1990, pp. 35–36).

10. See Goldman's treatment of "*in order to* explanations" (1970, pp. 77–78).

11. A misguided reply in defense of Wilson's claims should perhaps be anticipated. In a *variant* of the Q signal case, the man, before he gets to the top of the ladder, might cease intending (and desiring) to get x and might intend instead to start back down straightaway. Noticing that he is continuing to move upward, he might no longer take it to be true that he is moving himself up the ladder; and at any rate, he would not be intending of his movements that they satisfy his desire to fetch x. In light of the last point, the variant would not be a counterexample to the contention of Wilson's at issue. But the variant is one case and the original another. In the original Q signal case, things seem to the agent to be progressing quite normally, in accordance with what he desires and intends.

12. Incidentally, that *de re* intentions must be intentions about actions in progress is controversial. Davidson remarks, "Future actions, like any other entities, have unique descriptions, and so can be 'picked out' like other things. It is not even the case . . . that future actions can't be identified through the use of indexical devices. Of course they can: 'the next time I drink a Pernod in Paris' picks out . . . a unique future action" (1985a, p. 198). Cannot Davidson intend in Berkeley, of the next drinking of a Pernod by him in Paris, that it be done with Marcia?

13. This should not be understood as an endorsement of any of the claims about volition that I have reported. I discuss Ginet's position on volition in Mele n.d.(c).

References

Adams, Frederick. 1991. "Causal Contents." In Brian McLaughlin, ed., *Dretske and His Critics*. Boston: Routledge.
_____. 1989. "Tertiary Waywardness Tamed." *Critica* 21:117–25.
_____. 1986. "Intention and Intentional Action: The Simple View." *Mind and Language* 1:281–301.
Adams, Frederick, and A. Mele. 1989. "The Role of Intention in Intentional Action." *Canadian Journal of Philosophy* 19:511–31.
Ainslie, George. 1982. "A Behavioral Economic Approach to the Defense Mechanisms: Freud's Energy Theory Revisited." *Social Science Information* 21:735–80.
_____. 1975. "Specious Reward: A Behavioral Theory of Impulsiveness and Impulse Control." *Psychological Bulletin* 82:463–96.
Ainslie, George, and V. Haendel. 1982. "The Motives of the Will." In Edward Gottheil et al., eds. *Etiologic Aspects of Alcohol and Drug Abuse*. Springfield, Mass.: Thomas.
Ainslie, George, and R. Herrnstein. 1981. "Preference Reversal and Delayed Reinforcement." *Animal Learning and Behavior* 9:476–82.
Ajzen, Icek. 1985. "From Intentions to Actions: A Theory of Planned Behavior." In Julius Kuhl and J. Beckman, eds., *Action Control: From Cognition to Behavior*. Heidelberg: Springer.
Ajzen, Icek, and M. Fishbein, eds. 1980. *Understanding Attitudes and Predicting Social Behavior*. Englewood Cliffs, N.J.: Prentice–Hall.
Alston, William. 1986. "An Action-Plan Interpretation of Purposive Explanations of Actions." *Theory and Decision* 20:275–99.
_____. 1974. "Conceptual Prolegomena to a Psychological Theory of Intentional Action." In Stuart Brown, ed., *Philosophy of Psychology*. New York: Barnes & Noble.
_____. 1967. "Motives and Motivation." In Paul Edwards, ed., *The Encyclopedia of Philosophy*. New York: Macmillan.
Anscombe, G.E.M. 1963. *Intention*. 2d ed. Ithaca, N.Y.: Cornell University Press.
Antony, Louise. 1989. "Anomalous Monism and the Problem of Explanatory Force." *Philosophical Review* 98:153–87.

Aristotle. 1915. *Nicomachean Ethics.* Vol. 9 of William Ross, ed., *The Works of Aristotle.* London: Oxford University Press.

Armstrong, David. 1980. "Acting and Trying." In David Armstrong, *The Nature of Mind.* Ithaca, N.Y.: Cornell University Press.

Atkinson, John. 1957. "Motivational Determinants of Risk-taking Behavior." *Psychological Review* 64:359–72.

Audi, Robert. 1989. *Practical Reasoning.* London: Routledge & Kegan Paul.

———. 1988. "Deliberative Intentions and Willingness to Act: A Reply to Professor Mele." *Philosophia* 18:243–45.

———. 1986a. "Intending, Intentional Action, and Desire." In Joel Marks, ed., *The Ways of Desire.* Chicago: Precedent.

———. 1986b. "Acting for Reasons." *Philosophical Review* 95:511–46.

———. 1982a. "A Theory of Practical Reasoning." *American Philosophical Quarterly* 19:25–39.

———. 1982b. "Believing and Affirming." *Mind* 91:115–20.

———. 1980. "Wants and Intentions in the Explanation of Action." *Journal for the Theory of Social Behavior* 9:227–49.

———. 1979. "Weakness of Will and Practical Judgment." *Noûs* 13:173–96.

———. 1973. "Intending." *Journal of Philosophy* 70:387–402.

Bach, Kent. 1984. "Default Reasoning: Jumping to Conclusions and Knowing When To Think Twice." *Pacific Philosophical Quarterly* 65:37–58.

Baier, Annette. 1976. "Mixing Memory and Desire." *American Philosophical Quarterly* 13:213–20.

Beardsley, Monroe 1978. "Intending." In Alvin Goldman and J. Kim, eds., *Values and Morals.* Dordrecht: Reidel.

———. 1975. "Actions and Events: The Problem of Individuation." *American Philosophical Quarterly* 12:263–76.

Bishop, John. 1989. *Natural Agency.* Cambridge: Cambridge University Press.

Brand, Myles. 1984. *Intending and Acting.* Cambridge, Mass.: The MIT Press.

———. 1979. "The Fundamental Question in Action Theory." *Noûs* 13:131–51.

Brandt, Richard, and J. Kim. 1963. "Wants As Explanations of Actions." *Journal of Philosophy* 60:425–35.

Bratman, Michael. 1987. *Intention, Plans, and Practical Reason.* Cambridge, Mass.: Harvard University Press.

———. 1985. "Davidson's Theory of Intention." In Ernest LePore and Brian McLaughlin, eds., *Actions and Events.* Oxford: Basil Blackwell.

———. 1984. "Two Faces of Intention." *Philosophical Review* 93:375–405.

———. 1979. "Practical Reasoning and Weakness of the Will." *Noûs* 13: 153–71.

Bretherton, Inge, S. McNew, and M. Beeghly-Smith. 1981. "Early Person Knowledge As Expressed in Gestural and Verbal Communication: When Do Infants Acquire a 'Theory of Mind'?" In Michael Lamb, ed., *Infant Social Cognition: Empirical and Theoretical Considerations.* Hillsdale, N.J.: Lawrence Erlbaum.

Burge, Tyler. 1989. "Individuation and Causation in Psychology." *Pacific Philosophical Quarterly* 70:303–22.

———. 1986. "Individualism and Psychology." *Philosophical Review* 95:3–45.

———. 1979. "Individualism and the Mental." *Midwest Studies in Philosophy* 4:73–121.

Castañeda, Hector. 1975. *Thinking and Doing.* Dordrecht: Reidel.

Champlin, T.S. 1987. "Doing Something for Its Own Sake." *Philosophy* 62:31–47.

Charlton, William. 1988. *Weakness of Will.* Oxford: Basil Blackwell.

Chisholm, Roderick. 1964. "The Descriptive Element in the Concept of Action." *Journal of Philosophy* 61:613–25.

Davidson, Donald. 1992. "Thinking Causes." In John Heil and A. Mele, eds., *Mental Causation.* Oxford: Clarendon.

———. 1989. "The Myth of the Subjective." In Michael Krausz, ed., *Relativism: Interpretation and Confrontation.* Notre Dame, Ind.: University of Notre Dame Press.

———. 1987a. "Problems in the Explanation of Action." In Philip Pettit, R. Sylvan, and J. Norman, eds., *Metaphysics and Morality: Essays in Honour of J. J. C. Smart.* Oxford: Basil Blackwell.

———. 1987b. "Knowing One's Own Mind." *Proceedings and Addresses of the American Philosophical Association* 60:441–58

———. 1985a. "Replies to Essays I–IX." In Bruce Vermazen and M. Hintikka, eds., *Essays on Davidson.* Oxford: Clarendon.

———. 1985b. "Incoherence and Irrationality." *Dialectica* 39:345–54.

———. 1982a. "Rational Animals." *Dialectica* 36:318–27. Also in Ernest Lepore and B. McLaughlin, eds., *Actions and Events.* Oxford: Basil Blackwell, 1985.

———. 1982b. "Paradoxes of Irrationality." In Richard Wollheim and J. Hopkins, eds., *Philosophical Essays on Freud.* Cambridge: Cambridge University Press.

———. 1980. *Essays on Actions and Events.* Oxford: Clarendon.

———. 1970. "How is Weakness of the Will Possible?" In Joel Feinberg, ed. *Moral Concepts* Oxford: Clarendon. Reprinted in Davidson 1980.

———. 1967. "The Logical Form of Action Sentences." In Nicholas Rescher, ed. *The Logic of Decision and Action.* Pittsburgh, Pa.: University of Pittsburgh Press. Reprinted in Davidson 1980.

———. 1963. "Actions, Reasons, and Causes." *Journal of Philosophy* 60:685–700. Reprinted in Davidson 1980.

Davis, Lawrence. 1979. *Theory of Action.* Englewood Cliffs, N.J.: Prentice–Hall.

———. 1970. "Individuation of Action." *Journal of Philosophy* 67:520–30.

Davis, Wayne. 1984. "A Causal Theory of Intending." *American Philosophical Quarterly* 21:43–54.

Donagan, Alan. 1987. *Choice.* London: Routledge & Kegan Paul.

Dretske, Fred. 1988. *Explaining Behavior: Reasons in a World of Causes.* Cambridge, Mass.: The MIT Press.

Feather, Norman. 1982. *Expectations and Actions: Expectancy-Value Models in Psychology.* Hillsdale, N.J.: Lawrence Erlbaum.

Fishbein, Martin. 1980. "A Theory of Reasoned Action: Some Applications and Implications." In Herbert Howe and M. Page, eds., *Nebraska Symposium on Motivation.* Lincoln: University of Nebraska Press.

Fishbein, Martin, and I. Ajzen. 1975. *Belief, Attitude, Intention, and Behavior.* Reading, Mass.: Addison–Wesley.

Fodor, Jerry. 1991. "A Modal Argument for Narrow Content." *Journal of Philosophy* 88:5–26.

———. 1989. "Making Mind Matter More. *Philosophical Topics* 17:59–79.

———. 1987. *Psychosemantics.* Cambridge, Mass.: The MIT Press.

———. 1980. "Methodological Solipsism Considered As a Research Strategy in Cognitive Psychology." *Behavioral and Brain Sciences* 3:63–73.

Frankfurt, Harry. 1978. "The Problem of Action." *American Philosophical Quarterly* 15:157–62.

Gallistel, C.R. 1980. *The Organization of Action: A New Synthesis.* Hillsdale, N.J.: Lawrence Erlbaum.

Gibbard, Allan. 1990. *Wise Choices, Apt Feelings.* Cambridge, Mass.: Harvard University Press.

Ginet, Carl. 1990. *On Action.* Cambridge: Cambridge University Press.

Glover, Jonathan. 1970. *Responsibility.* London: Routledge & Kegan Paul.

Goldman, Alvin. 1970. *A Theory of Human Action.* Englewood Cliffs, N.J.: Prentice–Hall.

Gosling, Justin. 1990. *Weakness of the Will.* London: Routledge & Kegan Paul.

Grice, H.P. 1971. "Intention and Uncertainty." *Proceedings of the British Academy* 57:263–79.

Gustafson, Donald. 1986. *Intention and Agency.* Dordrecht: Reidel.

Harman, Gilbert. N.d. "Desired Desires." Forthcoming.

———. 1986a. *Change in View.* Cambridge, Mass.: The MIT Press.

———. 1986b. "Willing and Intending." In Richard Grandy and R. Warner, eds., *Philosophical Grounds of Rationality.* Oxford: Clarendon.

———. 1976. "Practical Reasoning." *Review of Metaphysics* 79:431–63.

Heckhausen, Heinz, and J. Beckmann. 1990. "Intentional Action and Action Slips." *Psychological Review* 97:36–48.

Heil, John, and A. Mele. 1991. "Mental Causes." *American Philosophical Quarterly* 28:49–59.

Honderich, Ted. 1988. *A Theory of Determinism.* Oxford: Clarendon.

Horgan, Terence. 1991. "Actions, Reasons, and the Explanatory Role of Content." In Brian McLaughlin, ed., *Dretske and His Critics.* Boston: Routledge & Kegan Paul.

———. 1989. "Mental Quausation." *Philosophical Perspectives* 3:47–76.

Hornsby, Jennifer. 1980. *Actions.* London: Routledge & Kegan Paul.

Hursthouse, Rosalind. 1991. "Arational Actions." *Journal of Philosophy* 87:57–68.

Jackson, Frank. 1985. "Internal Conflicts in Desires and Morals." *American Philosophical Quarterly* 22:105–14.

Jackson, Frank, and P. Pettit. 1990. "Program Explanation: A General Perspective." *Analysis* 50:107–17.

———. 1988. "Functionalism and Broad Content." *Mind* 97:381–400.

Jeffrey, Richard. 1985. "Animal Interpretation." In Ernest LePore and B. McLaughlin, eds., *Actions and Events*. Oxford: Basil Blackwell.

Kant, Immanuel. 1964. *Groundwork of the Metaphysic of Morals*. Trans. H. J. Paton. New York: Harper & Row.

Kavka, Gregory. 1983. "The Toxin Puzzle." *Analysis* 43:33–36.

Kim, Jaegwon. 1984. "Epiphenomenal and Supervenient Causation." *Midwest Studies in Philosophy* 9:257–70.

Klapp, Stuart, D. Grein, C. Mendicino, and R. Koenig. 1979. "Anatomical and Environmental Dimensions of Stimulus–Response Compatibility: Implication for Theories of Memory Coding." *Acta psychologica* 43:367–79.

Kruglanski, Ariel, and Y. Klar. 1985. "Knowing What To Do: On the Epistemology of Actions." In Julius Kuhl and J. Beckmann, eds., *Action Control: From Cognition to Behavior*. Berlin: Springer–Verlag.

Lashley, Karl. 1951. "The Problem of Serial Order in Behavior." In Lloyd Jeffress, ed., *Cerebral Mechanisms in Behavior*. New York: Wiley.

Lennon, Kathleen. 1990. *Explaining Human Action*. Peru, Ill.: Open Court.

Lewis, David. 1986. "Causation." In David Lewis, *Philosophical Papers,* vol. 2. Oxford: Oxford University Press.

———. 1973. *Counterfactuals*. Cambridge, Mass.: Harvard University Press.

Locke, Don. 1982. "Beliefs, Desires, and Reasons for Action." *American Philosophical Quarterly* 19:241–49.

———. 1974. "Reasons, Wants, and Causes." *American Philosophical Quarterly* 11:169–79.

Lycan, William. 1988. *Judgement and Justification*. Cambridge: Cambridge University Press.

McCann, Hugh. 1991. "Settled Objectives and Rational Constraints." *American Philosophical Quarterly*. 28:25–36.

———. 1989. "Intending and Planning: A Reply to Mele." *Philosophical Studies* 55:107–10.

———. 1986a. "Intrinsic Intentionality." *Theory and Decision* 20:247–73.

———. 1986b. "Rationality and the Range of Intention." *Midwest Studies in Philosophy* 10:191–211.

———. 1975. "Trying, Paralysis, and Volition." *Review of Metaphysics* 28:423–42.

———. 1972. "Is Raising One's Arm a Basic Action?" *Journal of Philosophy* 69:235–49.

McGinn, Colin. 1982. *The Character of Mind*. Oxford: Oxford University Press.

MacKay, Donald. 1981. "Behavioral Plasticity, Serial Order, and the Motor Program." *Behavioral and Brain Sciences* 4:630–31.

McLaughlin, Brian. 1985. "Anomalous Monism and the Irreducibility of the Mental." In Ernest LePore and B. McLaughlin, eds., *Actions and Events: Perspectives on the Philosophy of Donald Davidson.* Oxford: Basil Blackwell.

Malcolm, Norman. 1984. "Consciousness and Causality." In David Armstrong and Norman Malcolm, *Consciousness and Causality.* Oxford: Basil Blackwell.

———. 1968. "The Conceivability of Mechanism." *Philosophical Review* 77:45–72.

Mele, Alfred. N.d.(a). "Intentions, Reasons, and Beliefs: Morals of the Toxin Puzzle." Forthcoming.

———. N.d.(b). "*Akrasia,* Self-Control, and Second-Order Desires." *Noûs.* Forthcoming.

———. N.d.(c). Review of Carl Ginet, *On Action. Philosophy and Phenomenological Research.* Forthcoming.

———. 1990a. "Exciting Intentions." *Philosophical Studies* 59:289–312.

———. 1990b. "Irresistible Desires." *Noûs* 24:455–72.

———. 1990c. "He Wants To Try." *Analysis* 50:251–53.

———. 1990d. "Intending and Motivation: A Rejoinder." *Analysis* 50:194–97.

———. 1990e. "Errant Self-Control and the Self-Contolled Person." *Pacific Philosophical Quarterly* 71:47–59.

———. 1989a. "Intention, Belief, and Intentional Action." *American Philosophical Quarterly* 26:19–30.

———. 1989b. "Intentions by Default." *Pacific Philosophical Quarterly* 70:155–66.

———. 1989c. "She Intends To Try." *Philosophical Studies* 54:101–06.

———. 1989d. "Motivational Internalism: The Powers and Limits of Practical Reasoning." *Philosophia* 19:417–36.

———. 1988a. "Effective Reasons and Intrinsically Motivated Actions." *Philosophy and Phenomenological Research* 48:723–31.

———. 1988b. "Against a Belief/Desire Analysis of Intention." *Philosophia* 18:239–42.

———. 1987a. *Irrationality: An Essay on Akrasia, Self-Deception, and Self-Control.* New York: Oxford University Press.

———. 1987b. "Are Intentions Self-Referential?" *Philosophical Studies* 52:309–29.

———. 1987c. "Intentional Action and Wayward Causal Chains: The Problem of Tertiary Waywardness." *Philosophical Studies* 51:55–60.

———. 1984. "Intending and the Balance of Motivation." *Pacific Philosophical Quarterly* 66:370–76.

———. 1983. "*Akrasia,* Reasons, and Causes." *Philosophical Studies* 44:345–68.

Milgram, Stanley. 1974. *Obedience to Authority.* New York: Harper & Row.

Mischel, Harriet, and W. Mischel. 1983. "The Development of Children's Knowledge of Self-Control Strategies." *Child Development* 54:603–19.

Mischel, Walter, and N. Baker. 1975. "Cognitive Appraisals and Transformations in Delay Behavior." *Journal of Personality and Social Psychology* 31:254–61.

Mischel, Walter, and E. Ebbesen. "Attention in Delay of Gratification." *Journal of Personality and Social Psychology* 16:329–37.

Mischel, Walter, E. Ebbesen, and A. Zeiss, 1972. "Cognitive and Attentional Mechanisms in Delay of Gratification." *Journal of Personality and Social Psychology* 21:204–18.

Mischel, Walter, and H. Mischel. 1977. "Self-Control and the Self." In Theodore Mischel, ed., *The Self: Psychological and Philosophical Issues*. Oxford: Basil Blackwell.

Mischel, Walter, and B. Moore. 1980. "The Role of Ideation in Voluntary Delay for Symbolically Presented Rewards." *Cognitive Therapy and Research* 4:211–21.

Mischel, Walter, and B. Moore. 1973. "Effects of Attention to Symbolically-Presented Rewards on Self-Control." *Journal of Personality and Social Psychology* 28:172–79.

Mook, Douglas. 1987. *Motivation: The Organization of Action*. New York: Norton.

Moore, Bert, W. Mischel, and A. Zeiss. 1976. "Comparative Effects of the Reward Stimulus and Its Cognitive Representation in Voluntary Delay." *Journal of Personality and Social Psychology* 34:419–24.

Moya, Carlos. 1990. *The Philosophy of Action*. Cambridge: Polity Press.

Navarick, Douglas, and E. Fantino. 1976. "Self-Control and General Models of Choice." *Journal of Experimental Psychology: Animal Behavior Processes* 2:75–87.

Neely, Wright. 1974. "Freedom and Desire." *Philosophical Review* 83:32–54.

Nisbett, Richard, and T. Wilson. 1977. "Telling More Than We Can Know: Verbal Reports on Mental Processes." *Psychological Review* 84:231–59.

O'Shaughnessy, Brian. 1980. *The Will*. Cambridge: Cambridge University Press.

Patterson, Charlotte, and W. Mischel. 1976. "Effects of Temptation-inhibiting and Task-facilitating Plans on Self-Control." *Journal of Personality and Social Psychology* 33:209–17.

Peacocke, Christopher. 1985. "Intention and *Akrasia*." In Bruce Vermazen and M. Hintikka, eds., *Essays on Davidson*. Oxford: Clarendon.

Pears, David. 1985. "Intention and Belief." In Bruce Vermazen and M. Hintikka, eds., *Essays on Davidson*. Oxford: Clarendon.

———. 1984. *Motivated Irrationality*. Oxford: Oxford University Press.

Putnam, Hilary. 1981. *Reason, Truth, and History*. Cambridge: Cambridge University Press.

———. 1975. "The Meaning of 'Meaning'." In Hilary Putnam, *Mind, Language and Reality*. Cambridge: Cambridge University Press.

Rachlin, Howard, and L. Green. 1972. "Commitment, Choice, and Self-Control." *Journal of the Experimental Analysis of Behavior* 17:15–22.

Rorty, Amelie. 1980. "Where Does the Akratic Break Take Place?" *Australasian Journal of Philosophy* 58:333–46.

Searle, John. 1983. *Intentionality.* Cambridge: Cambridge University Press.

———. 1979. "The Intentionality of Intention and Action." *Inquiry* 22:253–80.

Sellars, Wilfred. 1973. "Action and Events." *Noûs.* 7:179–202.

Sheridan, Martin. 1984. "Planning and Controlling Simple Movements." In Mary Smyth and A. Wing, eds., *The Psychology of Human Movement.* London: Academic Press.

Solnick, Jay, C. Kannenberg, D. Eckerman, and M. Waller. 1980. "An Experimental Analysis of Impulsivity and Impulse Control in Humans." *Learning and Motivation* 11:61–77.

Sousa, Ronald de. 1987. *The Rationality of Emotion.* Cambridge, Mass.: The MIT Press.

Stalnaker, Robert. 1968. "A Theory of Conditionals." In Nicholas Rescher, ed., *Studies in Logical Theory.* New York: Oxford University Press.

Stich, Stephen. 1983. *From Folk Psychology to Cognitive Science.* Cambridge, Mass.: The MIT Press.

Stoutland, Frederick. 1980. "Oblique Causation and Reasons for Action." *Synthese* 43:351–67.

Thalberg, Irving. 1985. "Questions About Motivational Strength." In Ernest Lepore and B. Mclaughlin, eds., *Actions and Events.* Oxford: Basil Blackwell.

———. 1984. "Do Our Intentions Cause Our Intentional Actions?" *American Philosophical Quarterly* 21:249–60.

———. 1977. *Perception, Emotion, and Action.* Oxford: Basil Blackwell.

Thomson, Judith. 1977. *Acts and Other Events.* Ithaca, N.Y.: Cornell University Press.

———. 1971. "The Time of a Killing." *Journal of Philosophy* 68:115–32.

Tuomela, Raimo. 1989. "Methodological Solipsism and Explanation in Psychology." *Philosophy of Science* 56:23–47.

———. 1977. *Human Action and Its Explanation.* Dordrecht: Reidel.

Ullman-Margalit, Edna, and S. Morgenbesser. 1977. "Picking and Choosing." *Social Research* 44:757–85.

Van Gulick, Robert. 1992. "Who's in Charge Here? And Who's Doing All the Work?" In John Heil and A. Mele, eds., *Mental Causation.* Oxford: Clarendon.

Velleman, J. David. 1989. *Practical Reflection.* Princeton, N.J.: Princeton University Press.

Warshaw, Paul, and F. Davis. 1985. "Disentangling Behavioral Intention and Behavioral Expectation." *Journal of Experimental Social Psychology* 21:213–28.

Watson, Gary. 1977. "Skepticism About Weakness of Will." *Philosophical Review* 86:316–39.

Wellman, Henry. 1985. "The Child's Theory of the Mind: The Development of Theories of Cognition." In Steven Yussen, ed., *The Growth of Reflection in Children*. San Diego, Calif.: Academic Press.

Wilson, George. 1989. *The Intentionality of Human Action*. Stanford, Calif.: Stanford University Press.

Wilson, Timothy, and R. Nisbett. 1978. "The Accuracy of Verbal Reports About the Effects of Stimuli on Evaluations and Behavior." *Social Psychology Quarterly* 41:118–31.

Wittgenstein, Ludwig. 1953. *Philosophical Investigations*. Trans. G. Anscombe. New York: Macmillan.

Wright, G.H. von. 1963. *The Varieties of Goodness*. London: Routledge & Kegan Paul.

Yates, Brian, and W. Mischel. 1979. "Young Children's Preferred Attentional Strategies for Delaying Gratification." *Journal of Personality and Social Psychology* 37:286–300.

Index